MAO'S WAR AGAINST NATURE

Politics and the Environment
in Revolutionary China

JUDITH SHAPIRO

American University

CAMBRIDGE
UNIVERSITY PRESS

PUBLISHED BY THE PRESS SYNDICATE OF THE UNIVERSITY OF CAMBRIDGE
The Pitt Building, Trumpington Street, Cambridge, United Kingdom

CAMBRIDGE UNIVERSITY PRESS
The Edinburgh Building, Cambridge CB2 2RU, UK
40 West 20th Street, New York, NY 10011-4211, USA
10 Stamford Road, Oakleigh, VIC 3166, Australia
Ruiz de Alarcón 13, 28014, Madrid, Spain
Dock House, The Waterfront, Cape Town 8001, South Africa

http://www.cambridge.org

First published 2001

Printed in the United States of America

Typeface Garamond 3 11/13 pt.   *System* QuarkXPress   [HT]

A catalog record for this book is available from the British Library.

Library of Congress Cataloging in Publication Data

Shapiro, Judith, 1953–
Mao's war against nature : politics and the environment in Revolutionary China /
Judith Shapiro.
p.   cm – (Studies in environment and history)
Includes bibliographical references.
ISBN 0 521 78150 7 – ISBN 0 521 78680 0 (pb)
1. Environmental policy – China – History – 20th century.   2. Environmental
degradation – China – History – 20th century.   I. Title.   II. Series.
GE190.C6 S48 2001

363.7′00951′0904 – dc21   00-041420

ISBN 0 521 78150 7   hardback
ISBN 0 521 78680 0   paperback

Let's attack here!
Drive away the mountain gods,
Break down the stone walls
To bring out those 200 million tons of coal.

Let's strike here!
Let the Dragon King change his job,
Let the river climb the hills,
Let us ask it for 8000 *mu* of rice paddies.

Let that valley open its bosom
To yield 500 *jin* of oats every year.
Cut down the knoll
To make a plain over there...

Let's wage war against the great earth!
Let the mountains and rivers surrender under our feet.
March on Nature,
Let's take over the power of rain and wind.

We shall not tolerate a single inch of unused land!
Nor a single place harassed by disaster.
Make wet rice, wheat, and yellow corn grow on top of
    the mountain,
And beans, peanuts, and red gaoliang rise on sheer rocks...

Zhang Zhimin, *Personalities in the Commune*[1]

CONTENTS

Chinese Measurement Equivalents

100 *mu*	1 *qing*
6 *mu*	1 acre
15 *mu*	1 *ha* (hectare) or 2.47 acres
100 *qing*	16 acres
1 *li*	$^1/_3$ mile or $^1/_2$ kilometer
1 *jin* (catty)	1.33 pounds
16 *liang*	1 *jin*

PREFACE

This book is the product of my longstanding involvement with China and more recent interest in international environmental politics. The effort to understand the Maoist attempt to "conquer" nature has provided me with unexpected pleasure as well as enormous intellectual challenges. I have revisited the familiar terrain of Mao-era China with fresh perspective and explored the new territory of environmental politics with the aid of well-known landmarks. I remain fascinated by the interconnections between human and environmental politics under Mao and am gratified now to share my work.

Observers of global environmental politics are quick to point out that no solution to the earth's environmental problems is possible without the involvement of China. China is a major force in almost every global environmental issue, be it climate change, ozone depletion, biodiversity loss, world food security, human population growth, or overexploitation of the global commons. At the regional level, China is involved in trans-boundary air and water pollution, conflict over shared watercourses, international trade in endangered species, and cross-border fallout from nuclear weapons tests. With its enormous size, remarkable economic growth, and severe environmental degradation, China's importance to planetary health is overwhelming.

A legacy of political upheaval, only partially acknowledged by China's current leadership, has contributed to the current grave environmental situation in China. Uneasy reactions to the Mao era have intensified the negative effects of industrialization on the environment; the aftereffects of the tumultuous Mao years continue to undermine Communist Party claims to legitimacy, to promote corruption and disillusionment with public goals, and to hinder the Chinese people's search for national identity and pride. The dismal environmental record of the Mao years offers scant guidance as China seeks to meet new challenges raised by explosive economic development. China's cities are among the world's most polluted; much of the population struggles with falling water tables and unsafe drinking water; health problems due to environmental problems are so widespread that, if fully accounted for, they would negate much of the region's economic growth; erosion, salinization, and desertification plague much of China's arable land; sandstorms traced to deforestation and overgrazing torment northern China; and major floods connected to excessive logging and land reclamation are becoming more frequent. A comprehensive portrait of the causes and effects of contemporary Chinese environmental problems is beyond the scope of this book, and only some of China's current predicament is attributable to Mao's policies and legacy. However, this book seeks to inspire debate about the social and political causes of China's environmental difficulties and to challenge the received wisdom that China's environmental problems are attributable solely to post-Mao economic reforms and industrial growth.

Beyond China's importance to global environmental issues, there is an additional, even more compelling reason to investigate and explain the environmental dynamics of the Mao years: few cases of environmental degradation so clearly reveal the human and environmental costs incurred when human beings, particularly those who determine policy, view themselves as living in an oppositional relationship to nature – as well as to each other – and behave accordingly. The relationship between humans and nature under Mao is so transparent and extreme that it clearly indicates a link between abuse of people and abuse of the natural environment. As this book will show, coercive state behavior such as forcible relocations and suppression of intellectual and political freedoms contributed directly to a wide range of environmental problems ranging from deforestation and desertification to ill-conceived engineering projects that degraded major river courses. At numerous important junctures of Mao-era history, the connection between human suffering and the degradation of the natural world was very clear. Today, at a time when it has become critical to adopt more sustainable modes of human activity, the cautionary example of the Maoist "war against nature" may shed light on the human–nature relationship in other periods and parts of the world.

Preface

To write this book, I have assembled evidence of the environmental impact of Mao-era politics in representative cases, drawing on newspaper and magazine accounts, interviews, written memoirs, scholarly field studies, and journalistic accounts. I have built on the limited Western scholarly materials on the environment during the Mao years, as well as on analyses of the politics of the period. I have searched Chinese "reportage literature," or semifictionalized memoirs, as well as autobiographies by many who suffered during the era's political campaigns, for hints of the environmental story that was not usually their main focus. In an effort to understand the roots of Mao's war on nature, I have drawn on Mao's writings and speeches and on Chinese Communist Party statements. Informative and outspoken books published in China during the climate of greater intellectual openness of the late 1990s also provided insight and factual material, although political constraints remained evident, particularly with respect to the roles and responsibilities of Mao and other leaders whose reputations were still being protected. Finally, perhaps most importantly, I have plumbed the memories of ordinary Chinese who participated in Mao's massive nature-control experiments, whether they did so by terracing mountains or filling in lakes during the years of "learning from Dazhai" or by relocating to the frontiers to counter the Soviet threat. Out of respect for the law of unforeseen consequences, which this book illustrates well, I have protected the anonymity of these informants, except in a handful of cases in which disclosure of their identities added significantly to the memories they shared and I was able to obtain explicit permission for their names to be used.

Most official accounts were unreliable as descriptions of what happened, precisely because of the lack of freedom of expression and information of the Mao years. They were relevant, however, for the models they provided and for the attitudes and policies toward nature that they revealed. Even such obvious sources as the *People's Daily* and *China Pictorial* provided windows onto how China's policy-makers conceived national struggles and campaigns, and were excellent sources for charting the evolution of official discourse. Moreover, official sources pointed toward other versions of the truth, as acknowledgment of small problems suggested big ones, and announcements that problems had been resolved served to expose the problems. Because mass political campaigns touched almost all Chinese, and because many of those who lived through the period are still alive, an infinite base of experiences was available to be discovered and retold.

I made my first visit to China in 1977 and taught English in Changsha, in Hunan province, from 1979 to 1981, as one of the first forty Americans to work in China after U.S.-China relations were normalized. My Chinese students and colleagues were quick to disabuse me of any romanticism about Maoism and the Cultural Revolution; my wide travels and explorations of Chinese society confirmed that the Mao era had been a disaster for the country on numerous levels. In the early 1980s, that period was still poorly understood in the outside world, and upon my return to the United States, I worked to share what I had learned, collaborating with my former husband, Liang Heng, on a series of books about the Cultural Revolution and the ongoing constraints on intellectual freedom in China. I returned to China repeatedly, often spending time in out-of-the-way places where I came to know the arduous lives of rural Chinese and observe how closely they depended for survival on their interactions with the land. I heard much testimony about how much easier rural life has become since the end of the desperate Mao period. I also observed enduring political victimization and a host of environmental problems that originated under Mao. My instinct that these phenomena were connected helped suggest the hypothesis, explored in this book, that abuse of people and abuse of nature are often interrelated.

Research for this project was conducted during four visits in 1998, 1999, and 2000. My interest in China's environment led me to volunteer to lecture on environmental philosophy and international environmental politics at Southwest Agricultural University near Chongqing. Since I had been a teacher in China, I was familiar with this role and felt comfortable contributing to Chinese efforts to train environmental professionals at the same time that I developed my own work through conversations and interviews. I also traveled to other regions to collect exemplar stories, returning twice to Yunnan province, where several of the cases featured in this book are located. I sought out intellectuals who had been persecuted during the Anti-rightist movement, former schoolchildren who had participated in the campaign to get rid of the Four Pests, workers and peasants who had been mobilized to fill in a lake to grow grain, and former "educated youths" who had been sent to the frontier to "open the wasteland" and grow rubber. I made a special effort to speak with older Chinese engaged in environmental protection. Although their often-bitter experiences during the Mao years were typical of those of other Chinese intellectuals of their generation, their perspectives were unusually helpful, as they had often thought deeply about the themes investigated here. Their memories inform the core insights contained in this book. I also spoke to younger Chinese who did not live through the Mao years about their attitudes toward environmental issues, particularly during a May 2000 lecture tour on the role of nongovernmental organizations in environmental protection. Although contemporary attitudes were not the primary focus of my research, these conversations provided an important source of hope for the future, as reflected in this book's conclusion.

The illustrations for this book came primarily from magazines and books purchased in Chinese flea markets, which have become a rich source of Mao-era collectibles. Propaganda posters, back issues of *Zhongguo Huabao* (China Pictorial), *Zhongguo Sheying* (China Photography), and various provincial pictorials were readily available. Fortuitously, I also found a 1971 commemorative album depicting the building of the Chengdu-Kunming Railroad, several albums used in "learning from" Dazhai, a volume of wood-block prints designed to encourage youths to volunteer to "open up" the countryside and frontiers, and several sets of commemorative photographs of Chairman Mao. A journalist who had retained his 1960s negatives kindly gave me unpublished original photographs of Panzhihua, the Third Front steel base; hydro-engineer Huang Wanli and his children were generous with their family photographs, for which I am most grateful.

A few caveats about the limitations of this book: If the study of attitudes, values, culture, and ideas is always difficult, it is even more difficult to pin down their relationship to policy and behavior. Memory is slippery, especially as it seeks to retrieve and make sense of politically charged events that have caused personal dislocation or suffering. Much evidence was subjective, as is its interpretation; however, the memories of witnesses and participants are an essential part of this book. Moreover, no study of a country as large as China, covering as broad a time span as the Mao years, can possibly be comprehensive, and this book does not pretend to be an exhaustive history of the environment during the period. Rather, it is an attempt to tease out themes by investigating particularly telling cases, and thereby to draw a rich portrait of the complex human face of environmental degradation in China under Mao. In so doing, I hope to provide a historical context for China's current environmental problems. I hope also to advance our theoretical grasp of the connection between problems among humans, on the one hand, and problems between humans and nature, on the other, by providing detailed cases that demonstrate how this connection has been played out. The confluence of destructive interhuman relations and destructive human–nature relations in Maoist China is an extreme example of similar patterns and distortions that occur and have occurred in other settings. Further study of this congruence may have value for a broader understanding of the relationship between social and environmental activity.

This book has benefited from a wealth of expertise, ideas, experience, and support from colleagues, friends, family, and people known to me only electronically. Mary Child of Cambridge University Press believed in the project from the start, patiently and wisely improved the manuscript with numerous intelligent suggestions, and shepherded it through publication. Donald Worster, editor of Cambridge University Press's Studies in Environment and History, welcomed the project onto an exceedingly distinguished list and provided valuable guidance for revisions. Cathy Felgar, Nancy Hearst, Betty Pessagno, Larry Meyer, and Laura Ho contributed their expertise during the production process. A calligrapher who prefers to remain anonymous kindly wrote the slogans that open each chapter. Among the many other individuals who played pivotal roles are Paul Wapner, who helped conceptualize the project and read it in numerous incarnations, and Edward McCord, who invented the title and was responsible for essential conceptual modifications. Other West-based scholars who commented on all or parts of the manuscript include David Barrett, John Israel (who drew my attention to the Dianchi wetlands in-filling and persuaded me to meet him and his family in Kunming), Jacques deLisle, Roger Kasperson, Mark Elvin, Nicholas Menzies, Zhao Quansheng, Rick Edmonds, Ken Conca, Louis Goodman, Cao Zuoya, Marjorie Lightman, Robin Broad, Stacey Lance, Joan Lennox, Priscilla Grayson, and some very helpful anonymous reviewers for Cambridge University Press. Assistance with ideas, materials, and contacts in China was afforded by Jing Jun, Gan Che Ng, Jim Harkness, Dan Viederman, He Ping, Devra Kleiman, Walter Parham, Dave Cowhig, David Bleyle, Zhou Yuedong,

Liang Congjie, Fang Jing, Li Shuxian, Liu Binyan, Liu Lei, Tauna Szymanski, Hasan Arslan, Barry Naughton, Michael Schoenhals, Nick Young, Li Bo, Julia Su, Wayne and Pat Fisher, Cathy Cooper, and numerous others. E-mail dialogues with strangers who responded to queries posted to environmental history and Chinese environment listservs, and kind replies to requests for specific information from some of the leading lights of environmentalism helped make this project feel like an adventure. The School of International Service at American University provided support during much of the writing of this book and fostered a creative environment for pursuing multidisciplinary work. The Southwest Agricultural University in Chongqing provided a much-appreciated base during some of the research, as did the University of Aveiro in Portugal during the writing of both the first and final drafts. The Carnegie Council on Ethics and International Affairs and the U.S. State Department sent me to China for other projects that greatly enriched this book. I am also grateful to the many students and colleagues who supported this work in myriad ways.

My husband, Richard Shapiro, supported my decision to write a new book and kept me on track when my resolve wavered. He was often my first and most demanding reader, and he endured my writer's angst with patience and understanding. Others who played special roles include Tom McKain, who was reliably at the other end of the e-mail when I despaired, Michael Shapiro, my brother-in-law, who stepped in to help at a critical moment, and numerous others who know who they are.

Finally, a word about those to whom I owe the greatest thanks, the hundreds of Chinese who helped me by sharing memories, information, printed materials, introductions, and kindness. I am reluctant to bring possible inconvenience to them by naming them here. It saddens me to be unable to acknowledge them publicly. Some of them cautioned me to be circumspect in writing about political questions, but I could not implement this advice and also tell the story of the environment under Mao as I understand it, and I apologize if I have offended their sensibilities in any way. Others urged me to write what they cannot yet write openly. I hope that this book does them justice. I remain deeply grateful to all of these extraordinary, courageous, and generous individuals, and I hope that one day the views they expressed to me can be openly published in China.

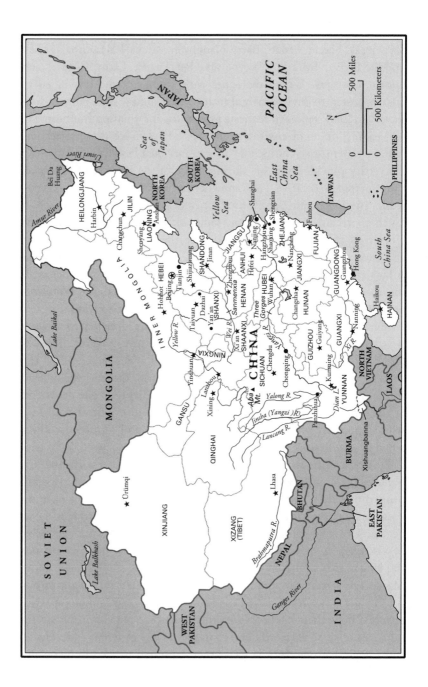

INTRODUCTION

Most environmental problems have roots in human relationships and are ultimately social, political, and cultural problems. Not all environmental degradation is human-induced: natural processes such as floods and droughts can also reduce the earth's productivity, and nonhuman species also alter and transform ecosystems. However, we human beings are far more effective than other species in altering our environments in an effort to satisfy our needs, and our very success often makes us a danger to others and to ourselves. Unlike other species, moreover, we make conscious, contestable choices about how resources are used, who uses them, and how we understand ourselves in relation to nature.

Maoist China provides an example of extreme human interference in the natural world in an era in which human relationships were also unusually distorted. The period illustrates the relationship between political repression and environmental degradation, demonstrating the tragedy of this interface under extreme conditions. The environmental dynamics of the period suggest a congruence between violence among human beings and violence by humans toward the nonhuman world. When the Chinese people mistreated each other through suppression of intellectual freedoms, tyrannical utopianism, political labeling, ostracism, punishment, terror, and forcible relocations, they also treated nature badly.

The political dynamics of the Mao period as they affected nature are complex, however; they do not simply involve coercion of political victims from among the urban intellectual or Communist elite. The degradation of the natural world in revolutionary China cannot be divorced from the often willing participation of millions of Chinese people, at all levels of society, whose traditional culture played a critical role in suppressing dissent and in promoting overambitious development projects. Confucian culture fostered obedience to superiors and a limited capacity on the part of both leaders and ordinary people to resist Mao's destructive utopian schemes; it thereby established a foundation for revolutionary excesses. On the other hand, traditional rural customs involved numerous sustainable practices of tilling, water control, nomadic use of grasslands, and sequential harvesting of forest products; local farmers were loath to relinquish these practices when imported "scientific" theories or revolutionary fervor held sway. While local values, knowledge, and practices ought not to be demonized or romanticized, their importance cannot be ignored; they made an important contribution to complicity in, and resistance to, Maoist development projects.

Few social experiments in history have had the scope and penetration of Chinese socialism. From 1949, when the Chinese Communist Party defeated the Guomindang, to 1976, when Mao died, Mao and the Communist Party sought to reengineer Chinese society by remolding human nature. Less well known is their effort to reshape the nonhuman world, with severe consequences both for human beings and for the natural environment. Numerous campaigns suppressed elite scientific knowledge and traditional grass-roots practices concerning the physical world, stifling dissent through political labels, ostracism, and labor camp sentences. In the early 1950s, Soviet-style plans for rapid development of heavy industry started the country down a path of environmental problems. By the late 1950s, Mao was repudiating economists' warnings of the dangers of overpopulation and exhorting the Chinese people to bear children so that, by dint of sheer numbers, they could increase production and withstand Western and Soviet threats. He thus created conditions for later coercive birth control policies and intensified struggles over land and resources. The 1958–60 Great Leap Forward raised farmers' hopes for national transformation through rapid industrialization of rural areas. Despite limited success in small-scale water conservancy and irrigation projects, the Leap failed to reach its goals, decimated China's forests, and caused widespread starvation. "Red experts" were in control, and the labors of rural "armies" were put at the service of utopian projects. Huge hydropower projects removed millions from their homes but were useless or caused disastrous floods when poorly constructed dams broke.

During the Cultural Revolution, projects and campaigns affecting the environment were driven less by utopianism than by coercion and chaos. Centrally launched earth-transforming campaigns such as "In Agriculture, Learn from Dazhai" (the model agricultural production brigade) were applied nationwide, with scant consideration for local topography and climate. Mao's parable of imperialism and feudalism, "The Foolish Old Man Who Removed the Mountains," a tale about the effectiveness of concerted manual labor, was required memorization; it exhorted the people to reshape the physical world radically, one bucket at a time. In the leadership vacuum that followed Red Guard attacks on Party officials, natural resources became fair game for all. Involuntarily resettled into wilderness and sparsely populated areas, disoriented urban relocatees were induced to carry out reclamation activities that often degraded land toward which they had little sense of connection or stewardship. Trained scientists who uttered words of dissent or caution were often exiled or persecuted to death. Class struggle, which created such adversity in human relationships, thus also created severe environmental damage. The state's battle against individualism, feudalism, capitalism, and revisionism was also a battle against nature.

The Maoist adversarial stance toward the natural world is an extreme case of the modernist conception of humans as fundamentally distinct and separate from nature. If it is true, as some environmentalists argue, that a core cause of contemporary environmental problems is the human failure to see ourselves as part of nature, seeing nature rather as something external to be harnessed or overcome, then this period provides a significant warning about the dangers of such schismatic views and the policies they generate.[2]

Mao's voluntarist philosophy held that through concentrated exertion of human will and energy, material conditions could be altered and all difficulties overcome in the struggle to achieve a socialist utopia.[3] In concert with the militarization of other aspects of life, Maoist ideology pitted the people against the natural environment in a fierce struggle. To conquer nature, the power of ideas was unleashed through mass mobilization in political campaigns, often accompanied by the use of military imagery. Official discourse was filled with references to a "war against nature." Nature was to be "conquered." Wheat was to be sown by "shock attack." "Shock troops" reclaimed the grasslands. "Victories" were won against flood and drought. Insects, rodents, and sparrows were "wiped out." This polarizing, adversarial language captures the core dynamic of environmental degradation of the era. The metaphor of a "war against nature" thus provides a compelling image for understanding human attitudes and behavior toward the environment in China during the Mao years. While this metaphor has characterized the human effort to dominate nature in other cases (such as the conquest of the American West, when the Army Corps of Engineers tried to "rationalize" the great rivers), the Chinese case involves a deprivation of human volition that makes it one of the most extreme cases of its kind.

The Mao era was nearly three decades long; China is vast and variegated, and its human population huge. As a means of explaining the dynamics of anthropogenic environmental degradation for such a great time span, space, and populace, four core themes can be used as analytical tools and organizing devices. They are: (1) *political repression,* including the repression of intellectuals, scientists, officials, and ordinary people who dissented from the Maoist vision of how humans should treat the natural environment; (2) *utopian urgency,* initiated by Mao and adopted by local leaders and peasants, to remold the landscape quickly and achieve socialism; (3) *dogmatic uniformity,* or imposition of "one-knife-cuts-all" [*yi dao qie*] models that ignored regional geographic variations and local practices toward nature; and (4) *state-ordered relocations,* or reconfigurations of society by administrative fiat, particularly those that sent people into "wasteland" areas in concentrated efforts to convert land into farmland, enhance military defense, and bolster national security by increasing the percentage of Han Chinese in minority areas. These characteristics and their environmental impacts, chronologically represented through a focus on successive political campaigns, provide the analytical and narrative structure for this book. Each of the coming chapters emphasizes one theme and one destructive political campaign. It should be noted, however, that the themes occur throughout the Mao period, with varying prominence, as will become clear.

Focusing on the theme of *political repression,* Chapter 1 treats the 1957 Anti-rightist movement and the political persecution of two distinguished thinkers, economist and Beijing University president Ma Yinchu, who warned China's top leadership about the country's population growth, and hydro-engineer Huang Wanli, who cautioned against a Soviet-influenced plan to dam the main stream of the Yellow River. Chapter 2 discusses *urgency to achieve utopian socialism* in connection with the 1958–60 Great Leap Forward, when the demand for fuel for "backyard furnaces" caused massive deforestation and Soviet-influenced agricultural schemes impoverished the land, resulting in the greatest human-created famine in history. *Dogmatic uniformity,* or central planning that ignored regional variation and local practices, provides the focus for Chapter 3, describing the misapplication of the Dazhai model during the early years of the Cultural Revolution, the lake in-filling, deforestation, and erosion resulting therefrom, and the human suffering created when the Chinese people were asked to emulate the ambitious projects described in Mao's essay, "The Foolish Old Man Who Removed the Mountains." Chapter 4 discusses the *state-ordered relocations* of the war preparation campaign of the late 1960s and early 1970s, when strategic industries were transferred by administrative fiat to the interior to form a defensive "Third Front" against the American "imperialists" and Russian "revisionists," and millions of "educated youth" were sent to the countryside and frontiers. This phase represents the climactic expression of Mao's war against nature, both literally and metaphorically, as all China came to resemble an army in a state of military alert, and the cult of the People's Liberation Army and Marshal Lin Biao, who was then Mao's designated successor, reached its height.

Military images – discipline, mobilization, regimentation, attack, and redeployment – carry the theme of the "war against nature" into the narrative. Social reorganization along military lines fueled much of the Mao-era drive to realize utopian socialism. With varying degrees of intensity, people were made to work collectively, eat in public dining halls, and sleep in dormitories. Civilians were often organized into detachments, regiments, platoons, brigades, and teams; even nonmilitary leaders were sometimes referred to as commanders, colonels, and lieutenants. During the Cultural Revolution, civilians and soldiers alike often wore olive green military uniforms. Both radical activists and political victims were induced to "volunteer" to relocate to frontier areas and remote rural areas of the interior, where they often slept in single-sex barracks and prepared for war. They dug air-raid shelters and were awakened during the night for military drills. In major cities, underground rivers were diverted to provide tunnels for use in war. During the height of the cult of Mao, there was strong social support for this state-led reorganization, with virtually no room for dissent. The notion was propagated that China would pick itself up after its long history of humiliation by imperialist powers, become self-reliant in the face of international isolation, and regain strength in the world. Since China lacked modern technology and wealth, the vehicles for its transformation were to be brute labor, defeat of internal enemies through class struggle, collective remolding of human nature through self-criticism, and study of Marxism–Leninism–Mao Zedong Thought.

The militarization of society had multiple purposes. It was one strategy in the Party's attempt to break up the traditional Confucian family structure and create a "new socialist man." It was part of an effort to use mass mobilization efficiently to overcome China's poverty and backwardness, deriving motivation through fear of real and imagined threats to China's security from without and within. "Continuous revolution" was a central tenet of Mao's brand of socialism, requiring constant social upheaval and reorganization. Finally, militarization was a coercion mechanism. Military-style social reorganization facilitated Party control and kept people too preoccupied with the transformations of their individual lives to question or resist Mao's rule. Over the course of the Mao years, the enemy shifted: it was variously said to be the Guomindang, the imperialist West, the revisionist Soviet Union, or land-hungry India. Meanwhile, the struggle against perceived internal threats from counterrevolutionaries, "rightists," and other "black" elements was at times so convulsing that it threatened to bring Chinese society into a state of collapse.

The contrast between the militarized Maoist approach toward the conquest of nature and traditional Chinese values of harmony and sustainability is sharp. Historically, wise leaders were considered to be those who conducted the human–nature relationship well, and legal codes from the Qin (221 B.C.–206 B.C.) to the Qing dynasties (A.D. 1644–A.D. 1911) contain provisions reflecting environmental concerns, such as those prohibiting poaching young animals and birds in springtime, restricting deforestation, and prescribing how land was to be used on hillsides.[4] The mulberry tree/fish farm system is often considered a model of sustainable agriculture, while terraces are often perceived to be efficient ways to maximize scarce arable land. These themes represent only the best-known examples of Chinese nature philosophy.

In traditional China, there were at least three major schools of thought about how humankind should behave in nature: a Daoist tradition that tended toward accommodation to nature's way, a Buddhist tradition of reverence for all living beings, and a Confucian tradition that actively sought to manage, utilize, and control nature.[5] These varied understandings of nature, by turn adaptive, respectful, and confrontational, are almost as old as Chinese civilization. Of the three, the anthropocentric Confucian tradition, which leans toward mastery of nature, has been by far the dominant one. While Confucianism has many principles prescribing what amounts to "wise use" of natural resources, its emphasis is on the regulation and ordering of the nonhuman environment for the good of human society.

China's geographical conditions help explain these preoccupations, for the country has long been at the mercy of natural disasters. Ancient legends speak of floods and droughts; China's legendary first ruler, Yu the Great, is said to have built hydro-projects for flood control more than four millennia ago. Vulnerability to the forces of nature helped establish the importance of water conservancy projects and granaries to ward against famine as primary responsibilities of imperial administrators. Early successes of engineering and coordination in the struggle against nature can be seen in massive waterworks projects such as the Dujiangyan irrigation works, built during the Qin dynasty, and the Grand Canal, built in the seventh century to link North and South China.

Despite China's many successes in tempering nature and molding landscapes to make them more suitable for human life, environmental degradation is far from a recent Chinese invention. A powerful national drive toward expansion, mastery, and resource exploitation, fueled by population growth and new technologies, has contributed for millennia to widespread destruction of nature and ecosystems. China's efforts to reshape lands and waters, open up forests, and feed a growing population extend into prerecorded time. A pattern of "exhausting the earth" through deforestation, erosion, siltation, desertification, land reclamations, habitat loss, and human-caused extinctions has been noted for centuries and has recently been the subject of innovative scholarly studies.[6] Even the notion of battling against nature, which provides the central image for this book, can be found in late imperial times:

The local peasants in defence of homesteads and of farms
Willingly commit themselves to contending with the waters:
From west to east, and east to west, along both river margins,
Dykes are constructed, strand by strand, the way they re-weave
    hawsers.[7]

By the Mao years, China's most fertile and readily arable land had been thoroughly transformed by centuries of human use, and large areas of China were parched and eroded from deforestation and overexploitation. Extinctions and pressures on rare species were already common. By the early eighteenth century, for example, tiger attacks were no longer recorded in Lingnan in southern China, as the tiger habitat had been destroyed.[8] Thus, official public values of sustainability and human–nature harmony did little to protect China from a pattern of overuse and destruction that predated the Mao years by millennia.

The Mao-era effort to conquer nature can thus be understood as an extreme form of a philosophical and behavioral tendency that has roots in traditional Confucian culture. Many of the themes sounded in this book – including state-sponsored resettlements and waterworks projects, extensive and excessive construction of dikes for land reclamation, political campaigns to change agricultural practices, and environmentally destructive land conversions in response to population shifts – can be found in imperial times.[9]

Despite such continuities with pre-Mao practices, however, the relationship between humans and nature during the Mao era was distinctive in Chinese history. Maoism rejected both Chinese tradition and modern Western science. The effort to conquer nature was highly concentrated and oppositional, motivated by utopianism to transform the face of the earth and build a socialist paradise, and characterized by coercion, mass mobilization, enormity of scale, and great human suffering. The articulation of Mao's war against nature is striking for its overtly adversarial expression and disregard of objective scientific principles, while its implementation stands out for focused destructiveness and mass coordination. Maoism strengthened problematic aspects of Chinese tradition, such as the tendency to see nature through a purely utilitarian lens. At the same time, through suppression of local knowledge, it undermined aspects of traditional practice that fostered sustainable relations with nature. In these respects, the Mao era represents a sharp departure from what came before and from what followed with the economic reforms.

A Chinese scholar from Yunnan province, a man in his sixties whose life has been buffeted by the numerous political campaigns of the Mao years and who has observed their environmental consequences at close hand, spoke in confidence to me about the role of Mao. He voiced what many thoughtful intellectuals of his generation say in private but cannot publish in the current political climate. His comments, as follow, are worth quoting at length, for they touch on many of the themes that will be treated in depth in the coming pages:

> Under the influence of the Soviet Union and his own peasant background, Mao adopted a series of unsuitable policies. Mao was always struggling in war, so he continued to struggle after the war ended. Class struggle – everything was a struggle. In his youth, he wrote a line of poetry, "To struggle against the heavens is endless joy, to struggle against the earth is endless joy, to struggle against people is endless joy" [*Yu tian dou, qi le wu qiong, yu di dou, qi le wu qiong, yu ren dou, qi le wu qiong*]. His whole philosophy was that of struggle. Not everyone in the Party thought as he did. Zhou Enlai opposed the population policy. Peng Dehuai opposed the Great Leap Forward.[10] Destruction of nature during the Mao years was connected to the cult of Mao.
>
> Traditional Chinese philosophy emphasizes moderation and adaptation, "Harmony between the Heavens and Humankind" [*Tian Ren Heyi*]. But Mao took another view: "Man Must Conquer Nature" [*Ren Ding Sheng Tian*]. For him, building China meant transforming China's face. To improve the lives of the poor, nature should be defeated [*zhansheng ziran*]. Mao didn't respect nature. This struggle mentality was there from the beginning, with Marxism. Marxism rests on struggle.
>
> Although Mao was supposedly a peasant, he had little farming experience. Mao's attitude toward nature was an oppositional relationship. It influenced China for decades. Population policy and national construction were influenced by his military mentality. With respect to population, Mao said, "With Many People, Strength is Great" [*Ren Duo, Liliang Da*], and he suppressed those who disagreed with him. The Great Leap Forward of 1958 did not

respect the laws of nature or science. Mao wanted to catch up with Great Britain in steel production, and many trees were cut down to fuel furnaces. By 1959, the people had no grain, and in 1960 and 1961 there was a great famine. So Mao said, "open the wilderness to plant grain" [*kaihuang zhong liangshi*], and it was another disaster for the forests. The forests were cut without restraint so as to plant grain in the mountains. During the Cultural Revolution, there were even more crazy things. Everything was collective and nature belonged to the country, so there was no individual responsibility to protect nature. Tradition was destroyed. Because of the "Take Grain as the Key Link" policy in agriculture, only grain was planted and other crops were destroyed. Officials were ordered to cut down fruit trees. If they resisted, it was terrible. Some cut down trees with tears in their eyes. The third great cutting took place in 1980–82, after Mao's death. The farmland that had been state-owned was contracted out to families, as were the forests. But people feared they wouldn't have the right to use the land for long, so there was terrible cutting.[11] So we can speak of "three great cuttings" [*san da fa*]: the Great Leap Forward, the Cultural Revolution, and the early 1980s.

Because of their lack of a democratic, scientific approach, and their philosophy of struggle, the leaders didn't know how to build China. They had ideals, but if you struggle against your own people and against nature, and don't allow people to express their opinions, it suppresses people and harms nature.

As this experienced and thoughtful Chinese intellectual indicates, the changes in attitude toward nature of the pre-Mao, Mao, and post-Mao periods can be conveyed, in broadest outline, by the set phrases of which Chinese are so fond. Traditional China is associated with *Tian Ren Heyi* [Harmony between the Heavens and Humankind]; this core apothegm yielded in the Mao era to *Ren Ding Sheng Tian* [Man Must Conquer Nature]. In reform-era China, both have been largely supplanted by the popular saying, *Yiqie Xiang Qian Kan* [Look Toward Money in Everything], as commercialization and the market have become predominant. Under Mao, conventional commitments toward mutual accommodation in human relations, and between humans and nature (however ineffective in practice) were publicly abrogated, and a "war" to bend the physical world to human will was launched. This war continued in altered form after the death of Mao, as the market replaced ideological mobilization as a driving force for the transformation of nature. As we will explore further in the final chapter, a vacuum in shared public values left people eager to seek meaning in material consumption and the pursuit of wealth. Although many rapidly developing societies engage in environmentally damaging behavior, the destructive influence of the Mao years on traditional values has facilitated China's plunge into the current phase of materialistic exploitation of nature. This story is not, therefore, merely a cautionary tale of historical significance, but also an exploration of the social and historical roots of behavior patterns that affect environmental health today, not only of China but of the world.

Since this book often stresses public discourse and Maoist philosophy, it must be cautioned that attitudes and values do not translate directly into policy or behavior. Other powerful influences such as geographic conditions, the inertia or activism of institutions, enforcement capabilities, population pressures, and economic incentives also shape the human–nature relationship. Clearly, philosophical traditions espousing harmony with nature have not saved other Asian countries from degrading the environment, even when they are embraced by the state; Asia's polluted and congested cities and exhausted natural resources warn against an easy equation between beliefs and behavior. However, values, attitudes, behaviors, and policy do interact and influence each other over time, even as they are constrained by the institutional structures and cultural frameworks within which they arise; behavior and policies can be indicators of attitudes and values, and vice versa.[12] In essence, this book is about how Maoist values came to dominate and govern the human–nature relationship, and about what happened as a result.

Environmental degradation under Mao can be linked to such problems as population explosion, arable land limits, poverty, misguided policies and mistaken beliefs, and irrational price structures due to state ownership. However, the underlying dynamics of such degradation lay in a nationwide war against nature expressed through a pattern comprised of the four motifs described above: political repression, utopian urgency, uniformity that ignored regional variation and time-tested local practices, and state-sponsored relocations into wilderness areas.

The militarization of Chinese society in a war against foreign and domestic enemies was matched by a militarization against nature that helped promote modernization projects that transformed the landscape and degraded the environment. This militarization included reorganization of society through attacks on traditional culture and the family structure.

Factors that allowed Maoism and political struggle to take root included a traditional culture of patronage and obedience to authority, a coercive organizational apparatus, the aspirations of the Chinese people to end their suffering at the hand of man and nature, and the disproportionately influential decisions and actions of a few individuals, particularly Mao and his loyalists. China's historically strong, centralized imperial system provided a generous entryway for Leninist party organization and its propensity for centrally orchestrated political movements. At the same time, in many parts of China, clan-based village institutions provided the foundation for a complex and personalized range of local and regional power centers that sometimes promoted and sometimes resisted the dictates of a center that was itself often wracked with dissension. A fear of lagging in political fervor worked in concert with belief and hope that Maoist development ambitions would at last raise China out of its poverty and achieve socialist paradise. These were key elements in a complex set of interactions between humans and the natural environment during which Mao-era utopian modernization projects were variously contested, implemented, and distorted by the Chinese leadership and people.

The effort to supplant traditional values and behavior with mass campaigns and Marxism–Leninism–Mao Zedong Thought represented an unprecedented intervention by the state, eclipsing previous attempts to harness nature and accelerating the degradation of China's natural resource base. Environmental degradation under Mao was likewise connected with Mao's growing sense of his own mortality as he weakened physically. His urgent wish to mold China to his revolutionary vision rode roughshod over tradition, politicizing agricultural and industrial activity and exacerbating environmental degradation. China's uneasy foreign relations, and Mao's conviction that China was surrounded by sworn enemies, led him for security reasons to promote imbalanced industrial development in China's remote areas. The ideology of Marxism–Leninism–Mao Zedong Thought, with the conviction that nature was conquerable through military mobilization, attack, and victory, shaped the human–nature relationship, as did a traditional culture that provided the conditions under which such models and leaders could take hold.

It should be noted that revolutionary China's environmental problems resulted primarily from overextraction of resources, impoverishment of the land's productivity through intensive farming schemes, and drastic reshaping of the physical landscape, often beyond the ability of ecosystems to recover or adapt. An exploding population and massive human transfers into wildlife habitat altered fragile ecosystems, while overhunting and overfishing further pressured the nonhuman living world. Intense efforts to increase arable land failed to compensate for declines in agricultural productivity due to other unsustainable activities such as deforestation, excessive well-digging, and reclamation schemes that led eventually to desertification. A 1982 *Beijing Review* article acknowledged, for example, that between 1957 and 1977, China had a net loss of 29 million hectares of farmland despite reclamation of 17 million hectares from "wasteland."[13] According to Qu Geping and Li Jinchang, "From 1957 to 1980, the annual net loss of cultivated land averaged 545,000 ha [hectares]."[14] Moreover, because of time lags between activities that degrade the environment and their consequences, subsequent generations are still paying for the effects of Mao's policies. Ironically, Mao's failure fully to realize his goals of industrialization may have spared his era some of the pollution that has become so severe since the economic reforms. Some have argued that, to the extent that it slowed down economic development, Maoism actually delayed degradation from rapid industrialization.[15] Mao's well-known vision of a Tiananmen Square filled with magnificent smokestacks is surely closer to being realized today than it ever was under his watch. Nonetheless, industrial contamination of air and water became pronounced in many areas under Mao. Party planners urged construction of heavy industry as a focus of development policy during the First Five-year Plan, while during the latter Mao period, industry was promoted in rural areas as a way to eradicate social differences, carry out a policy of regional and national self-reliance, and protect national security.[16]

Mao's death in 1976 and the institution of deep reforms a few years later brought a sharp change in the character of China's environmental problems, as explosive economic growth created what some analysts have called an environmental crisis.[17] Economic growth has supplanted Maoist authoritarianism as a central force in China's growing environmental difficulties. But without taking social conditions and historical background into account, economic growth alone cannot account for the high levels of environmental degradation that have plagued the country in recent years. The reaction to the Mao years has promoted disillusionment, uncertainty over land tenure and other property rights, and problems with corruption and enforcement that have often exacerbated the negative effects of industrialization and deterred investments in sustainable development. The Maoist experience continues to affect contemporary political life through the people's "crisis of belief" in socialism, their mistrust of Communist Party leadership, and their turn toward materialism, short-term profits, and apparent venality in human relations, all of which encourage rapid and unsustainable exploitation of nature. Despite China's public commitment to resolving its environmental problems, the shadow of the Mao era hangs over China's environmental policies, including the Three Gorges Dam on the Yangzi River, which some consider to be a monument to Communist Party hubris.

This effort to explain the dynamics of the environmental experience of the Mao years can be seen as part of an ongoing concern over the primary causes of ecological destruction.[18] Many contend that overpopulation, or exceeding carrying capacity, is the critical factor, whereas others emphasize industrialization and use of fossil fuels, arguing that technology facilitates depletion of natural resources at rates beyond nature's ability to replenish itself.[19] Paul and Ann Ehrlich have combined these elements into a famous IPAT equation: Impact = Population × Affluence × Technology.[20] Green economists emphasize faulty pricing, arguing that destructive practices can be curbed through valuations that include formerly ignored environmental services such as carbon-fixation and pollination, and through the use of accounting methods that credit conservation and debit degradation.[21] Others focus on poverty, desperation, and ignorance in the developing world, or on over-consumption in developed countries. A materialist school, drawing on Marxist insights, focuses on injustices in land and resource distribution and on position in the world economy, arguing that land reform, equal access to resources, and international justice can solve environmental problems. Disagreement over the role of ideas finds some suggesting that an ideology of greed and quick profit associated with capitalism has worked against sustainability.[22] Others contend that Judeo-Christian anthropocentrism has steered humankind toward an ethos of domination of nature, whereas biocentric traditions that respect all life, or ecocentric traditions that see humans as part of complex organic and inorganic systems, point the way toward a more harmonious path.[23]

For those who focus on human relationships, some factors mentioned above may be understood as proximate causes; ultimate causes can be better understood by examining social, political, and cultural issues. This book attempts to describe a contextual ecology that seeks explanations for environmental degradation in a complex interplay of political relationships, social structures, economic and geographic conditions, cultural traditions, linguistic understandings, and historical influences. During the Mao years, the core dynamic, delineated in the following pages, lay in the relationship between two sorts of mistreatment: the misuse and abuse of humans through exploitation and political repression, and the misuse and abuse of nature through misguided policies and interference with local practices.

Environmental case studies, whether historical or contemporary, enhance our understanding of both particular and general ways in which the human–nature relationship has been constructed. Identifying behavioral themes – such as the Mao-era effort to conquer nature through political repression, utopian urgency, dogmatic formalism, and state-sponsored relocations – may foster an inquiry into whether these themes occur in other settings, and if so, whether they can be understood as part of broader patterns. The Mao era is unique, with its specific set of historical factors, ideological influences, utopian dreams, and coercive political structures. However, many of its themes, such as the dangers inherent in constructing the human–nature relation in oppositional terms, shed light on other cases, including China's own imperial past and reform-era present, as well as numerous regions beyond China's borders. The transparency of Mao-era human–nature dynamics thus makes the period valuable both for insight into China's environmental past and present and as a starting point for reflection on environmental degradation in other societies and eras.

An additional preliminary reflection concerns the role of Mao Zedong. For many years, it was believed that the Chinese Communist

Party controlled the Chinese people from above, through intrusion into the totality of every aspect of life and thought. With the opening of China to foreign researchers after Mao's death and the publication of fieldwork and memoirs by Chinese scholars, this view has been discredited. The model of a top-down relationship between center and grass roots has yielded to one characterized by interaction and influence among numerous political actors at many levels, with centers of power and interests throughout the bureaucratic hierarchy. Policies and campaigns were distorted and rewritten in the service of rivalries and alliances, and were often resisted and modified according to local political conditions. While this book often focuses on the critical role of Mao and Maoism, I am not arguing that Mao alone was responsible. True, without Mao, environmental degradation in the era would not have taken the form that it did, but the implementation of his ideas varied according to the locale and the individuals living there. People resisted political repression and irrational policies that threatened their freedoms and livelihoods as best they could, even as they promoted such repression and policies when it furthered personal goals. Even at their weakest, peasants have always had "weapons" of passive resistance.[24] The central Party–state was not the only power center; government bureaucracies at various levels implemented, interpreted, and sometimes distorted policies to further their own interests.[25]

While the picture is more complex than that of a coercive system manipulating a pliant people into utopian or revolutionary insanity, there were powerful limits to resistance under Mao. As the story of the degradation of the environment shows, more often than not, people had little say in their fates or their behavior. The importance of these limits in creating conditions for environmental and social disaster has been suggested by James C. Scott, who has identified four key elements in some of history's greatest disasters of social engineering (including Soviet collectivization and Tanzanian "villagization"): the administrative ordering of society by the state, faith in modernist ideals of progress, an authoritarian regime prepared to use coercion to further the modernist project, and a civil society too weak to resist. Scott argues that while the former two elements can be found in most contemporary societies, the addition of the latter two provides a recipe for catastrophe.[26] In Maoist China, all four elements were present, and they actively contributed to the period's environmental disasters. By the late

1950s, political repression had silenced much dissent; utopian urgency, set in motion by Mao and supported by the desires of local leaders and people, swept away the voices of more realistic leaders and pulled most ordinary Chinese into the Great Leap Forward; dogmatic formalism in the implementation of the model Dazhai Brigade, which transformed a distinctive local landscape of ravines and rocky hillsides into terraces and fields, made it difficult to oppose the imitation of Dazhai's practices despite their frequent lack of relevance to local conditions; finally, state-sponsored relocations during the War Preparation campaign clearly demonstrate the coercive aspects of Mao-era environmental behavior, and the link between the degradation of nature and the Communist Party's willingness to reconfigure society by fiat.

The official success stories of these campaigns hide another narrative. Policies went woefully awry and local people resisted as well as collaborated. Behind the public discourse of battles and conquest, bumper harvests, and victory lie tales of displacement and human suffering, as well as a toll on nature still observable as in-filled lakes, silted rivers, increased flooding, and denuded and eroded hillsides. Stories of repression and coercion, as well as of cooperation and complicity, tell different versions of the truth than do official narratives of revolutionary sacrifice and glory. Although these stories show the strength of the Party's organizational control apparatus, they also reveal how a culture that stressed collectivity, social harmony, hierarchy, and obedience to authority sometimes acquiesced to, or even fostered, violations of the human and natural world.

Finally, it must be noted that although this is a book about the human–nature relationship under an authoritarian socialist system, the environmental records of capitalist and socialist systems indicate that neither form of government is inherently good or bad for the environment. Positive and negative examples of environmental behavior may be found across a range of political systems. Several social welfare states (particularly the Scandinavian countries) have impressive environmental records, while some capitalist countries, including the United States during its "conquest" of the West, have distinguished themselves for destruction of nature.[27] Strong property rights may also protect the right to degrade. While public property ownership, with its frequent link to public indifference and lack of sense of stewardship, is relevant to excessive resource exploitation during the Mao years, even more significant is the widespread disruption of land connections through forced migrations. The "tragedy of the commons"[28] may often have less to do with ownership than with lack of connection, responsibility, and good governance. Particularly important is whether the relationship to the land is perceived to be a lasting one. Elements often *associated with* democracies – such as intellectual freedom, political participation, government accountability and transparency, and local self-governance – are more important to sound environmental behavior than the form of government per se.

Environmentally responsible behavior appears to involve restraint and sacrifice. If human excess has caused the current level and rate of degradation, as some have argued, curtailment of human freedom to despoil and exploit seems to be called for.[29] This viewpoint implies a tension between Western-style political freedoms and environmentalism; Singapore, a politically, if not economically authoritarian state, can point to one of the greenest records in Asia. However, Singapore may be the exception that proves the rule. While coordination and central control indeed may have beneficial effects on the environment, this book aims to show how those tools can become dangerous when they fall into the wrong hands. Clearly, much remains to be learned about what modes and degrees of state involvement and intervention on environmental issues are desirable.

In general, the negative example of the Mao years points toward the importance of political participation, public deliberation and oversight, intellectual freedom and rule of law, respect for regional variation and local wisdom, and land tenure systems that give people an understanding of their responsibility for the land and of a shared future with it. These principles may not in themselves suffice to shift China, or any nation, from the destructive path that the growing global human population is pursuing. Nevertheless, more responsible behavior may be promoted by free speech, participation in land-use decision making that respects the principle of subsidiarity, development of civil protections and enforceable regulatory frameworks, and respect for learning and information. Clearly, the importance of these principles as conditions for environmental sustainability is not limited to China alone.

As this book's final chapter will show, China is increasingly concerned with pollution, water and food supply, deforestation, soil erosion, desertification, biodiversity loss, and a host of other environmental issues, and is attempting to take strong measures to deal with them. The four core themes around which this book is structured have become attenuated or transformed. Political repression has decreased, and there is more room for dissenting views. Urgency is no longer "utopian" – its source lies in the marketplace. Localities have more freedom of self-governance and are less likely to be forced to apply inappropriate development models to their own landscapes. The Chinese people are at far greater liberty to choose their occupations and places of residence. Nonetheless, the elements that contributed to environmental degradation under Mao remain present, if in different guises and to different degrees. They continue to contribute to China's environmental problems even as powerful new factors such as commercialization and the rush to development have emerged to hasten destruction of the natural world.

The issues raised by the Mao years thus remain deeply relevant. China's contemporary environmental problems are still linked to its authoritarian system, recent history, cultural traditions, and national character. The dynamics of the human–nature relationship in China under Mao provide important lessons for China to consider in its struggle toward a more "sustainable" relationship to nature. As we shall see in coming chapters, repression of expression and other intellectual freedoms, urgency to achieve progress, suppression of local traditions, and disruption of connections to the land exacted an enduring toll on the human and natural worlds. Maoist coercive, state-sponsored experiments for social improvement came at a dangerously high price.

"With Many People, Strength is Great"
Ren Duo, Liliang Da

"When a Great Man Emerges, the Yellow River
Will Run Clear"
Shangren Chu, Huanghe Qing

1

POPULATION, DAMS, AND POLITICAL REPRESSION

A Story of Two Environmental Disasters and the
Scientists Who Tried to Avert Them

Our story begins not in the physical world but in the political one – with a struggle among human beings. In the summer of 1957, just a few years after the 1949 Communist victory, hundreds of thousands of China's most distinguished scholars and scientists were criticized, harshly punished, ostracized, and silenced in an "Anti-rightist movement." By destroying those who sought simply to perform the Chinese intellectual's traditional duty to speak out in order to assist the country's leaders to govern better, China deprived itself of authoritative voices that might have cautioned against foolhardy schemes that ultimately destroyed the natural environment. People from many levels of society contributed to the events that will be described in the coming pages. However, as we shall see, Mao played a leading role in launching the Anti-rightist movement, as he did in numerous subsequent decisions that affected China's environment for the worse. His mistrust of intellectuals and reluctance to listen to differing opinions were essential preconditions for his efforts to transform China along lines that ignored the laws of natural science. The stories of any of hundreds of individuals might have illustrated the impact of the Anti-rightist movement on China's environment, but we focus on two senior intellectuals, economist Ma Yinchu and hydro-engineer Huang Wanli. Their "bitter love" of their country was typical of a generation whose patriotism caused them endless suffering and whose repression changed China's relationship with the natural world in important ways.[1]

On July 1, 1957, Beijing University president Ma Yinchu presented a report entitled "New Demography" [*Xin renkoulun*] to the National People's Congress. On July 5, the report was published in its entirety in the *People's Daily*. The product of several years of careful analysis of the

1953 census, the essay warned that China's rapidly growing population was jeopardizing the country's development.

Although Ma was motivated by concern for his country, his ideas were dangerously provocative in the prevailing political climate. Population control was associated with the English "reactionary," Reverend Thomas Robert Malthus (1766–1834). Malthus' rejection of England's social welfare laws and his apparent approval of the "positive checks" of war and famine on the working-class population made him an anathema in China.[2] The Chinese leadership was well aware that Soviet theorists, following Marx and Engels, had condemned Malthus as an apologist for the bourgeoisie, especially for using demographic analysis to explain away the capitalist exploitation at the root of working-class misery.[3] As we shall see, Mao himself forcefully argued that Malthus had been proven wrong in pointing to population rather than the capitalist political system as an explanation for the people's suffering.[4]

Ma Yinchu considered himself a Marxist, and his ideas differed significantly from those of Malthus. But within months of his July 1 report, national newspapers attacked him and his ideas. The following winter, tens of thousands of posters denouncing him as a dangerous Malthusian appeared on the walls of Beijing University. Pressure mounted, and in March 1960, he was forced to resign his university presidency; his numerous academic and government posts were gradually stripped away. For twenty years, from January 1960, when a final article protesting his innocence was published and then repudiated in the press, until his rehabilitation twenty years later at the remarkable age of 98, by which time population control had become a national priority, he was utterly silenced, unable to lecture or publish. Although Premier Zhou Enlai's intervention saved him from being formally labeled and stigmatized as a rightist, he remained banned from his university offices and from public life.[5]

The silencing of Ma Yinchu was one of the great mistakes of the Mao years. Had Ma continued to warn of the dangers of unchecked population growth, China might have engaged in wide public debate about the issue. The country might have adopted vigorous family planning programs in time to head off the population crisis. At the very least, the repression of Ma Yinchu robbed the country of its best and most thoughtful demographer. There was little chance that population issues could be openly discussed as long as Ma's ideas remained ideological heresy.

Another great Chinese intellectual, hydraulic engineer Huang Wanli, was also silenced during the Anti-rightist movement. Like Ma Yinchu, he had been educated in premier universities in the United States and had chosen to return to China to serve his country. When, in the early 1950s, China began to plan major flood control and hydro-electric projects under the tutelage of Soviet engineers, he submitted written opinions to the planning groups, expressing his opposition to the construction of the Sanmenxia [Three Gate Gorge] dam on the main stream of the Yellow River.[6] He foresaw correctly that siltation would choke the dam's mechanisms and cause widespread environmental damage and human suffering. Many years of his own practical research conducted on the Yellow and other major rivers had shaped his conviction that damming the main streams of large waterways ran contrary to the laws of nature.

For his opposition to the dam, Huang Wanli was labeled a rightist. His professional life was officially terminated. He was subjected to mass criticism meetings and made to conduct public self-examinations; then he was sent to a construction site to do hard labor. The dam was built, resettling 403,800 people and flooding 856,000 *mu* of land [one *mu* is about one-sixth of an acre].[7] The dam's mechanisms quickly silted up as Huang had predicted, and the resultant backup of silt caused enormous human hardship from flooding, salinization and alkalinization, ecosystem damage, and financial loss; today the dam is barely viable either for power generation or flood control. During Huang Wanli's years of enforced public silence, the unpublished research in which he persisted reaffirmed his views concerning the dangers of building large dams on major rivers, including the Three Gorges Dam on the Yangzi River. Knowledgeable Chinese admire Huang Wanli enormously, pointing out that his repression silenced an outstandingly courageous engineer whose integrity and depth of knowledge could have served China well.[8]

Huang Wanli fought the Sanmenxia Dam at around the same time that Ma Yinchu was speaking out about population; indeed, in an interesting historical convergence, one of Huang's "crimes" was his complaint that Ma's warnings on population were going unheeded. Like

Ma, Huang was silenced for challenging the prevailing Soviet and Maoist orthodoxy. And like Ma, he remained defiantly convinced of the integrity of his views, continuing to conduct scholarly research on his own even when there was no hope of publishing it. Both Ma Yinchu and Huang Wanli were rehabilitated as very old men, the political clouds over their names cleared away, and their reputations restored with fanfare and honors. But only in their longevity and prominence are Ma and Huang different from thousands of others who dared speak out in an era in which the only acceptable truth was Marxism–Leninism–Mao Zedong Thought. How the Maoist system treated these highly principled scholars is representative of the Mao era's broad repression of intellectuals. Other demographers were persecuted because they worried about China's growing population, and other engineers met their political demise because they fought against big dams.[9] Hundreds of thousands of less well-known thinkers, leaders, and ordinary Chinese were silenced for daring to disagree with Maoist orthodoxy, or thought better of airing their views when more prominent thinkers came under attack. In all, more than half a million outspoken individuals were labeled rightists for voicing their views.[10]

In Maoist China, lack of freedom of speech and of intellectual inquiry had grave consequences for the human relationship with nature. Expert views actively proffered to China's leadership were ignored or overruled. Had the opinions of just these two dedicated intellectuals been heeded, population would have become a social policy issue much earlier and the Sanmenxia would not have been built; but because these views were ignored, an existing problem was exacerbated and a new one was created. Through a more detailed examination of the ideas and lives of Ma and Huang, and of the historical context in which they sought to pursue their work, we may gain a deeper understanding of the connection between political repression and environmental degradation. If the suppression of two intellectuals had such grave consequences, it is easy to infer the broader consequences of the silencing of hundreds of thousands of China's best minds. These two men's stories also shed light on two of the greatest threats to the environment, overpopulation and misguided dam projects. Since Ma and Huang were first attacked during the early years of New China, their personal histories provide an appropriate beginning to the larger chronology of environmental degradation under Mao.

POSTREVOLUTION POLICY TOWARD INTELLECTUALS

At the outset of the Chinese Communist revolution, it was unclear how the new regime would treat intellectuals and how much freedom of speech would be permitted. Many educated Chinese had supported the revolution, some seeing great hope for China in communism, while others were so disillusioned with Guomindang corruption and lack of commitment to the war against Japan that they supported the Communists simply because they believed they could be no worse.[11] But the new regime came to power without a clear policy toward the elite groups on whose support had relied. There were theoretical disagreements, for example, over whether intellectuals should be considered members of the proletariat or the bourgeoisie, a class distinction that was critical to their fates under the new regime.[12] In the early years after the revolution, the Party tried to reassure supporters who were not obviously workers or poor or lower-middle peasants that the revolution would work with them. They held meetings to that effect, not only with intellectuals but also with wealthy capitalists and the middle class. So convincing were these overtures that many educated Chinese returned from overseas to help build New China. It became apparent soon enough, however, that the "United Front" was primarily a tactical invention intended to help the Communists consolidate power; intellectuals, particularly those with overseas connections, were viewed with suspicion, and by the time of the Cultural Revolution they were considered the "stinking ninth category," or the lowest of the low.

The murky status of intellectuals was paralleled by uncertainty over the role of free speech in the new society. Since Confucian times, Chinese intellectuals had understood their role in society as that of friendly critics, helping to inform paternalistic leaders about abuses and suffering at the grass roots, and enduring suffering and exile when their views were not heeded. By the Communists' years in their Yanan base, periodic repression of writers, artists, and other intellectuals as a prelude for political struggle had been established as a pattern. In 1951, however, it seemed briefly as if an era of free speech had begun: Vice-chairman Liu Shaoqi called for consolidation of a New People's Democracy as the main task of the new regime. Democratic centralism, with popular elections held at various levels of government, would provide a structure for the new government, and free discussion was to direct policy formulation.[13]

Soon enough, the newly close relationship between China and its Soviet "elder brother" helped put an end to China's foray toward intellectual freedom. The victorious Chinese leaders had turned reluctantly to the Soviet Union for guidance and aid, for "New China" needed economic support and a model for its development and had nowhere else to turn. The Chinese Communist Party entrusted Soviet leadership with considerable ideological authority because the Comintern had carried out the world's first successful socialist revolution, achieving industrialization of a backward country and creating a powerful state. Soviet influence helped to shift China away from the early vision of achieving people's democracy. At the Party's second organizational work conference in September–October 1953, Chairman Mao made it clear that the national goal of promoting people's democracy would be dropped in favor of achieving socialism, and then communism. The short-lived era of new democracy thus yielded to socialist transformation. Of course, Mao would soon reject the Soviet timetable as too conservative for China, and would impatiently launch China on its own urgent path to development.

Soviet dogma had a deeply constraining effect on Chinese intellectual life, determining which topics could be studied and which schools of thought were considered acceptable; the natural sciences were no exception. For example, China adopted Soviet adherence to the ideas of the geneticist Trofim Lysenko, who believed that acquired characteristics could be transmitted to offspring; these notions made a mockery of Chinese agricultural research.[14] In 1954, breeding expert Zhuang Qiaosheng's work on resistance to wheat stem corrosion was discredited, and in 1956, CalTech-trained geneticist Bao Wenkui's laboratory fields, which contained the results of years of work on black wheat genetics, were hoed up. In 1955, respected botanist Hu Xiansu criticized Lysenko in an essay in *Zhiwu fenleixue jianbian* [Plant Taxonomy Digest]; as a result, he was made a target of political criticism.[15] Only after Lysenko's ideas were rejected in the USSR after Stalin's death in 1953 could Chinese geneticists once again discuss the ideas of Gregor Mendel and Thomas Morgan.

A respite from this rigidity, one with consequences for the intellectual and artistic life of all China, arrived with the 1956–57 Hundred Flowers movement. As early as autumn 1955, Mao had expressed his surprising opposition to having a single Party history text.[16] Mao began to enjoin the Party to guard itself against excessive "leftism" as well as the usual threats from the right. Dogmatism, formalism, and orthodoxy were to be discouraged. The slogan, "Let a Hundred Flowers Bloom," which Mao had raised in connection with artistic creativity in 1951, was increasingly mentioned in connection with a second slogan about academic debate, "Let a Hundred Schools of Thought Contend." By spring 1956, the linked slogans were being widely disseminated. Then in February 1957, Mao made his famous speech to the State Council, "On the Correct Handling of Contradictions among the People," seemingly heralding an end to class struggle by defining most conflicts as "internal" tensions that could be resolved. In the more relaxed climate, free expression flourished as it had not since the founding of New China. Scholarly debate enjoyed a renaissance, and the literature and arts of the Hundred Flowers movement proved distinctively freer than what had preceded it.[17]

Just months later, however, on June 1 and 3, *People's Daily* editorials proclaimed a campaign to repel the attacks of "bourgeois rightists." It remains unclear whether Mao was taken by surprise by the vehemence of the spring debates and felt he had to clamp down for fear of confronting a disturbance like those of the previous year in Poland and Hungary, or whether the Hundred Flowers movement was a deliberate deception, as many victims and observers of the subsequent crackdown tend to believe. Former "rightist" journalist Liu Binyan, for example, has called the Anti-rightist movement "a trap laid for a million."[18] The popular perception that it was a trap may be more significant than the reality. It is likely that in launching the Hundred Flowers movement, the Party misjudged the political situation and later tried to save face by claiming it was a successful effort to ferret out rightists. In any event, the pillorying that was conducted with varying intensity for the next few years silenced tens of thousands of patriotic scientists, engineers, journalists, intellectuals, and ordinary people who might have encouraged China's leaders to be concerned about the environment. It also forced thousands more to become "red experts" afraid to mouth anything but what the Party wanted to hear. Potentially unruly thinkers were disciplined and brought into line to become foot-soldiers in Mao's war against nature, even when they saw clearly that his policies violated nature's own principles.

DEMOGRAPHER MA YINCHU

The relationship between human population numbers and degradation of the nonhuman world is indirect. More proximate causes of despoliation and contamination of nature include poor government policy, inequality in resource distribution, lack of certainty over land tenure, price subsidies, desperation born of poverty, and deep culture and tradition. Most leading Chinese environmentalists, however, view overpopulation as by far the most significant cause of the destruction of China's environment. (Those writing from within China must, for political reasons, avoid explicitly blaming the Communist Party for environmental problems.) Qu Geping, widely known as the father of Chinese environmentalism, articulates the fundamental population–degradation connection in his classic analysis (written with Li Jinchang), *Population and Environment in China*: "Population control and environmental protection are two sides of the same coin."[19] Studying the environmental impact of overpopulation as the root cause of other problems, Qu traces the population explosion to the Mao years and argues that population expansion leads, in an endless feedback loop, to increased economic activity, environmental degradation, "poor awareness," and continued population growth. Similarly, Ma Yinchu biographer Zhang Chunyuan writes as follows about the connection:

> Because of population expansion, it was necessary to increase the area of arable land, and, therefore, to conduct land reclamation, cut down forests and open wastelands, destroying the ecology's natural balance.[20]

Environmental activist Dai Qing agrees that the effect of overpopulation on China's environment has been profound:

> The policy of "larger population, greater labor force, and increased working morale" [*Ren Duo, Liliang Da, Reqi Gao*] led to the doubling of the Chinese population ... in 30 years. But it also led to the destruction of forests to make room for farmland to encourage "self-reliance."[21]

In the year 2000, as China struggled to curb its population with often-drastic measures, Chinese emphasis on the link remained clear: on a country wall in Jiangsu province, near Ma Yinchu's hometown of

Shengzhou, a slogan read: "Protect the Environment, Practice Family Planning."

There are several reasons for China's unwillingness to see population as a growing problem in the years immediately following the revolution: the straitjacket imposed by China's admiration of the USSR, then involved in postwar recovery; Chinese tradition; and limited world awareness of population issues. Each of these factors provides some context for the repression of Ma Yinchu. Nevertheless, ultimate responsibility for the explosion of China's population after the revolution must rest with Mao Zedong, whose belief in the raw power of unleashed labor remained constant through the years of his leadership and whose intervention at critical moments ensured that those who doubted the wisdom of unfettered population growth would be silenced.

The fundamental ideological restriction that Soviet orthodoxy imposed on demographic research was the Marxist precept that, by definition, there could be no population problem under socialism. By its very nature, socialism would release the forces of production so that all people would be provided for. Zhang Chunyuan writes:

[The question] whether or not a population problem would appear in socialism first clearly appeared in the Soviet theoretical world. They thought, "The socialist system guarantees that labor power be fully employed. Therefore, there is no, and can be no, surplus population. The population quickly increases, people's living standard rises, disease and death rates decrease, and at the same time labor power is appropriately and fully used. That is the essence of socialism."[22]

Articles from the early 1950s reflect the common belief in the positive power of greater population. "The more people there are, the earlier we can realize humanity's greatest ideal – communism." "Under socialism, there is no need to fear that population will increase at a rapid rate, but rather [the task is] to create advantageous conditions for the rapid increase in population."[23] Soviet influence on population issues was not limited to the ideological tenet that socialist countries could not experience population problems; the Soviet Union had suffered huge casualties in World War II from battle and starvation, and was desperately trying to restore lost numbers through financial and political rewards for "Mother Heroes." China came close to imitating this policy, deciding instead to award congratulatory flags to women with large families which read, "People will flourish, reap abundant grain" [*Ren ding xingwang, wu gu feng deng*].[24]

China's traditional clan-based social structure, in which wealth was often based on numbers, provided another powerful force for continued high fertility rates. "Four generations under one roof [equals] five generations of prosperity" [*Sishi tongtang, wushi qichang*], went the traditional aphorism.[25] High birth rates are key to survival in most developing countries because of high infant mortality rates and the dependency on children in old age, but the Confucian emphasis on the extended family or clan as the building block of social order made this tendency particularly strong in China. The practice of ancestor worship and valuation of many sons reflected deeply entrenched beliefs. Any discussion of population control thus conflicted with traditional values that endured despite the official postrevolutionary rejection of Confucianism and Maoist efforts to replace the traditional family with the Communist state.

Limited world awareness of the perils of overpopulation was one more factor contributing to contemporary attitudes. That China was a land of "great size, rich resources, and many people" [*di da, wu bo, ren duo*] was a source of national pride.[26] China's population had been expanding quickly since the early eighteenth century. (For several centuries prior it had risen and fallen cyclically but was relatively stable at around 150 million.) From around 1700 to 1850, the population virtually tripled due to the introduction of high-yield crops, the increase in the rate of reclamation of land for grain fields, and the prevalence of peace.[27] It continued thereafter to grow. In the 1940s, however, during the Anti-Japanese and civil wars, death rates as well as birth rates were high, making it unlikely that demographers would consider population a potential problem. Only with the cessation of fighting in 1949 did death rates go down, again spurring overall population growth.[28] In the mid-1950s, it was not yet apparent to most observers that China's population was growing at an alarming rate.

While all of these factors constrained discussion of population issues, the decisive deterrent was Mao's view of people as a great resource. Mao's tendency to value human numbers is not surprising coming from a military leader who grasped their importance in fighting technologically superior foes. Experience taught Mao that with proper leadership, the masses could overcome even the better-armed Guomindang and Japanese; a large population was understood as a form of military capital.[29] Mao's ideas on population were informed by military logic and were often expressed through military metaphors. His conviction about the value of having many people was made clear, for example, at the dawn of New China, in his 1949 speech, "On the Bankruptcy of the Idealist Conception of History":

> It is a very good thing that China has a big population. Even if China's population multiplies many times, she is fully capable of finding a solution; the solution is production. The absurd argument of bourgeois Western economists like Malthus that increases in food cannot keep up with increases in population was not only long ago thoroughly refuted in theory by Marxists, but has also been completely exploded by the realities in the Soviet Union and the liberated areas of China after their revolutions ... [r]evolution plus production can solve the problem of feeding the population...
>
> Of all things in the world, people are the most precious. Under the leadership of the Communist Party, as long as there are people, every kind of miracle can be performed.[30]

These sentiments were distilled into a five-character slogan, *Ren Duo, Liliang Da* [With Many People, Strength is Great]. Although it is unclear whether Mao used this phrase himself, many Chinese attribute it to him and see it as the essence of his views on the value of a large population. Mao's military attitude toward population was expressed on another occasion in which, using one of his surprising metaphors, he compared women with aircraft carriers: "Because they will have children after getting married, mothers will split off three or two, or even as many as ten or eight of them, much the same as an aircraft carrier splits off airplanes."[31]

Mao thus saw China's population as a source of military strength and survival on the world stage. He boasted to Nehru in 1954 that although America had nuclear weapons, China had 600 million people and 9,600,000 square kilometers of land. Even with the bomb, he claimed, America would be unable to wipe out China.[32] During a visit to

Moscow in November 1957, Moscow, Mao shocked Soviet Premier Nikita Khrushchev with his casual calculations about human life:

> We shouldn't be afraid of atomic missiles. No matter what kind of war breaks out – conventional or thermonuclear – we'll win. As for China, if the imperialists unleash war on us, we may lose more than three hundred million people. So what? War is war. The years will pass and we'll get to work producing more babies than ever before.[33]

As Khrushchev recalled the meeting, of all the leaders present only Mao seemed not to be seeking ways to avoid war. Mao's physician Li Zhisui remembered Mao's indifference to human life with revulsion:

> I did not immediately understand, because it was so hard to accept, how willing Mao was to sacrifice his own citizens in order to achieve his goals... It was not until the Great Leap Forward, when millions of Chinese began dying during the famine, that I became fully aware of how much Mao resembled the ruthless emperors he so admired. Mao knew that people were dying by the millions. He did not care.[34]

In the context of Mao's faith in numbers, there was little support in the early years after the revolution for any sort of family planning. Journalist Liu Binyan recalled this period as a great challenge for himself and his wife:

> Neither of us wanted to have a baby yet, but contraception was discouraged and abortion forbidden by government policy. By 1952, contraceptive devices had disappeared from the market. I remember a man who worked at the Youth League Central and whose wife kept on having children until she was completely exhausted. She had eleven, and for every new birth she received a stipend. Mao Zedong had said that socialism was not threatened by population growth, and so women having large families were rewarded.[35]

China's first national census under the new government was undertaken in 1953 as part of the First Five-year Plan. While the resultant count may not be exact, there is general agreement that in 1953 the population of Greater China stood at more than 600 million, including Chinese in Taiwan and overseas. The official figure of 583 million for China proper was greater than expected and was greeted with jubilation.[36] Only later did anxiety over the numbers begin to develop.[37] By 1964, approximately 700 million people crowded mainland China proper; by 1969, the number was more than 800 million.[38] During the early years after the revolution, then, China already had a population well in excess of the 500 million that may have been the maximum sustainable population for China at a high living standard.[39]

A former census official's recollections shed light on Mao's role in shaping postrevolutionary attitudes toward population:

> The 1953 census was intended to establish a basis for selecting representatives to the National People's Congress and for drafting the First Five-year Plan. The 600 million figure was much higher than anyone expected. We had been using a Guomindang figure of 475 million that dated to the 1930s. Even Chairman Mao had been using this figure. So the new number was a big shock. Most people thought it was good, though, because the war was over, and the government was talking about "mother heroes." If you had more children, you got more ration coupons. Only a small number, including Ma Yinchu, thought about the implications.
>
> Chairman Mao has direct responsibility for the population problem. As Party Chairman, policy depended on him. When he said, "With Many People, Strength is Great," that was the last word on the subject. If he had adopted the opinions of intellectuals like Ma Yinchu, the population wouldn't have grown so, and the environment wouldn't have been so damaged. If not for him, we wouldn't have so many people.
>
> When our 1964 census revealed a figure of 694 million people on the mainland and 720 million including overseas Chinese, Mao suppressed our findings. He refused to believe the figure, and we were not permitted to publish it. We were furious that our hard work had been for nothing.

During the Hundred Flowers movement, Mao wavered briefly in his conviction concerning the value of unlimited numbers of people, thereby creating a climate in which population issues could be discussed freely. Journalist Liu Binyan recalled that Mao remarked that there were getting to be so many people that it would soon be necessary to stand in line to take a walk. "I wrote an article about the crush of people I encountered when my wife and I took our daughter to the park," Liu told me. "I couldn't have published the article unless Mao had made that comment."

Demographers were briefly able to debate a number of subjects, including whether to raise the marriage age stipulated in the 1950 Marriage Law (18 for women and 20 for men).[40] A tentative family planning campaign began in 1956, advocating birth control and delayed marriage. In 1957, abortion and sterilization were legalized, and between 1955 and 1958, contraceptives were produced and distributed. Some contraceptives were imported from Japan, and four condom-manufacturing plants were built,[41] although the products were of inferior quality and sufficient for only a small percentage of childbearing-age couples.[42] According to the 1956–57 National Agricultural Development Plan, "except in the areas of the minority nationalities, birth control [should be] publicized and promoted in all densely populated places; planned childbearing [should] be encouraged."[43]

However, the attacks on Ma Yinchu during the Anti-rightist movement quelled discussion of population issues, and with the Great Leap Forward in the spring of 1958, family planning was virtually abandoned. Mao held that the only real limitation on the Leap was lack of manpower and that mass mobilization of labor would solve the problem of slow growth. In May 1958, he stated that population levels would stabilize of their own accord:

> We are not afraid of a population of 800 million or one billion. American reporters say that, after 100 years, the Chinese population will constitute 50 percent of the world population. By that time, our cultural level will be high. When all the people are college educated, they will naturally practice birth control.[44]

The slogan, "With Many People, Strength is Great" dominated public views of the population issue. Judith Banister writes, "Press and radio reports stopped encouraging birth control and began talking about the need for more people in China to carry out the labor-intensive work of development."[45] Lack of freedom of speech, debate, and publication meant that few dared protest when the tentative birth control program was swept away in the Leap. Few arguments were heard against the notion that only insufficient labor power was holding back China's development.

In subsequent years, even after the great famine shook the faith that socialism would automatically provide for all, and even after family planning programs were again implemented, Mao's emphasis on labor power continued as an imperative of Chinese political life. The notion that mass mobilization of manual labor could compensate for China's lack of advanced technology is reflected in Mao's essay, "The Foolish Old Man Who Removed the Mountains," which became required memorization for the whole country. The essay inspired numerous foolhardy projects to transform nature, discussed in subsequent chapters. Still, the great famine of the Three Hard Years (1959–61) forced leaders to reevaluate the question of whether food production could keep up with population growth, and a second family planning drive lasting from early 1962 to mid-1966 promoted later marriage.[46] Mao hinted at another change in his attitude toward population in his

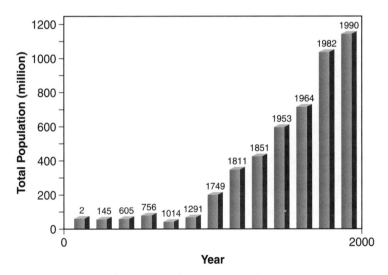

Figure 1.1. China's population increase.

1964 "Spring Festival Talk": "It is not certain we shall have a population of 720 million in 1965... There will be 800 million in 1970? This is serious."[47] The first national Family Planning Office was formed that year,[48] but family planning efforts were again thrown into disarray in 1966 with the chaos of the Cultural Revolution. Only with a new family planning campaign that began in 1971 was fertility finally substantially reduced, to 2.4 children per family.[49] By that year, the population was already more than 50 percent larger than it had been in 1949.[50]

Belatedly, the Party introduced a series of additional measures to control China's population growth. The legal age for marriage was raised to the mid-twenties, with regional variations, with the Fourth Five-year Plan (1971–75). The Family Planning Commission became part of the State Council in July 1973. A *wan xi shao,* or "later, sparser, fewer" campaign, meaning later marriage, more time between births, and fewer births, was launched in December of that year.[51] In January 1979, a draconian one-child family policy, born of urgency and desperation, was introduced.

The Life of Ma Yinchu

Ma Yinchu was born on June 24, 1882 in Zhejiang province, in the charming village of Pukou near the county seat of Shengxian (today's Shengzhou City). Today, Shengzhou is only a four-hour bus ride from Shanghai, but it was in Ma's youth a remote place accessible only by boat. Ma Yinchu was the fifth child of the owner of a small distillery that produced fermented rice liquor similar to the famous Shaoxing spirits.[52] His father wanted him to carry on the family business, but he wanted to study; the resulting rift between him and his father never healed, although he remained close to his mother and returned frequently to his home village to see her even after he attained great status and held heavy public responsibilities. Today, its traditional architecture little changed, Pukou remains populated by distant relatives and former neighbors who remember Ma Yinchu with fond admiration for his plain lifestyle and abiding concern for them. His former lane has been renamed "Famous Man Street," and his birth home, an ancient two-storey wooden structure surrounding a courtyard which still holds a few ceramic fermentation jars, is being renovated as a museum.

From such humble beginnings emerged a young man of fierce commitment to scholarship. At 16, Ma Yinchu attended middle school in Shanghai, at the Yuying Shuguan. Although his father cut him off financially, he found a way to study mining and metallurgy at Tianjin's Beiyang University. In 1907, the imperial government sponsored him to study economics at Yale University, where he obtained his M.A. before continuing to Columbia University for his doctorate. He obtained a joint degree in economics and philosophy with a dissertation on New York City finances. Columbia sought to retain him on its faculty, but in 1916, he chose to return to China.

In war-torn China, Ma Yinchu led a peripatetic life typical for public intellectuals of the era. When Beijing University President Cai Yuanpei hired him, he became chairman of the Economics Department. He was also banking advisor to his home province of Zhejiang. In 1928, he moved to Nanjing to become chairman of the Economics and Finance Committees of Chiang Kai-shek's government. When the Japanese invaded in 1937, he fled inland with the Guomindang to Chongqing, where he taught in the Chongqing University Economics Department and became president of the Commerce Institute. During this period, he met Zhou Enlai, a fellow countryman from Shaoxing, and grew close to the Communist Party. Ma became a critic of Guomindang corruption, and Chiang Kai-shek eventually had him arrested. On December 6, 1940, he was incarcerated in the notorious Xifeng concentration camp in Guizhou; he was later moved to Shangrao camp in Jiangxi. By his release on August 20, 1942, he had been in prison more than a year and eight months. He remained on probation in Chongqing until he was freed in 1945, with the help of Zhou Enlai and some American friends. After he was wounded in a military clash between the Guomindang and the Communists in February 1946, he began openly to call for the overthrow of the Guomindang. In April, he moved to Shanghai to teach, and in 1948 the Communist Party sent him briefly to Hong Kong.

After 1949, he held numerous positions in service to his country. In June 1951, he was named president of Beijing University, the first appointment to the position after the Communist victory. He also became the East China Administrative Committee vice-chair, Central People's Government Finance Committee vice-director, Zhejiang University president, Chinese Academy of Sciences Philosophy and

Social Science Division committee member, and the Chinese Demographers' Association honorary chair. He was a frequent member of the Standing Committee of the National People's Congress, and it was in this capacity that he presented his controversial 1957 report.

Those who were students at Beijing University in the early 1950s recall their president with great warmth. One such student was a physicist who entered Beijing University in the first class enrolled after the revolution; later she was herself labeled a rightist for advocating democracy, and she now lives in exile in the United States. She remembers Ma as an approachable old man who had great integrity. He could often be seen walking alone on campus in the days before leaders rode around in chauffeured cars. Short and stocky, with a red face and close-cropped hair, he had a friendly response for all who said hello. At the New Year, Ma warmly greeted the auditorium of students and teachers and invited them to begin the dance. It felt as if all Beijing University, were one family. The physicist recalled that Ma never spoke in clichés or put on airs; he seemed genuine in all aspects of his work. He arranged for prominent speakers, such as theoretician Yu Guangyuan, to speak on campus on Saturday afternoons, and even had plans to host his old friend Zhou Enlai. These lectures were never dull, since Ma was so well respected that he could secure almost anyone he liked. When the initial presentations were over, Ma always led the questions in such a way as to inspire debate. Beijing University was a happy place in those days, the physicist said, when student leaders were respected, not seen as Party spies, and intellectuals were considered valuable allies in developing New China.

A memoir of the history of Beijing University echoes this former student's recollections of the New Year celebrations, and points out that Ma's plain speaking in an age of slogans was in itself a sort of resistance to the dogmatism of the times:

His face was flushed, sometimes because of high spirits, sometimes because he was a little tipsy... It was all small talk, but it expressed a kind of freedom... At the time, slogans were rampant, but the college president's speech had very few political expressions; indeed, there was a kind of rare purity and freshness to it, as if the use of ordinary speech permitted common humanity to spill out. In those days, slogans were piled to the skies, and revolutionary redness was the color of China everywhere, so that when one could hear, from a podium, at a gathering of 10,000 people, those ordinary feelings and ordinary words, it meant that Beijing University was a place of freedom and democracy. In that uncompromising time, this showed a determined holding of one's ground ... that was even a wordless defiance of the current fashion.[53]

By the time he wrote *New Demography* in the mid-1950s, Ma Yinchu was at the professional peak of a life that had already spanned nearly three-quarters of a century. He enjoyed enormous prestige in academics and government, as well as the respect and affection of those whose daily lives he touched. But, according to a former neighbor interviewed in Pukou, Ma was becoming deeply worried about China's population growth. During a 1953 visit home to see his mother, he noticed the huge increase in the number of babies and toddlers in the village. An impoverished nephew named Ma Benna began borrowing money to support his growing brood, and Ma wrote him long letters urging him to stop having so many babies. Eventually, the nephew and his wife had eleven children. Ma's concern about demographic issues thus stemmed from these personal experiences as well as from scholarly analysis.

Ma greeted news of the Hundred Flowers movement with elation, seeing it as an opportunity to set forth to the public his ideas on population: "So many questions that we did not dare to discuss and could not discuss, now can be asked. I want to put the population question before you, in this great flowering springtime, so that everyone has a chance to study and discuss it."[54] In 1957, he wrote that he had waited for the right moment to present *New Demography:*

In 1955 ... I drafted a speech concerning the population question ... and planned to deliver it at the 1955 session of the National People's Congress... There were people who asserted that my statements were the same as Malthus'. There were also people who asserted that, though my phraseology differed from that of Malthus, the essence of my thought was of the same persuasion. ... I therefore withdrew the draft of the speech and waited quietly for the time to ripen enough for its presentation to the whole Congress.[55]

In the short-lived openness of the first period of population control, Ma had the courage to say what others were thinking but dared not say. According to Ma biographer Zhang Chunyuan, whether to confront the population question was "a test for every economist and sociologist." But Ma was unafraid to take on Mao and Soviet orthodoxy, and he dealt squarely with the question in his report: "What was new about *New Demography* was that it refuted the dogmatic point of view that in socialist societies no population problem exists."[56]

Ma's ideas gained the attention of the highest leaders, who had by then, as we have seen, begun to pay attention to family planning. In March 1957 a meeting of the State Council was convened in the inner sanctum of Zhongnanhai, with Mao Zedong, Liu Shaoqi, Zhou Enlai, and other top Party officials in attendance. Mao is said to have echoed the generally positive response to Ma's arguments for population control, commenting, "Whether population should be planned can certainly be researched and investigated. Ma Yinchu has spoken very well today."[57] Encouraged, Ma revised and expanded his draft for presentation to the July 1, 1957 Fourth Plenary Session of the First National People's Congress.

Ma's thesis was that a large population and high population growth rates would inevitably slow down China's development.[58] He advocated frequent census-taking, family planning campaigns, education for population control, later marriage, rewards for small families, administrative measures to discourage big families, and promotion of contraceptive use.[59] He saw population control as a means of alleviating pressure on limited food and raw materials and improving the Chinese people's lives. He warned of the negative impact of population on capital accumulation, advocating population growth only in accordance with planned development. His emphasis on contraception as the most scientific approach to population control differed sharply from Malthus' views, as Malthus opposed birth control on grounds that it would encourage indolence and contravene God's plan.[60] Interestingly, Ma strongly opposed abortion: "Most important is to broadly propagandize birth control, and avoid abortion at all costs."[61] Also interestingly, and presciently, in light of subsequent destructive land reclamation projects (to be discussed in later chapters), he rejected claims that China's food pressures could be solved by increasing arable land. He argued that much land not already in use as farmland was mountainous, dry, or occupied by minority groups who had been using it for grazing land for generations – land which "fundamentally cannot be reclaimed."[62]

In that era, however, any argument for population control was perceived as a form of Malthusianism. As became clearer as the Anti-rightist movement unfolded, no debate would be permitted on an issue that was fundamentally understood as black and white. Malthusians advocated population control, Marxists advocated population growth; everything was reduced to this simple formulation. As one scientist recalled in an interview, even middle school students were taught that Malthus was a reactionary for arguing that there was a contradiction between production and population. This contradiction was to be found only in capitalism, not socialism. In raising the specter of population problems in revolutionary China during the apparent freedom of the Hundred Flowers movement, Ma Yinchu violated a fundamental principle of socialist dogma. But what sealed his fate was disagreeing with Mao, whose enthusiasm for human capital rarely faltered. Under the conditions of the time, explains Zhang Chunyuan, "anyone who said there could be a surplus population under socialism became an enemy of Marxism."[63] Soon enough, Ma was accused of being "a dangerous Malthusian" and "a lifelong opponent of the Party, socialism, and Marxism-Leninism."[64]

On October 14, 1957, the *People's Daily* published a criticism which "names without naming" [*meiyou dianming de dianming*]:

> Someone has borrowed the population question to create a political conspiracy; [the person] speaks nominally of the population question, [and] the birth control question, but this is not a question of scholarship, it is in fact a question of genuine class struggle, a question of serious political struggle.[65]

As the Anti-rightist movement intensified, only the intervention of Zhou Enlai, who had supported China's early birth control program and had known Ma since the Chongqing years, saved Ma from being given the formal "rightist" label.

In 1958, the first issue of the Party theoretical journal, *Red Flag*, published Mao's April 1957 speech, "Introduction to a Cooperative" [Jieshao yige hezuoshe]. In this speech, Mao mentioned China's growing population: "Aside from the leadership of the Communist Party, a population of 600 million people is the decisive factor: with many people, there is much debate, heat is high, and enthusiasm great." A Ma biographer writes, "When people read those words, they had one feeling: Ma Yinchu and his *New Demography* were in trouble."[66]

The highest echelons of Party leadership soon became involved in the Ma Yinchu case. Chen Boda spoke on May 4, 1958 at Beijing University, suggesting that Ma make a criticism of *New Demography.* Liu Shaoqi, who had articulated the notion that man was primarily a producer, not a consumer,[67] criticized Ma indirectly the following day. By the end of the month, Ma was attacked by name at the national level, following which Beijing University began explicitly to attack him in university publications. Eighteen such articles were published in the latter half of 1958. Multiple nationwide denunciations followed, with nearly sixty articles published in such nationally distributed newspapers as *Guangming Ribao, Wenhui Bao, Beijing Ribao, Xin Jianshe,* and *Jingji Yanjiu.*[68] The criticisms continued even after the crest of the Anti-rightist movement had passed. In 1959 they were still appearing, although they were once again confined primarily to the scholarly world.

Ma Yinchu acknowledged the criticisms which he judged to have merit, but he stood fast on his conclusions. He refused to retract the fundamental judgment that China's population growth rates were on a disaster course. Defiantly, he stated, "I never consider myself or my reputation, I only consider the country and truth. For the sake of truth, if I must sacrifice my own life it would not be wrong."[69] Although he held temporarily onto his position as president of Beijing University, a turning point came in December 1959, when he sent an article defending his position to *Xin Jianshe,* entitled "I Repeat My Request" [Chongshen wo de qingqiu]. Ma concluded, "No matter how numerous the difficulties and obstacles, I will not retreat half a step." This article, published in January, is said to have fallen into the hands of notorious internal security director Kang Sheng, who ordered Ma thoroughly criticized. From mid-December 1959 to mid-January 1960, Beijing University conducted three university-wide criticism sessions and numerous small-scale ones. Campus students and professors were mobilized to hand-ink and paste up nearly 10,000 "big character posters" denouncing him, and eighty-two more articles were published.[70] A former mathematics student recalled that the campus had a quota of posters, and he participated in writing and posting them along with everyone else, unable to refuse:

> We copied what the newspapers said about him, we copied other posters, grabbing up any available scrap of paper. I wrote a poster that said, "Chairman Mao says that with many people, enthusiasm is great, but Ma Yinchu claims that people have only mouths, he doesn't see that every mouth has a pair of hands." In the university criticism meetings, every time he tried to defend himself they cut him off. He wasn't even allowed to speak.

The Chinese syllable *Ma* is not only Ma Yinchu's family name but is also used to render the names of both Marx and Malthus into Chinese. In a typically Chinese manipulation of puns, Kang Sheng is said to have remarked:

> As for Ma Yinchu's *New Demography,* does it really belong to the *Ma* family of Marx {*Ma-ke-si*} or to the *Ma* family of Malthus {*Ma-er-sai-si*} ... I think without a doubt that Ma Yinchu's *New Demography* belongs to the *Ma* family of Malthus!

The Malthusian label was a huge political "cap." Although Ma Yinchu is said to have defended himself by claiming, "the *Ma* of Ma Yinchu is from the *Ma* family of Marx," this proclamation of loyalty to the dominant ideology could do nothing to prevent the termination of his political and academic career.[71]

Ironically, Ma had often dissociated himself from Malthusian views before he was criticized. Like most of Malthus' critics, he noted that Malthus had erred in comparing ratios of population expansion and food supply. Malthus had not considered technological advances when he argued that population growth would advance geometrically while food supply would increase only arithmetically. In fact, food supply had also grown geometrically. Nor had Malthus foreseen that population would be checked as living standards rose. Ma wrote, somewhat quaintly,

> The increase in knowledge has promoted both the rise of labor productivity and the fall in reproduction rates. For example,

[among] society's upper levels and mental workers, recreational aspects became greater, such as playing ball, boating, riding horses, hunting, and other such activities, which reduced their sex drive.[72]

Moreover, Ma argued, like the Soviet theorists, that Malthus had erred in blaming food shortages and overpopulation for worker unrest in Britain, rather than the capitalist system which exploited workers and kept them in poverty and misery while the upper classes profited from their labor. In Ma's words, Malthus' purpose was

> to support control by the capitalist system and its government, and cover up the British government's wrong measures. His population theory told workers that their common poverty was not because of the government's excesses, but mainly because the population increased too quickly and food increased too slowly. This was the starting point for *Principles of Population,* and this was its basic mistake.[73]

Ma argued further that Malthus was cold-hearted to stress the "positive checks" of hunger and war on population, and he was reactionary to advocate moral suasion as the only "preventive check" for deterring workers from having more children, while exempting upper classes from such restraints.[74] Perhaps most importantly, Ma critiqued Malthus' rejection of contraception. Malthus favored "restraint," while Ma considered contraception to be the most scientific method of population control.[75]

Ma's writings did not convince critics that there were fundamental differences between him and Malthus, and on January 4, 1960, Ma was pressured into resigning from the presidency of Beijing University; he was forced to vacate his university offices and remove to his home at Number 32, Dongzongbu Alley. In January 1962, he made his last appearance as member of the Standing Committee of the National People's Congress, a position formally withdrawn in 1963. Unable to publish, he attempted to continue his research, at one point returning to a chilly reception in his ancestral village, for his old neighbors were afraid to cooperate with a man in such deep political disgrace. He remained at home from 1963 to 1965 writing *Nongshu,* a manuscript of more than a million and a half words on China's rural economy. But during the Cultural Revolution, after Red Guards raided the homes of two close friends, Ma told his family it would be safer to destroy potentially "counterrevolutionary" material before the rebels arrived. All day, the family smashed and burned items that might bring trouble – clothing and shoes, gifts from foreigners of porcelain and jade, calligraphy, and even personal letters from Mao Zedong, Zhou Enlai, and Zhu De. Finally, Ma burned the research materials from his safe, including the precious unpublished *Nongshu* manuscript on the rural economy. Had he not done so, he feared, he and his family might have been subjected to the beatings, humiliations, and exile that so many other intellectuals suffered. We will never know the full value of what was lost.[76]

Ma Yinchu was rehabilitated on September 11, 1979 at the age of 98, in an era when the "rectification of wrong verdicts" of the Anti-rightist movement and Cultural Revolution was a priority for Deng Xiaoping's post-Mao regime. All charges against Ma were retracted, and on September 14, he was made honorary president of Beijing University.[77] In November 1979, the Beijing Publishing Company printed 120,000 copies of *New Demography,* which had not previously appeared in book form. (It has now appeared in several editions, including one that is part of a "Green Classics" series on environmental issues.) Ma died soon after, on May 10, 1982, of heart and lung disease and pneumonia.

Ma Yinchu lived for a century. In Shengzhou City near his home village, a larger-than-life-sized statue stands outside a middle school named in his honor. Inside the school, a memorial exhibition dedicated to his life and work warns viewers about "a harsh lesson of history: 'Criticize one person, give birth to several million additional people'" [*pi yige ren, duo sheng ji yi ren*]. In 1997, on the fortieth anniversary of the publication of *New Democracy,* a nine-part television series about his life was broadcast nationally. Primary and middle school textbooks introduce students to "Uncle Ma" and his contribution to population control and environmental protection.[78] But if his scholarly achievements were extraordinary, his search for solutions to the suffering of the Chinese people was typical of that of many Chinese intellectuals. Ma believed that the Communist Party was China's best hope, and he sought to use his courage and scholarly rigor in its service. Mao and the Party chose instead to persecute him.

Ma Yinchu's Legacy

Zhang Chunyuan writes, "History ... finally proclaimed that Ma's [idea that] under socialism there can also be population problems was correct, and the dogmatism, 'if the Soviet Union hasn't discussed it, we can't discuss it either' about 'the bigger the population the better,' was wrong."[79] By then it was too late. Overpopulation had become China's great nightmare, with implications not only for the environment but also for every aspect of the country's development. The Chinese people are still paying a heavy price for Mao's shortsightedness. They also continue to suffer the loss of a generation of intellectuals suppressed for raising questions in an effort to serve their country. Ma's demographic analysis, and the efforts of those who might have pursued the implications of his reasoning, might earlier have helped China to achieve a reduction in rates of population growth. His humane approach might have helped China to develop population policies that relied less on punitive measures and abortions and more on contraceptives, improvements in living standards, and positive incentives.[80]

Many years later, in a conversation, a thoughtful journalist from Chongqing reflected on Mao's attitudes toward Ma Yinchu and population as follows:

> Mao tried to use the power of will as a substitute for a scientific relationship between humans and nature. When Ma Yinchu was persecuted, Mao didn't think there were a lot of people. He said China was like a blank sheet of paper. England and the United States were already drawn, but we had nothing, so we could draw whatever we liked. Mao thought that if there were a lot of people, it was better for making war. It was a military attitude left over from his victory over Chiang Kai-shek. In April 1957, when Mao spoke of introducing the cooperatives, he said we needed lots of people. This wasn't targeted at Ma Yinchu specifically. The lack of political freedom determined the lack of intellectual freedom. It was impossible to have a different position from Chairman Mao. As soon as Chairman Mao said your opinion was wrong, you were finished.

The repression of Ma Yinchu is widely considered to have had an enormous impact on China's population, encouraging reproduction with little regard for consequences. One of Ma's biographers makes generous extrapolations concerning Ma's influence: "People have roughly calculated that if Ma Yinchu's opinions and suggestions had been implemented and sustained, China's population today would at least be 300 million fewer."[81] The Party secretary at the Ma Yinchu Lower Middle School, an outspoken middle-aged woman, blamed Mao directly: "If Mao hadn't suppressed Ma, we wouldn't be having such problems with family planning." Qu Geping, China's preeminent environmentalist, describes Ma's fate as a deeply unfortunate mistake:

> Ma warned that if China permitted its population to grow unchecked the problem would certainly hamper – not help – its path of development. Ma's and others' outcries were unfortunately gagged by subsequent movements in China's modern history. In the late 1950s, Ma's view was under attack from all corners of the country.[82]

Popular perceptions of the impact of the Ma case are even starker: journalist Liu Binyan told me that many Chinese believe that if Mao had not silenced Ma Yinchu, China's population would be half its size. A young Chinese girl, a temporary worker in a Chongqing guesthouse, commented to me sadly, "If only we had listened to Ma Yinchu, I wouldn't be unemployed today." Such remarks reflect the perception of ordinary Chinese that overpopulation exacts a heavy toll in every area of their lives, and indicate Ma Yinchu's endurance in public memory.

The silencing of Ma Yinchu demonstrates the connection between suppression of intellectual freedom, population explosion, and the imbalance in human–nature relationships during the Mao years. These links are clearly drawn in a recent Chinese essay published by philosophy professor Yuan Weishi in the outspoken *Nanfang Zhoumo* [Southern Weekend]. The essay is entitled, "Why Did the Chinese Environment Get So Badly Messed Up?"

> The most important reason [for the degradation of China's environment] is that there is no strong guarantee of freedom to express one's views. When National People's Congress representative Ma Yinchu brought up the problem of population, he became regarded as a terrible criminal. During all the following turmoil,

a few hundred more hundred million Chinese were born. How to provide for them? Make more farmland! And so the lakes, rivers, mountains and grasslands of China were devastated.[83]

Political repression meant that people were afraid to speak in opposition to policies that promoted population growth. When Ma Yinchu was publicizing his ideas, there was only one acceptable view of population growth: It was good to have more people because more people would succeed in bending nature to their will. The collective force of many would lift China out of its poverty and humiliation to achieve a new socialist paradise. This rigid understanding of reality did not permit population problems or myriad other scientific issues to be aired. The belief in the triumphal human domination of nature thus mirrored the totalitarian impulse in the human political world. And so, China's population grew rapidly, increasing pressure on the land to provide resources and human habitat, and promoting extensive damage to ecosystems and eco-services.

HYDRO-ENGINEER HUANG WANLI

For thousands of years, it was considered the responsibility of China's emperors to manage China's great waterways and provide irrigation and transport by building reservoirs, dikes, and canals. An early legendary ruler, Yu the Great, founder of the Xia dynasty (2200–1750 B.C.), is still revered for dredging and diking the rivers after a nine-year flood. The country's battle with its great rivers has been so important to its national character that an influential Western scholar once attributed China's imperial system to the need to coordinate multitudes of workers for waterworks projects.[84] While this view of the genesis of Chinese bureaucratic authoritarianism has been challenged as simplistic, China's effort to control the waterways has been a perennial and central task, given the life-and-death importance of the great rivers to the nation.

After the fall of the Qing dynasty, in accordance with the ancient mandate of Yu the Great, Sun Yat-sen envisioned great plans for water control, including a 30 million horsepower dam across the Yangzi. However, the Guomindang government failed to realize these plans in the chaos of war with Japan and civil war with the Communists.[85] The management of China's waterways was even more of a priority for the early Communist regime. The Communist Party's ambition to conquer the waters, and nature in general, marked a definitive break with more accommodating approaches. Indeed, the effort to unleash popular energy in a war against nature is one of the distinctive characteristics of Maoism.[86]

Investigative reports on harnessing the rivers were conducted even before the formal announcement of the birth of New China, particularly in North China where the Communists had their base.[87] Among China's great rivers, the most persistently flood-prone and potentially most valuable as a resource was the Yellow River. This famously muddy river runs 5,500 kilometers from the edge of the Qinghai-Tibet Plateau through the loess plateau to the sea. The third-longest river in the world, the Yellow is considered the cradle of Chinese civilization and is also known as "China's sorrow" for its tendency toward floods. Sediment is so thick that the riverbed rises year after year, spilling over into the plains and necessitating the construction of higher and higher dikes. In some areas, the river flows 8 meters above the floodplain and runs 40 percent silt; in the early 1950s, it carried about 1.3 billion tons of sediment per year.[88] A traditional folk saying describes the river's murky muddiness as enduring until the advent of a miraculous leader: *Shangren Chu, Huanghe Qing* [When a Great Man Emerges, the Yellow River Will Run Clear]. It was believed that changes in the physical world would mirror a new political era, just as it was commonly believed that earthquakes and floods signaled a dynasty's loss of the right to govern, or Mandate of Heaven. Chairman Mao would certainly have known the folk saying. Political posters depicted him as sitting by the riverside dreaming of clean waters, and long-term opponents of damming the river suspect that he may have been trying to make the saying come true by containing sediment in the upper reaches.[89] Indeed, according to a former journalist, after the Sanmenxia Dam was built, the newspapers tried to make Mao happy by reporting that the river was running clear for the first time, although it clouded up again within a few months.

Communist China wanted electricity for development, and the farmers living on the riverbanks wanted relief from floods; new dams would undoubtedly be built. Yet in the case of the Yellow River, as with other rivers, such as the Yangzi, there was disagreement over whether to build one huge dam or several smaller dams on the great river's tributaries, a debate that echoed traditional philosophical rifts between "Daoist" engineers who sought to use only low levees and the natural flow of rivers to accommodate human activity to the river, and "Confucian" engineers who sought to control the waters through high dikes and other major civil works projects.[90] Officials in the Yellow River Commission and in the Ministry of Water Resources and Electric Power to which the Commission reported were the key players in these debates. Their arguments revealed problems with both approaches. A large dam meant large-scale resettlement, major engineering challenges, and high costs. Smaller dams meant questionable flood control benefits and the greater combined cost of harnessing so many tributaries.[91] Chairman Mao's public position was frustratingly ambiguous: in October 1952, he visited the river and declared simply, "Work on the Yellow River must be carried out well." In actuality, in terms of traditional Chinese culture, Mao was closest neither to Confucians nor Daoists, but to the less well-known Legalists, whose statist philosophy is associated with the despotic Qin Shi Huangdi (221–207 B.C.), founder of the Qin dynasty and unifier of China. Mao frequently compared himself to this book-burning and Great Wall–building emperor, and greatly admired him.[92]

In an essay, "A Lamentation for the Yellow River," Shang Wei explains that the outcome rested in the hands of Soviet advisors, whose authority in ideological and technical matters was enormous in the early 1950s. Soviet engineers who had built major hydropower projects in Siberia were predisposed toward grandiose plans, and a Soviet delegation inspected a proposed site on the main stream of the Yellow River at Sanmenxia in spring 1952. This visit led to formation of a Soviet Experts Yellow River Planning Group, which visited Beijing in January 1954. After a group of 120 Chinese and Soviet experts conducted another field visit in spring of that year, they recommended the Sanmenxia site as appropriate for a master dam and reservoir that would hold sediment upriver, control floods, and generate hydroelectric power. The Soviet engineers were authorized to draw the designs, and their first report, delivered in December, called for a pool level of 350 meters and a total reservoir capacity of 360 million cubic meters. This would have involved submerging 2.07 million *mu* of fertile farmland and relocating 600,000 people. However, as planned, the dam would have lasted only twenty-five to thirty years, and Chinese officials requested a plan for a dam with a longer life. In April 1956, Soviet engineers from the Leningrad Branch of the Soviet Power Stations Water and Electricity Design Institute submitted a design for a pool level of 360 meters with a projected one-hundred-year life, which would require flooding 3.33 million *mu* and relocating 900,000 people. This design was approved before decisions on how to handle the sediment had been made. Should it be flushed through the dam? Or should it be contained upriver so that those downstream would at last be free of the endless rising of the riverbed, and the prediction concerning the emergence of a great man would come true?[93]

When work began in April 1957, sluice gates were included in the design to permit sediment flow. But with Soviet approval, Chinese engineers decided to block these gates with cement, perhaps hoping, as dam critics have speculated, to build a monument to Party greatness and to please Mao. By June 1960, the dam was 340 meters high; by April 1961, it was 353 meters. By February 1962 it was complete, and the first 150,000-kilowatt generator was in operation. But, as we shall see, problems with sedimentation in the generators began almost immediately. Not even the eventual reopening of the sluice gates resolved the problems that have plagued the dam to the present day.[94]

The Life of Huang Wanli

Huang Wanli was born in Shanghai in 1911, the year the Qing dynasty fell. His father, Huang Yanpei, was a prominent revolutionary whose high position and international reputation later provided Huang Wanli with a modicum of protection when he came under attack. Huang Wanli trained in China as an engineer. He witnessed the 1931 flood of the Han River and the 1933 collapse of a dam on the Yellow River and concluded that, while China had many civil engineers, it needed hydrology and geomorphology specialists.[95] He went to the United States to study meteorology, first at Cornell and then at the University of Iowa. After working as an engineering aide at the Norris Dam with the Tennessee Valley Authority, he obtained a doctorate in engineering at the University of Illinois in Urbana-Champaign. On graduation, he made an extensive tour of dams in the United States, and then, in 1937, he chose to return to China to serve his country as a hydraulic engineer.

He worked in Sichuan province, whence he fled the Japanese, and then in Gansu province, where he was chief engineer at the Bureau of Reclamation. His many official positions included chief water engineering technology advisor to the State Commission on Economic Affairs. After the Communist revolution, he became chief advisor to the Northeast China General Bureau of Water Resources,[96] and in 1953, he became a professor at Qinghua University in the Hydraulic Engineering Department, a position which allowed him to pursue his love of fieldwork. He surveyed 3,000 kilometers of Chinese rivers on foot. His extensive study of geomorphology and geography gave him insight that was unusual among those trained in civil engineering, particularly into the interrelation between dams, sediment, and water flow.[97]

Now 88 years of age, his mind still crystal clear, Professor Huang Wanli recalled his opposition to the dam and his subsequent political persecution in conversations at his home on the campus of Qinghua University. In separate conversations in the U.S., his children confirmed his recollections and supplemented them with their own. In the mid-1950s, Huang Wanli became deeply concerned about the planned Sanmenxia Dam and submitted a position paper to the Yellow River Planning Commission challenging the design. In particular, he opposed the choice of a main watercourse for the dam and the effort to contain sediment, which he saw as "an attempt to fiddle around with the laws of nature." During a June 1957 meeting of more than seventy experts, Huang Wanli again asserted that the goal of a clear Yellow River "distorted the laws of nature."[98] Huang's eldest son, Huang Guanhong, recalled his father's steadfast opposition to the dam despite enormous pressure to accede to Soviet experts. Huang eventually became the lone dissenter, sometimes banging on the table to emphasize the strength of his convictions. His wife, more cautious than he, often begged him to express his reservations less stridently, but Huang insisted on stating the truth as he saw it. This was consistent with his most closely held values; his son recalls that he always instructed his children about the great virtue of honesty and would punish them if he thought they had lied.

In the tradition of older Chinese intellectuals, Huang Wanli was a poet and writer as well as a scientist. In an essay, he described his passion for writing as a complement to the mechanistic aspects of his work:

When I research how to manage the Yellow River, it is with deep feeling. Although technical research is absorbing, it is always dull by itself. A human being will always have an emotional life. Especially when you encounter a disadvantageous situation, it is good to practice some art.[99]

And so, it was ostensibly a short story that got him into trouble, although everyone knew that Huang was singled out for political persecution because of his opposition to the dam at Sanmenxia. His allegorical tale, "The Road Turns Over" [*Malu Fanjiang*], about a road with a broken foundation, was published in a Qinghua University journal. The story criticized toadies who said whatever the Party wanted to hear. Huang labeled those who mouthed socialist pieties to Communist Party leaders as the "Goethe faction" (translating "Goethe" as *Gede,* using Chinese characters that mean "Singing about Virtue,") and the "Dante faction" (translated as *Dangding,* with characters meaning "assume" [office] and "follow"). He used transparent code names for public figures he wished to praise and ridicule. Fang Sheng was meant to represent Huang himself (he took brushstrokes off two characters of his name); another figure was hydropower leader Zhang Hanying. Appreciative professors and students easily decoded the story, the main point of which was that something was fundamentally wrong with China's political system. Huang noted that in the United States, by contrast, people could remove elected officials from office. Mentioning Ma Yinchu, he complained that, while China was supposed to have family planning, the supply of contraceptives was erratic, changing suddenly according to official attitudes toward population growth; Ma Yinchu's wisdom was useless, he argued, because leaders controlled the contraceptive supply, whereas those who really understood the issue were powerless.

On June 8, 1957, the *People's Daily* published a devastating critique headlined with Chairman Mao's own angry words, *Shenme Hua?* ("What Is This [Trash]?"). Huang's text was reprinted next to the headline; the critique was an early signal of the beginning of the Anti-rightist movement. Ten charges were listed against Huang, among them allegations that he had attacked Chairman Mao, admired foreign countries, harmed the relationship between the Party and the masses, propagated bourgeois democracy, complained that intellectuals could not pursue scientific truth in China, and attacked China's population policy. But the key charge noted Huang's opposition to the Sanmenxia Dam. Huang's alleged assertion, "a clear-running Yellow River is an imaginary political ideal, impossible to be achieved scientifically," was clearly at the root of his troubles.[100]

Huang Wanli's daughter, Huang Xiaolu, who now lives in Maryland, recalled that when the *People's Daily* article came out, it was a big surprise to Huang and his family, since the university had encouraged everyone to speak freely as part of the Hundred Flowers campaign.

Maybe Chairman Mao thought China's intellectuals would rebel as they had in Hungary. They voiced their complaints and inner thoughts, and when Chairman Mao heard them, he got angry. My father didn't care about politics. But because his ideas on the Sanmenxia Dam differed from those of the leaders, he was singled out. I was only eleven at the time, but I remember my older sister and father talking about how good the story was, and then I remember my parents worrying that he would be criticized.

That summer, the university denounced my father. It was a very hot day, and he was made to sit in the center of a big crowd. Everyone had a fan except for him. My brother made the bitter joke that our father was enjoying the breeze from everyone's fans. Later, there was a meeting to criticize all the Qinghua University rightists. There were more at Qinghua than at Beijing University, because at Beijing University the Party Secretary, Jiang Longji, protected the professors. Jiang got in trouble for it during the Cultural Revolution and was beaten to death.

Unlike other intellectuals in similar positions, many of whom began to doubt their own sanity and to believe that perhaps they had made mistakes or had flaws in their way of thinking, Huang Wanli's conviction in the correctness of his views never wavered. His son, still bemused and a little resentful forty years later, recalled that after a long day of criticism meetings, Huang Wanli would come home and fall right to sleep, snoring loudly as the rest of the family tossed about in fear and worry.

Huang had been a high-ranking professor, second level, but after the criticisms he was no longer permitted to teach. His salary was reduced by two grades, from 289 *yuan* per month to 207, and he was sent to the Mi Yun reservoir construction site to do hard labor. He was the only "rightist" at the site. His daughter recalled her father's resilience and hardships:

> My father is a very adaptable person, he likes to make friends with all kinds of people. He had made friends among the laborers. The leaders complained to my mother that he was always going out to eat with them. The labor was very hard, but he was still fairly young, only forty-seven. Sometimes they had to work twenty-four hours a day making bricks, filling carts with stones and dirt. This was during the Great Leap Forward, and once they had to work thirty-six hours without stopping.

Huang was allowed to visit his family only during holidays, but after he had surgery for a growth in his neck, he was allowed to stay home. His father, Huang Yanpei, once conveyed a message from Chairman Mao, asking him to write a self-criticism so that his rightist label could be removed. Instead, Huang Wanli wrote an appeal in which he reiterated his opposition to the Sanmenxia Dam and argued that China's real problem was lack of freedom of speech. Why, he demanded, despite the lengthy training of so many intellectuals, was he the only one who dared express the truth? This stifling of views, he wrote to Mao, was China's real problem. In his appeal, Huang included some poetry. He later learned that Mao, a fellow poet, had appreciated his verse: "I used poetry and literature to express my ideas, and Mao saw that and was angry. He told my father, 'Huang Wanli's poems are good but his ideas are reactionary.' After those words were published, everyone thought I must be a great poet."[101] He laughed, and his wife added, "So only after Chairman Mao's death was the label removed. In fact," she added, "we were lucky because I had a brother in Taiwan, and they didn't label me a counterrevolutionary."

Unlike some spouses who submitted to pressure to "draw a clear line of demarcation," Huang Wanli's wife, an employee of Qinghua University hospital, remained loyal to her husband. Huang's children were victimized because of his rightist status, causing him great sorrow. His second daughter was assigned to a second-rate university, despite her high marks. His second son was barred from taking the university entrance examinations because a class monitor had made a "not qualified" notation in his file. The young man worked raising horses for a year, when, suddenly, the leadership relented and he was notified to take the exams. At the time, all China was wracked with food scarcity, and he had only three days in which to prepare. Despite his empty belly and the short notice, he managed to win a place at Qinghua University. Huang's youngest daughter was victimized as an elementary school student when, in 1958, she was suddenly barred from representing her class at a Children's Day ceremony because she was a "Little Rightist." She didn't blame her father for her suffering then, although later she could not help doing so when the family suffered even more severely under political pressure:

> At the time, no one had experienced such things. We felt that Chairman Mao was unfair. He had asked the people to speak, and then he turned on them. We felt unlucky, but not wrong. Later, during the Cultural Revolution, it was different. We had more years of "Party education" by then, and we began to wonder if my father's ideas were incorrect because he had been influenced by his experience and education in the United States.

On August 24, 1966, after the Cultural Revolution began, Red Guards from twelve high schools came to rightists' homes to conduct searches for the Four Olds – old ideas, culture, customs, and habits – anything that belonged to the old society or hinted at bourgeois values. Only Huang's youngest daughter, Huang Xiaolu, was still living with her parents, because she had not been admitted to the university because of her father's background:

> They took everything from the drawers and wardrobes and threw it on the floor in a great pile. They took away our old photo albums and put them in a display of counterrevolutionary items. They took away anything of value, good books, gold and silver, our stamp collections. I don't know where those things went. Then they put up a Big Character Poster announcing that the Red Guards had searched the home of Rightist Huang Wanli. We didn't dare put anything away lest they come again. It was terrifying.

On another Red Guard visit, Huang Wanli was home. It was a tempo-rary respite after the "August Red Terror," and Huang Wanli had just been issued his 207 *yuan* salary. The family was eating dinner when a group of Red Guards rushed in. Huang Xiaolu recalled, "They forced my father to stand up and bow his head. They shouted at him and forced him to turn over the money, saying that he was a rightist who did not deserve such a high salary."

Pressured to "draw a clear line of demarcation" with their father, Huang Wanli's children were eventually forced to denounce him in uni-versity criticism meetings. Huang Guanhong, the eldest son, had to repeat charges made when Huang Wanli was first labeled a rightist, such as the accusation that he had harmed the feeling between the Party and the masses. Such exercises were terribly painful for the whole fam-ily, but the Communist Party did not succeed in driving a rift between Huang and his loved ones. Then, in September 1969, Huang and his wife were sent to a May 7th cadre school in Liyüzhou in West Hunan for reeducation. These were thought-reform institutions, usually located in the countryside, where intellectuals and officials conducted heavy farm-work when not engaged in political study.[102] At first, Huang and his wife saw each other often, then only once a month. They were there for two years, Huang laboring in the fields and his wife raising chickens. It was exhausting for old people; once Huang Wanli almost died from heat exhaustion. Another time, he was accused of being a Guomindang spy. The leaders called a large meeting and proclaimed, "Within three min-utes, the great spy will stand up and reveal himself." Huang Wanli thought he knew which old man would stand up. When his own name was called out, he could hardly contain his laughter. Eventually, the camp was shut down because so many internees got schistosomiasis.

The irrepressible Huang Wanli never stopped thinking and writing. Even with little hope of publishing anything, he wrote letters to the lead-ership and completed a manuscript on Yellow River management.[103] In 1973, at the age of 62, while still undergoing labor reform, he managed to be assigned to work near Sanmenxia, where he labored by day and investigated siltation problems by night. After his rehabilitation follow-ing Mao's death, he criticized a plan to divert water from South China to the North along an eastern route that was supposed to restore the old Grand Canal, arguing that creating new channels for the upper reaches of river tributaries was more feasible.[104] He also became an outspoken opponent of the Three Gorges Dam on the Yangzi, writing three letters to Jiang Zemin and one to President Clinton. He believes that his letter to Clinton was decisive in persuading him not to support the dam.

Because of his stubbornness, Huang Wanli was one of the last Qinghua University rightists to be rehabilitated after Mao's death, resisting even when the "rightist" category no longer existed and Party Branch leaders came begging for a few face-saving sentences of remorse. He refused, saying, "The earth will always circle the sun, not the other way around. This will not change because of anything you have to say." His political label was finally removed, albeit with the qualification that he had made incorrect statements that belonged to the (relatively mild) category of "internal contradictions among the people." Later, the university apologized, after a fashion. At Huang's request, for his eightieth birthday, they copied a sheaf of his poetry for distribution to his colleagues. These included poems about the Sanmenxia and Three Gorges dams, as well as about his labor reform experiences. Three Gorges Dam opponent Dai Qing is preparing these poems for publication, with notes about the conditions under which they were written.

Today, Huang Wanli stands erect and alert at the age of 88. Tall and distinguished-looking, with thick white hair swept back from a broad forehead, he seems full of life, ready to laugh, and utterly confident of his views. When I went to visit him and his wife, he was wearing a formal gray Mao jacket. His home, a spacious first-floor apartment in an older university building, was decorated with potted plants, traditional calligraphy, and family photos. He reflected on his career and tribulations as follows:

I have no regrets about what I did. They knew they were wrong when they criticized me, but they had to go along with the government. There was a notion that the USSR couldn't be wrong, that it was somehow anti-Communist or counterrevolutionary to disagree with them. The others had no backbone. I was certain there would be trouble, but no one dared agree with me. In fact, it was clear that I was right as early as 1964, two years after the dam was completed. A town was completely flooded because of all the silt. Now they've apologized. Mao himself was the main reason that I was labeled a rightist. He thought that through collective will society could raise itself up. He didn't admit that people were basically selfish, even though he himself was so selfish. He used propaganda to force people to change their beliefs. In fact, Mao was the greatest criminal in history even if you look at just one thing: he instituted a policy that required peasants to sell all their grain to the government at a government-determined price [*tonggou, tongxiao*]. This policy destroyed the peasants' enthusiasm. My father debated Mao on the issue in the People's Congress. In 1960, even after people were dying, he still refused to listen. He said it was because their determination wasn't strong enough. Two of my younger brothers and my older sister were labeled "rightists" because our father spoke the truth about this grain purchasing policy.

He laughed. "I was the only 'rightist' in my own right."

Despite Huang's good humor, his daughter describes him as very angry at his treatment and all the lost years of professional life. When, in 1987, Huang toured the United States for four months, giving talks at twelve universities, he argued that Communist Party policy toward the great rivers had been a failure. The Party permitted only those who agreed with them to speak; they cast science aside in the service of their political ends. Huang's daughter reflected on the Party's failure to come to terms with their responsibility:

The *"Shenme Hua?"* [What Is This (Trash)?] headline in the *People's Daily* was Chairman Mao's own words, and even today the Party has not admitted they were wrong to ignore my father's concerns about the Sanmenxia Dam. Father was opposed to any kind of dam on the main stream of the Yellow River. But he said that if the dam must be built, at least there should be sluice gates.

She sighed. "Of all China's leaders, only Yu the Great managed the Yellow River well."

Despite all that he has suffered, Huang Wanli is still in many ways a typically patriotic older-generation Chinese intellectual. To the discomfiture of his children, four out of five of whom have chosen to live abroad (a sixth child was adopted by a childless brother), he has repeatedly urged them to return to China, arguing in letters that China's intellectuals are too precious a treasure not to serve their motherland.

Huang Wanli once explained that he was labeled a rightist in 1957 because of Mao's disregard of tested theories and suspicion of systematic knowledge. In Huang's view, it was up to engineers to apply scientists' theories:

> Mao Zedong proposed to relate theory to reality in the 1940s, saying that doctrines were useless and that only the kind of Marxism-Leninism that was produced in the rural hinterland could solve China's real problems. In the 1950s, following this "great teaching," a batch of people started to use "reality" as an excuse for theoretical ignorance. I said: "There is no theory that cannot be related to reality, only realities that one fails to explain in theory."[105]

In the name of promoting practical experience, Mao and his followers all too often fell into the trap of believing that because they declared something possible or true, it would be so. "Knowledge" based primarily on wishful thinking was given primacy over the tested understandings of scientists. Huang Wanli reproached university Party officials for precisely this delusion when he said that they could not simply order the sun to orbit the earth. The building of the Sanmenxia Dam is an example of how projects could be launched for political reasons even though Chinese scientists understood that they were not feasible or safe. Marxist orthodoxy and rigid adherence to the words of Mao fueled the notion that humans had an almost unlimited capacity to remold the natural world.

China's deference to the Soviet Union and to Chairman Mao's ambitions, vanity, and poor judgment about China's capabilities contributed to the conditions under which the Sanmenxia Dam was promoted and built. The project also attests to the power of popular legend and to the age-old desire of Yellow River basin farmers for freedom from siltation and floods. Ultimately, the dam was an enormous waste of resources that altered the river's dynamics with little to show for this interference in terms of hydropower or flood control.

We have seen how the abuse of Huang Wanli and the abuse of the Yellow River were entwined, and we have used their linked stories as a way to focus on the environmental consequences of political repression, particularly during the Anti-rightist movement. But the dam caused far greater human suffering than that of one man, and we may now briefly turn our attention beyond Huang Wanli's particular case to consider the many people dislocated because of state-sponsored relocations. This theme will be addressed in greater detail in the final chapter.

To prepare for the dam, 280,000 farmers from Shaanxi, Shanxi, and Henan were forced to leave the fertile lands they and their ancestors had farmed for centuries and were resettled in Ningxia and Gansu provinces' inhospitable lands. More than 1 million *mu,* including 750,000 *mu* of arable land, was flooded, including two county seats, 21 townships, and 253 villages. The story of the suffering of the relocatees and their battle to get back their land has recently been published by Leng Meng, a writer who collected their oral histories.[106] Highlights of the story follow here.

Resettlement began in 1956, with the slogan, "relocate one family, save ten thousand families" [*qian yijia jiu wanjia*].[107] At first, peasants believed the state's promises that they would be better off if they moved, and they vied to be in the first group of 5,208 migrants, who were handed red flowers and sent off with big celebrations. But the pioneers were shocked when they arrived five days later at what was to be their new home on the border of the Gobi Desert. One group of 800 sent to Taole County in Ningxia were so distressed at the barren and windswept appearance of the land that 361 of them tried immediately to go home. They were blocked at the crossing of the Yellow River, but 46 of them found their way across the Inner Mongolian deserts and mountains to report to their fellow villagers what lay in store for them. Their homes torn down, the peasants were forced to go along with the government's plans. They never adjusted to their new homes, and severe conflicts over water and land broke out with local people, most of whom were Hui, a Chinese Muslim minority group with very different customs from the Han.

Because of problems with dam construction, less land was inundated than planned. But rather than returning the land to the farmers, the government allowed the State Farm and Land Reclamation Bureau and the People's Liberation Army to establish huge farms on the vacated territory. The peasants agitated to get their land back, demonstrating by the thousands in 1961 for the right to cross the Yellow River and return home. They took their petitions to the central government in Beijing and to the Shaanxi provincial government. When they finally got permission to return to Shaanxi in late 1961, they found their land had been expropriated. For years, they continued to struggle for their homelands, using petitions, demonstrations, and guerrilla farming, often skirmishing with workers from the government units occupying the land. In the 1970s, conflicts between peasants and state farm workers decreased. The workers, many of whom were sent from the cities to work in the countryside during the Cultural Revolution, realized that if the peasants got their land back, they themselves would be allowed to go home. It wasn't until 1982, more than two and a half decades later, that the peasants won back about a third of their land. By then, many of the original relocatees had died.

The Aftermath

Today, many environmentalists see great dams as exacting excessive costs in human resettlement and destruction of ecosystems. At a time when coexistence with nature has become a paramount concern, mega-dams are coming to be seen as products of an outmoded ethos, relics that should in some cases even be torn down.[108] Ahead of his time, Huang Wanli argued in the 1950s that to block the central stream of a river system was in effect a violation of the laws of nature. He foresaw that by holding the Yellow River's sediment upriver so that the lower reaches would run clear, the mechanisms of the new structure would be clogged within a short time, and communities above the dam would be flooded. In his view, if a dam on the main waterway were built in the face of these considerations, sluice gates would be required to permit the sediment to pass through. But if this were to be done, the Chinese would have had to break with Soviet gigantism, something they were not willing to do, and the age-old prediction concerning a great leader and a clear river assuredly could not be made to come true. Huang's arguments were thus met with political disfavor, persecution, and punishment.

As Huang predicted, the Sanmenxia Dam silted up in only a few years. The sluice gates included in the original construction had to be reopened at a cost of 10 million *yuan* each to permit sediment to flow through. Accumulated sediment deposits rapidly extended into the Wei River tributary, raising the channel of the inlet so that the waters threatened to spill over and flood the densely populated industrial city of Xi'an. Underground water tables rose, increasing salinization and alkalinization of farmlands. In 1962, the dam had to be reconfigured with a lower pool level of 340 meters, and operations had to be shifted to sediment-flushing and releasing flood waters. The dam's generators were removed to another site, at enormous cost.[109] As rising water continued to threaten Xi'an, Mao is said to have told Zhou Enlai, "If nothing works, then just blow up the dam."[110] The dam was repeatedly reconstructed with tubes at the base to increase silt discharge capacity, but in 1969, again there were floods in Xi'an. Eventually, the dam was so pierced with holes that it became virtually worthless for either flood control or electricity generation.[111] Today, the Yellow River runs as muddy as ever, so exploited for irrigation and manufacturing that it often fails to reach the sea, while the dam's legacies of increased river turbulence, frequent dike collapses, sediment buildup, and ecological changes continue to cause problems for local people, some of whom must leave their homes every flood season when the dam's gates are closed.[112] Another dam, the Xiaolangdi, was completed in 2000 in an effort to produce the electricity that the Sanmenxia could not. Yet the Sanmenxia Dam was still being hailed as a success at its thirtieth anniversary, heralded as having transformed the river "from a dragon that brought perpetual disasters to the people to one that now provides them with benefits and aids the task of socialist construction."[113]

The silencing of Huang Wanli and others meant that few dared to dissent when "red experts" pressed forward other grandiose water conservancy projects. With the advent of the Great Leap Forward in 1958, work intensified on both large dams and small water conservancy projects, often involving millions of laborers. Remaining voices of caution were dealt with expeditiously. A hydrologist named Chen Xing, for example, argued that the overaccumulation of water in Henan province would cause the land to become waterlogged, leading to salinity and alkalinization. For his pains and for voicing concerns about other aspects of the Leap, he was labeled a "right opportunist."[114] Li Rui, Mao's much-admired personal secretary and a leading opponent of the Three Gorges Dam, was purged in 1959 at the Lushan Plenum for supporting Marshal Peng Dehuai's efforts to tell Mao that the Leap was a mistake.

Ill-considered and poorly executed interference with river courses was widespread. Big dams built hastily during the Leap included the Banqiao and Shimantan in Henan province at Zhumadian, which broke catastrophically in August 1975, resulting in the deaths of 86,000 (the official figure) to 230,000 people (an estimate by Chinese opponents of big dams).[115] In Henan province, more than 110 dams were built, but by 1966, half these dams had collapsed; many had been built only with earth and designed by untrained peasants.[116]

The tale of Huang Wanli's opposition to the Sanmenxia Dam, and the punishment he received for his courage, is a prominent example of what happened to scientists who opposed Mao-era dam projects. Shui Fu, a writer who has chronicled dam-building since 1949 and its frequently disastrous consequences, provides the larger picture. Before 1949, he writes, there were only 23 big and medium-sized dams in China; 80,000 have been built in the last forty years. In 1973 alone 554 dams collapsed. By 1980, 2,976 dams had collapsed, including two large ones. Shui Fu quotes Henan's chief Water Resources Bureau engineer: "The crap from that era [the Great Leap Forward] has not yet been cleaned up."[117] The erosion, siltation, and deforestation caused by such failed dam projects have been enormous. The scale and depth of human suffering in resettlement projects have also been vast. By the mid-1980s, there were at least 10.2 million "reservoir relocatees" in China, many still deeply impoverished.[118] Many Chinese engineers knew there were problems with the conceptualization and design of these dams. Some of them dared not speak out, and some were already undergoing "reeducation" and had no opportunity to make their views known; others were punished for expressing a dissenting point of view.

Today, journalist and nuclear scientist Dai Qing continues the tradition of Huang Wanli in her fight against the Three Gorges Dam, and the Party continues its tradition of repressing those who speak out against grandiose hydro-projects. Dai Qing was incarcerated for a year for her outspokenness about the dam and the June 4 incident. Today she is closely watched, and those who contact her are often questioned. On November 9,1997, when announcing the completion of the cofferdam and diversion of the Yangzi River at the Three Gorges, President Jiang Zemin joined the lineage of Chinese leaders who have dreamed of the great dam, from Sun Yat-sen and Mao Zedong to its strongest contemporary advocate, Li Peng, a Soviet-trained engineer and the chairman of the National People's Congress Standing Committee. Jiang stunned Chinese intellectuals by using Maoist phrases and slogans at the cofferdam ceremony: "Man Must Conquer Nature," he proclaimed. "This is a victory for the spirit of the Foolish Old Man Who Removed the Mountains."[119] Some intellectuals were furious at this reversion to the old language. "This reflects a polarized relationship to nature, not adjusting to it," one veteran told me. "This is trying to change nature, not acting in accordance with its laws. The Yangzi River floods are nature punishing China."

For many Chinese, the high price of suppressing Huang's ideas on the Sanmenxia Dam is analogous to that of suppressing Ma Yinchu's ideas on population.[120] Huang and Ma have together captured the Chinese historical imagination through their steadfast integrity. They have become twin symbols of the costs of repression of intellectual freedom. In Mao's "war against nature," the Anti-rightist movement that terminated their professional lives can be understood metaphorically as a moment in which the troops were disciplined and brought into order. The message was sounded that dissent was impermissible; the disobedient would be pilloried and made into examples of the perils of independent thought. No opinions that differed from Maoism's marching orders would be tolerated, either from elite cadres like Ma Yinchu and Huang Wanli or from the rank-and-file who would so often provide labor in the war to remold nature, society, and themselves. Discipline, the first requirement of any army, was thus established early in the Mao years as an essential prerequisite to subsequent military-style mobilizations and assaults on the natural world.

It is possible to imagine a society in which discussion and debate are not necessary to a harmonious relationship between humans and nature. In natural systems heavily populated by human beings, however, where resources are limited and decisions to use and transform nature for human purposes are being made constantly, freedom of speech and inquiry may be critical to a less destructive human–nature relationship. While it is far from clear that only democracies can create sustainable relations with nature, pluralism permits the expression of ideas in open public settings and in print, promoting criticism and debate. It allows people the opportunity to disagree, to seek and offer additional information, to deliberate, and to modify and improve proposals that have impact on the natural world. With such freedoms, moreover, there is a better chance that the unintended consequences of human activity will be revealed in a timely fashion. Basic intellectual freedoms thus deeply affect human actions vis-à-vis the nonhuman world. By silencing human voices, repressing the fundamental drive toward expression and understanding, and declaring certain subjects and interpretations off limits, Maoist leaders suppressed the human quest for understanding and created conditions for altering the earth's processes beyond nature's ability to recover.

"Man Must Conquer Nature"
Ren Ding Sheng Tian

"Greater, Faster, Better, More Economical"
Duo, Kuai, Hao, Sheng

2

DEFORESTATION, FAMINE, AND UTOPIAN URGENCY

How the Great Leap Forward Mobilized the Chinese People to Attack Nature

The Anti-rightist movement quashed freedom of speech by turning more than half a million people into political pariahs and allowed Mao to pursue the Great Leap Forward virtually unopposed.[1] The growing population about which Ma Yinchu had cautioned was seen as providing extra hands to catapult China toward a brilliant socialist destiny. Construction of the dams Huang Wanli and others had opposed went forward rapidly, intended to harness the great rivers once and for all. Smaller water conservancy projects such as reservoirs, holding pools, wells, and irrigation canals also engaged the labor power of millions; in 1958 alone, some 580 million cubic meters of earth were moved.[2] Urgently and rapidly, through extraordinary efforts, the Chinese people were tasked with overtaking Britain in steel production within fifteen years, raising agricultural yields, and achieving socialist transformation in the countryside by combining rural collectives into vast People's Communes. The conquest of nature and prosperity of humankind were believed to be at hand through the miracle of socialism.

With the Great Leap Forward, the Maoist philosophy of voluntarism was given full expression in a great social mobilization. Although, like Marx, Mao held that human consciousness was shaped by material conditions, Mao also saw ideas as having the power to mobilize efforts to transform the material world.[3] In the struggle for development, the will and energy of the masses would compensate for China's lack of sophisticated technology and equipment; ideas would unleash raw labor to conquer and remold nature. "Man Must Conquer Nature" [*Ren Ding Sheng Tian*], Mao declared, sounding the phrase that many Chinese mention as the core of Mao's attitude toward the natural world. "Great Courage

Brings Forth Great Yields" [*Ren You Duo Da Dan, Di You Duo Da Chan*]. High yields were held to depend only on the human capacity to imagine them.[4]

A song often sung in the countryside in 1958 captures the voluntarist spirit of the time:

> In heaven, there is no Jade Emperor,
> On earth, there is no Dragon King.
> I am the Jade Emperor, I am the Dragon King.
> I order the three mountains and five peaks:
> "Make way, here I come!"[5]

Mao often proclaimed his conviction that humans could force nature into obedience. In May 1958, he commented, "'Make the high mountain bow its head; make the river yield the way.' It is an excellent sentence. When we ask the high mountain to bow its head, it has to do so! When we ask the river to yield the way, it must yield!"[6] In November, he remarked, "We have always maintained that we must give [Taiwan] serious attention tactically but regard it with contempt strategically. This holds true in the struggle against nature as well as in the class struggle."[7] Similarly, in a critique of an essay by Stalin stating that men could not affect astronomy, geology, and other natural processes, Mao argued, "This argument is incorrect. Man's ability to know and change Nature is unlimited."[8] His acolytes apparently admired him for this: General Yang Shangkun is said to have boasted, "No other world leader looks down with such disdain on great mountains and powerful rivers."[9]

The belief that nature must yield to human will was a central fallacy in Mao's thinking. Jasper Becker describes Mao's shortcomings in this matter:

> Mao wanted to modernize China but could not grasp the basis of modern thought, the scientific method: that the way in which the natural universe behaves can be proved or disproved by objective tests, independent of ideology or individual will.[10]

Mao's politically persecuted former secretary, Li Rui, describes Mao as a military strategist who found systematic scientific knowledge annoying and constricting. In Li's view, contemporary research on the Leap should focus on how and why China cast aside the scientific spirit and violated objective laws, and the tragic consequences that unfolded when it did.[11]

The military analogy may help to illuminate the adversarial dynamics of the human–nature relationship during the Leap. As we saw in the preceding chapter, the Anti-rightist movement brought the "troops" into order by disciplining dissenters. The Leap then marshaled the troops into formation and mobilized them in an urgent campaign of conquest. Even as political initiatives became more centralized, local public works projects such as water conservancy and regional flood control were decentralized to free local leaders to find efficient ways to overfulfill targets and unleash the enthusiasm and creativity of the masses.[12] Efficiency is critical in permitting armies to achieve rapid mobilization and deployment. During the Leap, the Great People's Communes reshaped rural society by combining agricultural collectives into enormous social and territorial units. These units were intended to serve both as a military rear guard and as engines of socialist construction. Projects were often conducted under the Chinese flag, military style. Families and villages were disbanded and peasants were moved into barracks, while collective dining halls and day care centers assumed household duties. Laborers were divided into companies and platoons and made to line up like soldiers to march to the fields. "Work Armies" acted as mobile units available for deployment by local leaders.[13] In one Hebei village, four hundred women and six hundred men were organized into a "labor shock brigade" to promote, in Mao's words, "militarization, combatization, and disciplinization."[14] Militia were promoted throughout the country, and in some places, laborers carried guns to their work sites.

Britain, China's traditional enemy and a symbol of Western imperialism, was one nominal adversary, but victory was to be won not by military engagement but by "catching up" in industry, as measured in tons of steel. Nature was the other great enemy, to be conquered and forced to yield grain in a rapid agricultural transformation. A "war against nature" was propagandized in explicitly military terms.

The first important campaign, begun in the spring of 1958, was the "battle" to build irrigation and large hydropower projects.[15] Mass labor continued day and night. Huge water conservancy projects included the Red Flag Canal, about which the extraordinary claim was made that twelve times more earth was moved in the single week beginning December 12, 1959 than was moved to build the whole Panama Canal.[16] Forced resettlement to make way for a dam for the Xin'an power station project in Zhejiang province was carried out so suddenly that people were told to "bring along more good ideology and less old furniture," and form "combat-ready military-style organizations" to expedite the march from their homes.[17] Edward Friedman, Paul Pickowicz, and Mark Selden describe how the cultural establishment was harnessed to instill the Leap's military mind-set:

> People were called on to defend the nation and destroy its enemies... With militarization a central goal of the Leap, writer Ouyang Shan was attacked for writing as if there were a common human nature, instead of distinguishing enemies from friends by building on notions of class war so that people would learn to hate the enemy.[18]

Utopian urgency to modernize was a core characteristic of the Great Leap Forward, as reflected in the campaign's name, which conveys a jump across time to a more advanced stage of national development. The Maoist press to improve the lot of the Chinese people immediately and to provide China with a utopian future found a ready response among farmers eager to emerge from extreme poverty and leave the suffering of decades of war behind them. Provincial and local leaders, eager for capital investment in their regions, supported Mao's wish for speed when other leaders called for caution.[19] The rhythm of urgency provides a focal theme for the environmental story of this period.[20]

CAMPAIGNS AS COMPRESSED TIME AND THE LANGUAGE OF URGENCY: "RUSHING AHEAD," "OPPOSING RUSHING AHEAD," "OPPOSING 'OPPOSING RUSHING AHEAD,'" AND "LEAPING AHEAD"[21]

Maoist *yundong,* or political campaigns, were a distinctive phenomenon of the Mao years, and the Great Leap Forward is among the most dramatic and far-reaching examples.[22] The goals of these mass mobilizations for rapid change varied from sociopolitical transformation to economic development, and the campaigns served variously to introduce new policies, change attitudes, rectify malpractice, and purge class enemies. *Yundong* were orchestrated competitions designed to achieve targets established by superiors in the bureaucratic hierarchy; targets were often adjusted upward as campaigns continued. *Yundong* enforced compliance and participation through fear, even as they provided career advancement for political activists. Conventional codes of conduct were temporarily suspended, in Michael Schoenhals' words, through "flux, uncertainty and the negation of that which was 'regular,'" as campaigns put forward the notion that Chinese society was progressing toward a bright future.[23] Campaigns kept people busy, stifled dissent, and pitted people against each other by identifying some as front-runners and others as laggards. They often involved destruction of the existing social order as a way to facilitate transformation; stability was understood as a temporary condition, with campaigns providing the dialectic of continuous revolution for China's progress toward socialism. In short, campaigns vaulted participants into extranormal states where time and change were compressed and great energy was expended for the achievement of rapid transformation. Slogans – short, easily repeated phrases that could be painted on buildings or displayed at work sites – informed the masses about current policy, whipped up enthusiasm, and fostered conformity. The Great Leap Forward was one of China's most wide-ranging and convulsing campaigns. Its defining characteristic was speed: urgency in reorganizing society, urgency in catching up with Britain in industry, urgency in raising agricultural yields, urgency in building water conservancy projects, urgency in ridding China of pests, and so on. Mao sought to use the Leap to vault China toward a future utopia, realize his revolutionary vision, and capture his place in history.

Disagreements over the pace and rate of social transformation split the Party repeatedly during the pre-Leap period and are commonly known as the "two-line struggle."[24] Discussions centered precisely on the question of speed.[25] As Mao critic Li Rui writes of the 1955–56 period, "the speed of the original development model already dissatisfied [Mao], and he wanted to explore an 'unusual' road and speed; that is to say, he wanted to use a different method, to surpass the Soviet Union, to go faster than the Soviet Union."[26] The split eventually crystallized around a contested slogan, *Duo, Kuai, Hao, Sheng* [Greater, Faster, Better, More Economical]. With the launch of the Leap in the winter of 1957–58, arguments over the slogan were resolved in favor of Mao and urgency rather than in favor of Zhou Enlai, Chen Yun, Li Xiannian, Bo Yibo, and a more measured pace.[27]

The slogan appeared publicly on January 1, 1956 in a *People's Daily* editorial urging the achievement of goals of the Second Five-year Plan ahead of time and above target.[28] Mao claimed that China could leapfrog over conventional steps in development by increasing grain output and capital construction through a great burst of energy; it could hasten the achievement of socialism by stepping up the pace of collectivization. But during the next few months, Zhou Enlai, Chen Yun, Bo Yibo, and others protested that China was going too fast. They contended that economic development should come before increased collectivization, rather than the other way around. The moderates thus became associated with the need to *fanmaojin* [oppose rushing ahead], arguing that some goals, such as building large water conservancy projects and achieving rural communal ownership, were not achievable in a short time. In the latter half of 1956, when China's economic conditions were sound, Zhou Enlai excised the urgency slogan from the draft of the Second Five-year Plan. A replacement slogan current during much of 1957 encouraged a middle path, guarding against both "left opportunism" and "rushing ahead." But Chairman Mao remained discontented with the slower pace.

Mao counterattacked in October 1957 at the Third Plenum of the Eighth Communist Party Central Committee, when he managed to have the *Duo, Kuai, Hao, Sheng* slogan restored. He argued that "deceleration" [*cuitui*] was wrong, and that those who "opposed rushing ahead" were letting the people down. He substituted another phrase, *yuejin,* or leaping ahead, for *maojin,* rushing ahead.[29] While it had been easy to oppose *maojin,* which has a connotation of careening forth regardless of the consequences, few dared oppose *yuejin,* or making a leap forward, especially in light of Mao's accusations that those who "opposed rushing ahead" were linked with rightists. Then, in Moscow, on November 18, 1957, while Mao was in the Soviet Union celebrating the fortieth anniversary of the October Revolution with other representatives of world Communist parties, he made his famous statement that if the Soviet Union could catch up with the United States in steel output, then surely, within fifteen years, China could catch up with Britain. By the end of 1957, with press statistics heralding great advances in every development area, the Great Leap Forward was *de facto* under way.[30]

At meetings in the cities of Hangzhou, Nanning, and Chengdu in spring 1958, Mao continued to "oppose opposing-rushing-ahead" [*fan fanmaojin*], obtaining provincial support for his views and circumventing central-level naysayers, who were portrayed as throwing cold water on the enthusiasm of the masses. In Nanning on January 13, he sharply criticized Zhou Enlai, very nearly calling him a rightist.[31] He argued, "the rightists launched full-scale opposition to 'rushing ahead' asserting that 'the present is inferior to the past'... The opposition to 'rushing ahead' discouraged 600 million people."[32] Participants in the meeting agreed to ban the phrase *fanmaojin*, thereby creating what Michael Schoenhals has called an "act of semantic self-incapacitation" by those with reservations about the Leap.[33] On March 18, Chen Boda lent support for Mao's press for urgency with the statement that China was entering a period in which "a day equals twenty years."[34]

Chen Yun, Zhou Enlai, Bo Yibo, and other doubters were forced to conduct self-examinations, and the timetable issue was resolved decisively in Mao's favor at the May 5–23, 1958 Second Session of the Eighth Party Congress. Publicly acknowledging his disgrace, Zhou Enlai offered repeated self-criticisms and even proffered his resignation from the premiership, a gesture that was rejected.[35] By now, the Party was publicly unified behind the notion that a Great Leap was possible. (In the "1981 Resolution on Certain Questions in the History of Our Party Since the Founding of the State," the post-Mao document evaluating the Party's performance after 1949, the Party publicly accepted collective guilt for going along with Mao in this.) Confident that his vision of rapid socialist transformation could be realized, Mao referred often to the question of speed. For example:

Why is the speed of our construction faster than the Soviet Union? Because our conditions are different. We have 600 million people. We follow the road traveled by the Soviet Union; we have its technical aid. Therefore, we should develop faster than the Soviet Union.[36]

The fifteen-year timetable for catching up with Britain had apparently become compressed in Mao's mind since the preceding November:

> With 11 million tons of steel next year and 17 million tons the year after, the world will be shaken. If we can reach 40 million tons in five years, we may possibly catch up with Great Britain in seven years. Add another eight years and we will catch up with the U.S.[37]

By June, Mao was claiming that two or three years would be enough for China to catch Great Britain. When Khrushchev visited China at the end of July and betrayed reservations about Mao's timetable, Mao expressed even greater confidence in his boast that China would produce 10,700,000 tons of steel by year's end – a doubling of the previous year's output. By September, it seemed to Mao that China would catch up by the following year.[38] As Li Rui has pointed out, there is nothing wrong with speed in itself, depending on the circumstances. Yet at the very time in its development that China most needed to be careful because of inexperience, "Mao Zedong became prouder by the day... With this attitude, Mao Zedong increased China's economic development speed to such a level that it couldn't have gotten any faster and had no constraints."[39]

Together with two other slogans, "Go All Out" and "Aim High" [*Guzu Ganjin, and Lizheng Shangyou*], the *Duo, Kuai, Hao, Sheng* slogan was officially adopted as the Central Line [*Zong Luxian*]. The Central Line then came to be known as the first of Three Red Banners, the other two of which were the Great Leap Forward and the Great People's Communes. Speed was the soul of the Central Line. Still, even in May 1958, at the height of his victory over those more cautious, Mao occasionally backed off pressing for a breakneck pace: "The Great Leap Forward should not be pushed too urgently. The students of red and expert schools dozed off in class. This won't do at all."[40]

The Leap's outcome is well known. In spring and summer of 1958, agricultural production targets shot up to the skies as local leaders sought to outdo one another in grain yields, casting common sense and time-tested planting techniques into shambles in the process. The leadership boasted that China had so transformed nature that the people could not possibly harvest and store all the grain the earth had produced. Then in September, the whole country was set to smelting iron and steel in primitive "backyard furnaces" to meet an enormous target for the year, with even poor, minimally industrialized provinces given high production goals. After the banner yields of the summer, energy was shifted to industrial production. That autumn, China's masses smelted 10,700,000 tons of worthless "steel," destroying many useful tools and utensils and unable to focus on storing the grain. Even in December, although production statistics were already indicating that the Leap might be in trouble, the timetable issue remained at the forefront of Mao's concern:

> The issue of "basically transforming the entire country after three years of hard struggle." Is this slogan appropriate? Can it be done in three years?... Transforming a nation of over 600 million at such a speed seems incredible... Maybe we can strive for basic transformation in five years and thorough transformation in 10–15 years. What is the best?... The sooner we achieve our goal in advance of plans, the sooner we will get the results.[41]

Within months, China was in the grip of the greatest human-created famine in history.[42] As we shall see, the Leap's impact on the environment was also devastating.

The war against nature during the Leap can be separated into various modes of battle. Elements of nature were made variously into targets of transformation, casualties in the crossfire of other battles, and targets of direct attack. In agriculture, close planting and deep plowing techniques were conscious efforts to modify the land's capacity and force it to produce more grain. Forest destruction was primarily a byproduct of the need to fuel steel furnaces; that so much of this steel proved useless makes the deforestation more poignant. The Leap's most direct, military-style assault on nature was the attack on China's sparrows, which were believed to be eating too much grain. These modes of destruction are elements in the larger pattern of war.

NATURE AS TARGET OF TRANSFORMATION:
THE LEAP IN AGRICULTURE

The People's Communes were intended to increase grain production, but their highly coordinated efforts to transform nature often led instead to the degradation of arable lands. Close planting of seedlings, deep planting, the double-blade plow, peculiar fertilization techniques, and other dubious innovations introduced in the name of science often had adverse effects on agricultural productivity or wasted farmers' energy. Efforts to expand land for grain sometimes caused tea and fruit trees to be uprooted and fragile grasslands to be destroyed.[43] Widespread well-digging sometimes caused water tables to drop and land to become salinated and alkalinized, a consequence of the Leap that affects water availability and land quality even today.[44] Moreover, as some Chinese thinkers have recently argued, because the land no longer belonged to peasant cooperatives or collectives but rather to the Commune, the people had less incentive to care for it.[45]

Mao's faith in the innovations of Soviet agricultural specialists, propagandized to the peasants, helps explain why even those experienced with the land's capacities rarely resisted these experiments. Farmers gave the pseudoscience promoted by their Great Helmsman the benefit of the doubt in the hope that it would enable them to wrest more from the land and end their poverty. The deep desire for an improvement in harsh living standards often overcame the skepticism of local leaders and ordinary farmers. Moreover, as we have seen, dissenters were harshly punished. Desire, hope, and fear thus conspired to gain widespread acquiescence in ill-conceived schemes.

In summer 1958, competitions to produce higher yields led to wild boasts and false figures. Leaders claimed that grain surpluses were so large that only a third of all arable land needed to be farmed. Breaking prior records was humorously nicknamed "sending up satellites" (after the Soviet achievement), and local rivalries induced leaders to announce higher and higher results.[46] Claims grew frenzied and targets extreme; the State Statistical Bureau was virtually dismantled in the rush to decentralize and use target numbers to whip up enthusiasm; accurate figures were abandoned.[47] Doctored photographs of a Hunan field with grain so thick that children could sit and stand on top of it were published, inducing others to try for the same results. It was later revealed that the children were actually supported by a hidden bench. Grain choked, failed to grow, and rotted.

Yet Mao apparently remained convinced that Soviet theories were correct, even though he had already broken with the Soviet urban development model and was emphasizing rural development for China. In the case of close planting, for example, Mao asserted that seeds of the same type would not compete with each other for light and nutrients: "With company they grow easily, when they grow together they will be comfortable."[48] In Guangzhou, people were ordered to plant more than ten times the normal number of seedlings in their fields.[49] In Hebei's Wugong County, where cotton yields were normally 74 *jin* per *mu,* 5,000 seeds per *mu* were planted in an effort to attain 1,000-*jin* yields. Twenty thousand sweet potato plants per *mu* were planted, and 12,000 corn plants. Of course, the crops did not do well.[50] A former student, now a retired professor of plant nutrition, recalled her agricultural college's efforts to comply with the pressure quickly to achieve higher targets:

> There was a saying about Daqing, the model oilfield, "When the oil workers shout with all their might, the great earth will shake and tremble." This slogan says the earth must listen to the orders of humans. It is wrong. It violates the laws of nature. That's what they tried to do during the Leap. There was a photograph of some children standing on top of a field of rice. It was impossible, but that's how dense our rice was supposed to be. Our university also falsified figures. By the university gate there is a field about a *mu* large. The local leaders were "launching satellites," and as an agricultural college, we felt a lot of pressure. The leaders decided that this one little piece of land should produce 10,000 *jin* of rice. We students had to take the rice shoots from several *mu* of fields, and, all day and all night, even by lamplight, bind them together and squeeze them into the field, although they were already rotting. The peasants came from the surrounding farmland to see what on earth we could be doing – after all we were an agricultural college! But even the professors had no way of resisting, because everyone was competing with each other to produce higher figures. It was not a normal time. There was pressure everywhere.

There was a notion that human will could conquer nature. If you resisted, they would criticize you. A college dean named Li Shijun, an old revolutionary, resisted the policies and he was labeled as having rightist tendencies. So even though we knew it was impossible to grow 10,000 *jin* on that field, we had to go along with it. Afterwards, for many years, there was too much hydrogen sulfate [H_2S], and we couldn't grow anything. The field was black up to our knees.

She laughed. "Even today we call it the "10,000-*jin* field.""

The effort to raise grain yields through deep plowing derived from the ideas of Soviet expert Terenty Malstev. In some cases, furrows ten feet deep were dug by hand in exhausting and senseless marathon efforts to force the earth to become more fertile. Where topsoil was thin, as in parts of Anhui province, the land's productivity was almost entirely destroyed when overturning the earth caused the soil to erode to bedrock.[51] Another agriculture professor recalled the deep ploughing campaign as a senseless waste of effort:

During the Leap, the leaders mixed political and scientific questions up together. You could only report high figures, or you would be labeled as right-leaning. Some county leaders were purged for "being suspicious of rushing ahead." We were told to plough deeply, the deeper the better. In fact, it wasn't necessary to plough deep, but we didn't dare to say or publish anything.

The professor described a Sichuan teacher, Professor Hou Guangjun, who had designed research experiments in accordance with traditional practices, advocating "natural nonploughing" [*ziran miangeng*] or "no till" agriculture. In the 1950s, after seeing his research plot in Yibin Prefecture, Changling County, a Party leader became convinced of the efficacy of his methods and gave him a large piece of low-yield land for his work. Yields rose through the no-till method. After the Leap began and his ideas became heresy, Hou escaped persecution only because he had a political patron. The agriculture professor sighed at the lost opportunity:

If Professor Hou's methods had been adopted nationally, much wasted labor could have been avoided. The whole question of "taking grain as the key link" to raise agricultural yields could have been addressed in a more moderate way. But what leaders said counted, and what intellectuals said was ignored. We were targets for reform.

Hou's noninvasive approach, reminiscent of Daoist attitudes of oneness with nature and harmonious accommodation to its ways, was the very antithesis of the Leap's coercive, labor-intensive interventionism.

For those local leaders who dared resist the intense pressures to send up "satellites" during the summer of 1958, the consequences were severe. In Wenjiang District near Chengdu, for example, a vice-Party secretary named Zeng Jia dared voice his skepticism about the claims of neighboring regions that they were producing more than 10,000 *jin* of rice per *mu,* based on a yield of 250 grains per shoot. Zeng himself climbed into the fields to count and could discover no plant with more than 80 or 90 grains.

Writer Wang Dongfu describes Zeng Jia's superiors as urging him to see the light: "Whoever doesn't believe that rice fields can produce 10,000 *jin* is not a real Party member. The Communist Party has made it possible for a field to produce 10,000 *jin.* If you do not believe it, where has your Party spirit gone?" Zeng Jia was accused of the grave crime of making a "class" mistake. He defended himself with common sense: "If a 10,000-*jin* field exists, it exists; if it doesn't, it doesn't. What does that have to do with class?" But on January 7, 1959, the *Sichuan Daily* published an article criticizing the "Accountant Faction" [*suanzhang pai*], naming Zeng as a key representative.

In fact, when Zeng's colleagues investigated one well-publicized field, it was producing 600 *jin,* not ten thousand. But Zeng was forced to confess that his outlook was faulty and that he had failed to believe in the Party and the masses. He was sent off to perform heavy labor. His only consolation came when higher authorities reduced Wenjiang District's quota of 10,000-*jin* fields from 4 million *mu* to 1.4 million *mu.* On November 8, 1959, Zeng was labeled a "right opportunist," guilty of seven political crimes. He lay sick in bed, spitting blood; whenever he felt somewhat better he was brought out for criticism/self-criticism meetings. In 1962, his superiors relented, saying that his serious errors of capitalism and individualism had largely been corrected. However, he was never permitted to resume his professional duties. When he retired in the 1980s, he was given his first raise in decades. He died in 1999 at the age of 82, yet another victim of Mao-era leaders' determination to disregard the evidence of science and replace it with a wishful version of reality that better suited their goals.[52]

Perhaps the oddest challenges to nature's laws arose from the effort to "break through superstition" by encouraging untrained people, even schoolchildren, to conduct far-fetched experiments in grafting and interbreeding. Claims reached the fantastic. In Shaanxi, a rooster was made to bear chicks; at Northwest Agricultural University, a pig was created without ears or tail. A sheep was caused to bear five lambs instead of the usual one, two, or three. A bean was weighed at more than seven *liang* [one *liang* is 50 grams],[53] and a pumpkin was as heavy as a man. Persimmon trees bore grapes, pear trees yielded apples. Rabbits were bred with pigs and pigs with cows. Crossing cotton and tomato plants produced red cotton.[54] Meanwhile, trained agricultural scientists were in constant danger of being accused of following the "white road" of bourgeois knowledge and were forced to cede respect and power to an army of "red experts."

NATURE CAUGHT IN THE CROSSFIRE: STEEL-MAKING AND DEFORESTATION

To fuel "backyard furnaces" in areas where coal was unavailable, peasants cut down trees in a concentrated countrywide deforestation so devastating that the Leap became known as the first of "three great cuttings" [*san da fa*], the second and third being the Cultural Revolution and the uncertain period after land was redistributed in the economic reforms.[55] Erosion, sedimentation, desertification, and changes in microclimate followed hard on the heels of deforestation, resulting in a protracted loss of arable land.

Peasant enthusiasm for the steel-making project is understandable, given the glowing utopian descriptions of the promised future society and the belief that some of the steel would be used to mechanize agriculture. In this respect, the Great Leap Forward was intensely popular. Before 1958, there was hardly a tractor factory in China, but now, to read the newspapers, paradise was at hand: "Lumber mills will spring up in our district, and a railway too, and our trees will be sprayed by insecticide from airplanes, and we will have a big reservoir."[56] Trustful peasants thus went all out for the campaign, enthusiastically constructing furnaces out of earthen bricks, seeking fuel wherever they could find it, and sacrificing pots, woks, knives, ladles, and iron gates to the flames. By the end of October 1958, 60 million people had participated in the smelting, and furnaces built at the grass roots numbered several million. By the end of the year, 90 million people had taken part. If those in supporting roles are included, 100 million were involved in the campaign to smelt iron and steel, or one Chinese person in six.[57] Many useful items were being melted down to provide raw material for the manufacture of identical items, but the irony was lost.

While neither the forests of China nor its people were intended victims of the Leap, collateral damage from the steel-making campaign had severe and long-lasting consequences for both nature and human beings. In the short term, people suffered physically from the grueling work and from the loss of their household implements. In the longer term, the steel-making campaign diverted attention from bringing in the rich harvest and was a direct cause of the Great Famine that began that winter.

Like the "rightist" hydro-engineer Huang Wanli, who worked with his fellow laborers for thirty-six hours without rest to build a reservoir, the Chinese people were asked to push themselves beyond the exhaustion point. Accidents were common, as exemplified in a fictional account in the well-known 1994 Zhang Yimou film, *Huozhe* [To Live], based on a novel of the same name. A schoolchild, exhausted from day-and-night steel-smelting, is carried sleeping to his school's backyard furnace by his father, who is afraid the family will be perceived as political laggards if his son drops out. The child crawls off to sleep behind a wall. The District Chief, also exhausted from his own frantic work, backs a car into the wall, toppling it and killing the child.[58]

While people were suffering from exhaustion and accidents, China's forests were being decimated, many beyond recovery. (In many cities and parts of the countryside where coal was available, steel-smelting led less to deforestation than to waste and exhaustion.) Reliable figures on the extent of forests felled as fuel for backyard furnaces are scarce. The Chinese are just now calculating forest cover change; available figures are inconsistent and cannot be isolated for the Leap. Qu Geping and Li Jinchang write that by the 1970s forest cover had fallen to 12 percent, and David Lampton notes that by 1979, three years after Mao's death, China ranked 120th in the world in percentage of forested land, at 12.7 percent. In the late 1980s, He Bochuan, using remote-sensing images, found that China's forested areas had dropped to about 8 percent of land area, down from 13 percent in 1949, although he acknowledged that official statistics claimed that 13 percent remained forested.[59]

S. D. Richardson explains statistical difficulties as follows: "A continuing problem in China lies with statistical definition... Statistics of forest areas deriving from 'percentage cover of land surface' lack precision... Moreover, definitions change."[60] Beginning in 1986, for example, canopy cover of only 30 percent was suddenly counted among "forest resources," whereas they had previously been limited to 40 percent or more.[61] Nevertheless, Richardson has determined that, at least for human-planted forests, the Leap's impact can be measured: "There was a sharp drop in afforested area between 1957 and 1964 – due in part to felling of young shelter plantations to fuel the backyard industries called for by the Great Leap Forward." He then cites figures for the same period, provided in 1985 by the Ministry of Forestry, to show a drop in shelter forests from 993,000 to 437,000 hectares and in total man-made forests (including timber forests and economic crops) from 4,355,000 to 2,911,000.[62] A more recent study of deforestation in China, by Chinese scholar Wang Hongchang, extrapolates, "The proportion of growing stock destroyed in [the studied] provinces during the Great Leap Forward ranges from one third (Hunan, Hubei) to one tenth (Sichuan)."[63]

Despite such statistical difficulties, many Chinese analysts to whom I spoke concurred that at least 10 percent of China's forests were cut down within a few short months during the Leap. In Yunnan, for example, a geography professor was confident of his figures:

> The eastern part of the province had coal, but in the west there was very little electricity. So they had to cut trees during the Leap

for fuel. From Liberation until 1958, the area was 48 percent forested. They deforested about 10 percent of that during the Leap, so between 30,000 and 40,000 square kilometers were degraded, to different degrees.

Not all the deforestation of the Leap was due to backyard furnaces, of course. Large meetings at the commune headquarters sometimes involved huge bonfires, and the collective dining halls' giant woks also consumed great amounts of firewood.[64] Additional deforestation, as well as grassland erosion, occurred during the Leap when new croplands were opened up. However, as we shall see, conversion of wilderness to croplands became even more intensive after the Great Famine.

Many Chinese were unhappy about the rapidity and scope of the cutting. A Sichuan sociologist informed me that during his fieldwork in 1963, farmers expressed great anger at the cutting of trees they had known since childhood. They denounced policies that deprived them of trees, animals, and land, then left them starving. During subsequent "speak bitterness" campaigns intended to rally sentiment about the evils of prerevolutionary society, he said, peasants kept speaking about the Great Famine, and about their anger at the destruction of so many of the trees that had provided them with shade, hunting-grounds, firewood, and chestnuts.[65]

Lei Da Shi, a small mountain several hours' distance from Chongqing, was covered with huge trees until 1958, when the whole forest was cut down to fuel the steel furnaces. Although the peasants there expressed nostalgia for the great forests, they remembered that they had supported the steel-making campaign with all their hearts. A middle-aged woman and her neighbors sat in an open courtyard facing the mountain and reminisced:

Before, this was all virgin forest, with pines a foot thick. It was so dense that I was afraid to go there at night. The brush and branches we gathered were enough for all our firewood needs. We never had to cut the trees. There were small animals, rabbits and pheasants. I was only ten or eleven during the Leap. We collected scrap metal and pots while the grownups cut the trees. The result was a big mess of melted metal. We turned it over to the local steel factories to process further. This was supposed to be the first step. But the temperature was too low. Wood can never burn hot enough to make steel.

During subsequent campaigns, the peasants of Lei Da Shi were directed to plant grain on the mountain, but their efforts met with little success. Only after Mao's death were they permitted to reforest the mountain. But the new trees have been planted with an eye toward future harvests, and the old growth forest has been lost forever. The middle-aged woman revealed another element in the Leap's destructiveness when she remarked, "There used to be a monastery up there, on a flat rock. There was an old monk. Then he died and there was no one. So we took it down during the Leap to burn the wood and make steel." Similarly, the last Buddhist and Daoist temples of the Hebei village of Raoyang were destroyed during the steel campaign, when ramparts and rafters were taken down to fuel the furnaces.[66]

A man at Lei Da Shi commented, "I never heard of any opposition to the steel-making. Everyone was patriotic. We never thought about the long-term effects of cutting the trees." An old man who had been the Production Team leader during the Mao years summed up the spirit of the times: "Everyone was of one heart to make steel."

Others' memories indicate a mix of obedience, ignorance, patriotism, and helplessness among the participants. A former student at Meihua Mountain Middle School helped to build small furnaces, fueling them with wood from houses in the countryside:

Whatever the teachers told us to do, we did. We went to the Jinyun Mountains to mine iron ore. We spent more than ten days there, until the rains came and it got too cold. We also used scrap metal and old woks that weren't needed because of the collective dining halls. We made steel for about a month in the second half of 1958, after school started. We used a bellows. There was a sprayer for *lulufen* [benzene hexachloride], a pesticide now banned because it is too toxic, and it made a great bellows. What we made was unusable, waste metal. But we reported it all anyway. We were trying to help reach the national goal of 10,700,000 tons.

A Sichuan journalist recalled feeling powerless to stop perpetrating a lie. He and his newspaper colleagues had to make steel too, twenty-four hours a day:

> We worked on the sports field for about twenty days. We put out the newspaper and smelted steel in shifts. We melted iron railings. As soon as we made the steel, we could all see that it was no good. Years later, I was asked to write an article on a steel factory, and it became even more clear to me how bad our product was. But at the height of the movement, everyone had to compile figures. Our paper had to collect the statistics on how many tons were being produced in our district. We could see the campaign wasn't working, but we had to publish the numbers. Many millions of people went to the mountains to cut trees. At the end of 1958, we achieved the goal, but most of the steel was useless.

Even Chairman Mao acknowledged as early as December 1958 that all this effort had produced only a little more than 6 million tons of usable steel, after refining.[67] It is unclear how much was of any value at all, and the effort cost China 2 billion *yuan.* Nonetheless, Mao argued that this expenditure was "tuition" for the nation's newly acquired skills in steel-making.[68]

A woman told me the following story about her regret for her role during the Leap, when she was sent to help widen roads and "vehicularize" (*gao chezihua*) the countryside so as to facilitate steel transport:

> We were supposed to build wheeled push-carts to increase efficiency, and we were supposed to build them quickly. We knew that this push-cart was supposed to have one wheel and two frames, but we had never seen one and had no idea how to make it. The *wutong* tree is hollow, so it occurred to me that we could use it to make wheels, and we could use bamboo for the frame. So my classmates and I cut down an ancient *wutong* tree. No one told us we couldn't. The first turned out to be too small, so we cut down another one. Then we cut so much bamboo to try to make these carts! In the end, of course, the carts couldn't carry a thing. They

fell apart as we pushed them. We made dozens and dozens, and put them out for display. Later, they were burned as firewood. Even now I feel sad to think that those trees had grown for decades and decades, but no one stopped us from cutting them down.

Despite this tale, she and others insisted that successes can be attributed to the Leap, particularly some small irrigation and water conservancy projects:

A small family can't irrigate, they're always arguing with others over water use. The government organized water projects; the Red Flag Canal is a famous example. In 1959, I helped to build a pond called the Student Pond. We were so proud. We used broken pottery to put the name on the dike. It's still there.

Later, she was told, in my presence, that the pond today is clogged with garbage. She said sadly, "Maybe not all the ponds were maintained. But in my memory it seemed it was a success. Some people may have taken away the stones to build pigsties."

NATURE AS ENEMY: THE BATTLE AGAINST SPARROWS

If nature could be a target for transformation, like farmlands, or a collateral casualty, like the forests, it could also be understood as an enemy to be destroyed. The Leap's most directly targeted attack on nature was a nationwide assault on sparrows. As we have seen, the Leap envisioned a utopian socialist future; this included a vision of a society in which cleanliness and hygiene would be the norm.[69] To this end, the Four Pests – rats, sparrows, flies, and mosquitoes – would have to be eradicated. A slogan, "Wipe out the Four Pests" [*Chu Si Hai*] was propagated, and a concerted, highly coordinated, and synchronized campaign to eliminate the birds was conducted throughout the country.[70] Unlike the destruction of forests or the degradation of arable land, the campaign against sparrows was truly an effort to kill.

The assault against sparrows enlisted child-soldiers in the war against nature, for schoolchildren were among the main participants in the anti-pest drive. Chairman Mao himself established a tender age for participation when he spoke at the Second Session of the Eighth Party

Congress on May 18, 1958: "The whole people, including five-year old children, must be mobilized to eliminate the four pests."[71]

Many then in elementary school remember the campaign as a wonderful diversion from the classroom. In Sichuan, a former schoolchild recalled his sparrow-killing activities:

> It was fun to "Wipe out the Four Pests." The whole school went to kill sparrows. We made ladders to knock down their nests, and beat gongs in the evenings, when they were coming home to roost. It was many years before we knew that sparrows are good birds. At the time, we only knew they ate grain.

As with a real military campaign, coordination was of the essence. Participants had to attack simultaneously or the sparrows would simply fly away to more tranquil places. But when millions of Chinese of all ages dispersed to the hillsides at the same hour to raise a ruckus, the sparrows had nowhere to alight. The degree of synchronicity achieved is almost as striking as the campaign's self-destructiveness. An agricultural chemistry specialist at Chongqing's Southwest Agricultural University recalled that all Beibei District went to the hills at dusk.

> We had to bang on pots until the poor sparrows were exhausted. We did it for several days. There were many fewer sparrows after that. I remember a famous restaurant, the Lugaojian, that had moved from Suzhou to Chongqing during the Anti-Japanese war. Their speciality was two salted sparrows on a stick for a *jiao*. But after the Four Pests campaign, you couldn't buy them any more. And in 1959, there were more insects. It wasn't something you could notice for yourself, but our Plant Protection Department measured more infestations in the grain.

She remembered that the Four Pests were made to seem like enemies: "There was a painter who specialized in painting sparrows, the way others specialize in painting horses, shrimp, or fish. After the campaign to get rid of the Four Pests, he no longer dared to show his paintings to anyone!" The impact of the campaign in her area was long-lasting, exacerbated, she believes, by excessive pesticide use. "I didn't see sparrows for years. This year, for the first time, there's a nest outside my window."

Too late, the farmers learned that sparrows were their greatest allies in insect control. By April 1960, bedbugs had been substituted for sparrows, but by then the sparrow population in parts of China had been decimated. In Yunnan, a botanist recalled how Mao himself raised the call to do away with the sparrows and then just as suddenly put a stop to it:

We took down their nests, broke their eggs, and killed their nestlings. Later, scientists pointed out that sparrows also eat insects, and the National Academy of Sciences issued reports on how many insects they ate compared to how many seeds. So we stopped killing sparrows. Chairman Mao just said, *suanle* ["forget it"]. In those days, one man's word counted for everything.

Mao's sudden countermanding of orders without explanation, and his apparent expectation that no one would question these reversals, was, of course, classic military behavior.

For all its foolhardiness, the spirit of the Four Pests campaign has not completely disappeared from China. A poster dated June 19, 1998 spotted on a public wall at Southwest Agricultural University exhorted, "Get Rid of the Four Pests," just like the slogan used during the Leap. Cockroaches had been substituted for sparrows or bedbugs, but the other "pests" were the same – rats, flies, and mosquitoes. Ninety-five percent of households and workplaces were ordered to rid themselves of a certain percentage of pests by a certain deadline. It seemed unlikely that these targets could be enforced or that the local people would respond well to this campaign-style approach. A similar announcement was spotted on an alley wall in Beijing in the spring of 1998.[72]

It is not possible to quantify how much grain was lost due to insect infestations after the sparrow-killings, especially considering other factors influencing grain harvest figures such as the state's neglect of the 1958 crop because of the steel production drive and excessive levying of grain for the cities. The loss was significant enough, however, that Chinese often mention the Four Pests campaign as causing a lasting ecological imbalance. The simultaneous, highly coordinated, and compulsory mass slaughter of sparrows was a singularly foolish episode of wasteful mobilization of human energy in an effort to alter the natural world. It is also an unusually clear example of how Mao-era adversarial attitudes toward nature were translated into action.

CONSEQUENCES

The voluntarism, impetuosity, and military-style mobilization of Mao's Great Leap Forward led to the greatest famine in history, with common estimates ranging from thirty-five million to as many as fifty million deaths from starvation during 1959 to 1961. As the "launching satellites" phase of the Leap grew more and more detached from reality, state officials increased levies and extracted too much grain. Fields were degraded through unscientific practices, and some land was allowed to lie fallow because propaganda had it that the agricultural question had been resolved. In some places, as much as one-third of the land was abandoned, following the ideas of Soviet agronomist Vasilii Robertovich Villiams.[73] Meanwhile, peasants were encouraged to gorge themselves in collective dining halls, and local grain reserves were soon exhausted.[74] During the first autumn of the Leap, the harvest was all but abandoned for steel-smelting, and grain lay rotting in the fields. When China was confronted by drought during the second summer of the Leap, starvation had already begun in the countryside. Mao's enthusiasm for the Leap was momentarily shaken in the period before the August 1959 Lushan Plenum. However, he failed to seize the opportunity to reverse himself, ignoring evidence of the famine. Instead, he purged Peng Dehuai and other close advisors for trying to tell him the truth.[75] As the famine worsened, other leaders dared not speak. Several, including Chen Yun, Deng Xiaoping, and Liu Shaoqi, went into seclusion. The state extracted even more grain from villagers. Coffers full of grain stood locked, while local leaders launched a campaign of terror to ferret out hidden grain. Despite isolated protests and efforts to wrest grain from trains and state storehouses, resistance was effectively paralyzed, and people were forbidden to leave their villages even to beg. The famine reached its height in the first months of 1960. The Sino-Soviet split of July 1960 and loss of Soviet aid seemed only to strengthen Mao's denials. However, he did at last back away from the Leap, and at the July 15–August 10, 1960 Beidaihe work conference, emphasis was once again given to grain production and feeding the people.[76]

The Great Famine was an environmental and human disaster, for the Three Hard Years of 1959 to 1961 witnessed the breakdown of the systems on which people depended. The Great Leap Forward disrupted the ecological balance of many of China's agricultural regions. As people starved throughout China – from labor camps of the Great Northwest to country villages of the interior – the living creatures on whom they depended were hunted down and eaten.[77] Plant life, too, was decimated, as tree bark, seeds, roots, and anything remotely edible was consumed. Jasper Becker quotes an informant's recollection: "There were no birds left in the trees, and the trees themselves had been stripped of their leaves and bark. At night there was no longer even the scratching of rats and mice, for they too had been eaten or had starved to death."[78] Hebei farmers saw the ecological connections clearly when, remembering the famine, they told Friedman, Pickowicz, and Selden, "If people cheat the land, the land will cheat people's stomachs."[79] In some areas, such as Anhui and Henan provinces, ecological breakdown and famine were more severe than in other areas, in part because of local farming conditions and in part because local political leaders were guilty of egregious mismanagement and cruelty.[80]

Asked to reflect on their experiences of the Leap and its aftermath, several scholars focused on the campaign as an all-out attack on the laws of nature. One scientist commented,

> In my opinion, if you use scientific methods and principles, it's all right to "struggle" with nature, but if you violate those laws, the struggle will fail. People can discover natural laws and use them, but they cannot create them. That's the proper relationship between man and nature.

Another informant blamed Mao's views of nature and his departure from traditional culture for the Leap and subsequent disasters:

> In our country, the language of struggle against nature has become a habit. When the newspapers talk about the struggle against drought and flood, and about challenging and conquering flood, for us, this does not seem strange. It is said that in traditional China, people waited for the Heavens to decide their fate. *Ren Ding Sheng Tian* [Man Must Conquer Nature] was Chairman

Mao's idea. In fact, I'm against it. Human strength is limited. A person is small. How can we control and master nature? How is it possible to place a person above nature? It's not scientific. Chinese tradition has great respect for nature. A person is tiny in the face of nature. According to custom, we should respect the heavens, the earth, the emperor, our relatives, and our teachers. But during the Mao years, our great culture was so turned upside down you could no longer recognize it.

Dai Qing, the well-known opponent of the Three Gorges Dam, argues that traditions of balance and order were repeatedly violated through Mao-era mobilizations to conquer nature:

> The "red specialists" have never managed to grasp the concept of fundamental order and balance in the relationship between humankind and nature. At every turn – from its preference for a planned economy with a focus on iron and steel production, to its promotion of grain production, population growth, and large-scale dam construction – the Chinese leadership has made decisions which run counter to the Chinese philosophical concepts of maintaining order and balance between humankind and nature. Not surprisingly, each of these decisions has caused immense damage to the country's environment and natural resources. For political reasons, however, those scholars and intellectuals who are in touch with this philosophical tradition have had very little opportunity to speak up.[81]

To these scholars' reflections we may add some thoughts about the role that urgency played in this great project to transform nature, inviting harm both to people and to the environment. In the short term, haste caused exhaustion and accidents; in the long term, it disrupted the balances on which the people depended for sustenance and deprived nature of time to recover. Of course, natural systems are always changing, even without human intervention, and nature is often remarkably resilient. However, as the example of the 1958–60 Great Leap Forward demonstrates, human activity can alter mutual dependencies more rapidly than nature can adapt, sometimes causing the collapse of entire ecosystems. Implemented as the Leap was in a competitive political mode that rejected scientific objectivity, the campaign caused enormous environmental and human destruction. Actions taken in accordance with the Maoist understanding of the natural world as something that could be bent to the human will through force ended up destroying the people's very basis for subsistence.

With the country in the throes of deep famine, urgency was given a temporary rest; mobilization yielded to consolidation. The totalitarian politics of utopianism retreated into somber authoritarianism.[82] The famine discredited the left-wing approach and chastened the Leap's advocates. Mao himself enjoyed some "quiet years" in the early 1960s, reading history and basically ignored by the rest of the leadership.[83] Mao explained the need for periods of retreat in terms of dialectics, perhaps in an attempt to save face:

> One wave comes in as another crests. This is the unity of the opposites of high speech and low speed... If there are high speed and labor only, it will be one-sided. If it is labor alone and no rest, then how can it be! In doing anything there has to be a period of high speed and a period of low speed. In fighting a war in the past, there had to be periods of consolidation, replenishment and rest between two campaigns... In fighting a war there also has to be a tempo... High speed turns into low speed, and low speed turns into high speed.[84]

In this fashion, Mao conducted a tactical retreat and licked his wounds, quietly preparing for his political recovery.

The economy moved onto a sounder footing, and ordinary people enjoyed a breathing spell from major political campaigns. The natural world, too, enjoyed a respite from extreme human intervention; for a few short years, there were no conquest-style campaigns against nature. But urgency was again unleashed with the Cultural Revolution, as Mao reemerged in full control of China's political life, setting Red Guards against his enemies and again placing China on a headlong course toward political, social, and physical transformation. The "More, Faster, Better, More Economical" [*Duo, Kuai, Hao, Sheng*] slogan reappeared. Great dams were again hastily built; the 1970

Gezhou Dam groundbreaking, for example, was rushed to coincide with Mao's birthday; the plans were so hastily designed that the dam had to be rebuilt within two years.[85] All too quickly, the Chinese people were once again asked to labor night and day to transform nature and themselves.

"The Foolish Old Man Who Removed the Mountains"
Yugong Yi Shan

"Encircle the Lakes, Create Farmland"
Weihu, Zaotian

3

GRAINFIELDS IN LAKES AND DOGMATIC UNIFORMITY

How "Learning from Dazhai" Became an Exercise in Excess

After the famine of the Three Hard Years, concern about feeding China's growing population dominated agricultural policy, as captured in a slogan, "Take Grain as the Key Link" [*Yi Liang Wei Gang*]. The chastened Mao Zedong settled into a quieter mode, allowing other leaders to emphasize the production of consumer staples. Peasants were again permitted to grow vegetables on small private plots and to trade their surplus in free markets, and the rural economy gradually rejuvenated. The abrupt withdrawal of Soviet aid in July 1960, which soon resulted in a full split between the two socialist powers, had cast China into deep isolation. In reaction, China's leaders promoted "self-reliance" [*zili gengsheng*]. Although the phrase expressed defiance toward the outside world, it also described a domestic policy of regional self-sufficiency, as localities were asked to support themselves in grain and other supplies. This was both a security precaution to guard against distribution problems in the event of war and a way of reducing the impoverished state government's responsibility to provide relief.

By 1964, Mao was beginning a political comeback. He called on the entire country to imitate the Dazhai Brigade of the Dazhai People's Commune, which had overcome natural disaster through self-reliance.[1] Located in Shanxi's mountainous Xiyang County, not far from the historic Communist Party base at Yanan in neighboring Shaanxi, Dazhai first attracted notice in August 1963, after a week of flooding caused by heavy rainfall. Fruit trees, tools, and fields were swept away, and the homes of almost all 160 families were destroyed. When local Party secretary Chen Yonggui announced the principle of the "three nos" – refusing state grain, refusing state funds, and refusing state relief materials – Dazhai's future as a model of self-reliance was assured. Chen Yonggui declared that not only would Dazhai rebuild without help, it would even contribute grain to the state. As has been captured in countless propaganda posters and articles, the Dazhai peasants worked hard to make good on this promise; white-turbaned Chen Yonggui labored prominently in the fields among them. On February 10, 1964, the *People's Daily* raised the call to follow "the Dazhai Road" and use heroic will and revolutionary spirit to "change the face of rivers and mountains" [*he shan yi se*]. This article also resurrected the infamous Three Banners – the Central Line (including the slogan, "More, Faster, Better, More Economical"), the People's Communes, and the Great Leap Forward – which Mao had not given up despite their association with the Great Famine. (He even compared blaming the Three Hard Years on the Banners to blaming the sun when a demon appears on a sunny day.) In June 1964, Dazhai was made a national model for agriculture, and by Mao's seventy-first birthday in December 1964, Chen Yonggui was sitting at the head table while moderate leaders Zhou Enlai, Deng Xiaoping, and Liu Shaoqi were ostracized to lesser positions.[2] Photographs of Chen and Mao together were published on the first page of the *People's Daily* above the slogan, "In Agriculture, Learn from Dazhai."[3] This slogan, one of the most tenacious of the Mao years, would endure until a few years after Mao's death.

Dazhai was initially promoted as an embodiment of the spirit of independence, hard work, and close relations between Party leaders and ordinary peasants, who were depicted laboring together to terrace mountainsides and fill gullies with earth. But an aging Mao Zedong was soon presenting Dazhai as a universal political paradigm for the revolutionary rigor and fervor that he claimed China had lost. This formerly ordinary brigade of peasants scraping out an existence in an inhospitable part of China became a key part of his strategy to return to prominence and once again make ideology and class struggle paramount.

After laying the groundwork, Mao made his big move in 1966, at the age of 73, when he launched the great upheaval of the Cultural Revolution, calling on adoring "masses" to attack his enemies within the Party. On July 16, he proclaimed his youthful vigor and full-fledged return to the political stage through a symbolic, nature-conquering swim in the Yangzi River, during which he was reported to have covered vast distances at implausible speeds.[4] Mao's motives for the Cultural Revolution were complex: He sought to awaken the revolution from what he saw as its revisionist torpor; he wanted to wrest power from moderate leaders and reclaim his central role in political life; and he felt pressure to realize his revolutionary vision within the limited time remaining to him. "Continuing revolution" and rapid transformation again threw China into the chaos and upheaval of multiple *yundong,* or political campaigns. "Learning from Dazhai" became an exercise in political fervor:

> The principle of placing politics in command and proletarian ideology in the forefront, the spirit of self-reliance and hard work, and the communist style of loving the motherland and the collective is, in brief, the [D]achai spirit which is so worthy of being widely promoted.[5]

An ideological struggle over how to reward peasants for labor was resolved, through the Dazhai example, in favor of an ultra-leftist solution of assigning "work points" based on political performance, exchangeable for grain after the harvest. Dazhai peasants were compelled to demonstrate to all of China how laborers should be evaluated and rewarded according to their "political attitudes" [*zhengzhi biaoxian*].[6] The works of Chairman Mao were heralded as powerful weapons for the transformation of individual consciousness, society, and the physical world. Mao Zedong Thought was portrayed as overcoming the limitations of difficult terrain, as Dazhai peasants took political study into the fields and paused during meals to read and discuss the Little Red Book. Armed with this powerful ideological weapon, it was claimed, they could terrace steep rocky mountains and recover farmland from rivers and lakes, often with only the most primitive of tools. With the eyes of China upon them, Dazhai peasants demonstrated how grainfields could be carved into the most unlikely of landscapes. All China was exhorted to follow suit.

The Dazhai model embodied Mao's belief that the unleashed power of ideas could transform and conquer nature for the betterment of humankind. Instead, the philosophy brought enormous suffering both to the people of Dazhai and to a nation forced to follow their example. It also degraded and destroyed the natural world. Although rooted in the Great Leap Forward notion that the power of will could conquer nature, the Dazhai model took the Maoist relationship with nature in a new direction, as it was applied mechanistically in scenarios where it could not possibly succeed because it was inappropriate for local conditions. (Moreover, unbeknownst to its obedient imitators, Dazhai was a carefully tended and constructed fantasy universe whose "success" was predicated, as we shall see, upon central subsidies and military assistance.) In the Dazhai-driven stage of the Maoist relationship with nature, dogmatic uniformity – using a single pattern without consideration for local conditions, or cutting everything with one slice of the knife [*yi dao qie*] – ran roughshod over regional differences and customs, and usurped the power of decision-makers experienced with proven local practices. The effort to "get grain from the mountaintops, get grain from the lakes" [*xiang shan yao liang, xiang hupo yao liang*] often had disastrous ecological consequences. As we shall see in this section, inappropriate terracing on steep slopes and areas with thin topsoils brought deforestation, erosion, and sedimentation, while encroachments on lakes and rivers led to ecosystem imbalance, microclimate changes, and increased flooding.[7] The Dazhai model, its applications elsewhere in China, and its environmental impact are exemplified in a highly revealing example of dogmatic uniformity gone awry, the 1970 filling of wetlands in Lake Dian in Yunnan province.

MAO-ERA USE OF MODELS

Although models are standard teaching tools, they can be used to coerce. Authoritarian leaders value their efficiency, for models facilitate uniformity, centralization, regimentation, coordination, and mobilization while working to suppress the spontaneity, individualism, and airing of alternatives that might interfere with government control. Models foster conformity by exalting a place, an individual, or a method as an ideal to be studied and imitated, and by making that study and imitation compulsory. As Roderick MacFarquhar notes of the Mao years, "models encouraged the centrally led campaign pattern of development, and the speed it engendered."[8] For Mao, using the Dazhai model was also a way to bypass forces within China's bureaucracy who did not share his political vision.

Maoist models included exemplary individuals chosen – and essentially created – to embody characteristics considered desirable for imitation countrywide, as well as model workers and students singled out for study at the local level. The model soldier Lei Feng, whose "lost" diary detailed endless selfless acts performed in obscurity without desire for recognition or reward, is the most famous example of the latter. His elevation to model status inspired a generation of Chinese to pen similar diaries and lose them in prominent places in hopes of achieving political glory. Dazhai laborer Jia Jincai was depicted on a postage stamp, while Daqing oil worker "iron man" Wang Jingxi was featured in numerous articles and propaganda posters. Communes, factories, and schools, publicized through propaganda posters and the media, also became models for study and duplication. Such work units were required to receive guests on study visits and demonstrate their methods and successes.

During the Cultural Revolution, study visits to Dazhai took on the aura of pilgrimages to shrines.[9] At the height of Red Guard activity in autumn 1966, Dazhai was a major destination for China's revolutionary youth. One group walked fourteen days to see the calluses on the hands of model laborer Jia Jincai. Thousands of world political leaders as well as local leaders from far-flung corners of China were escorted to Dazhai to admire its achievements.

(In post-Mao China, leaders have continued to use models to promote social and political goals. A disabled, once-disheartened-but-now-hopeful young woman named Zhang Haidi was selected as a model for China's disillusioned youth in a Party effort to counterbalance post-Mao cynicism,[10] and Lei Feng made several comebacks. More recently, the city of Xiamen has been singled out as an environmental model for its cleanliness. However, nothing since the Mao years has approached Dazhai in universality of application and level of dogmatism and coercion.)

The use of Maoist models to transform the natural world had the strong potential to damage the environment because terrain was indiscriminately treated like that of the model, regardless of variations in topography, climate, soil conditions, rainfall, or local practice. Increasingly, as imitation of Dazhai came to be seen as a measure of loyalty to Chairman Mao, the slightest departure from the pattern invited attack and exile, if not worse. Dogmatism, literalism, and formalism, born of zeal and fear, overtook China as the Cultural Revolution progressed; whatever the people of Dazhai did to their land was imitated, to the letter, in rural areas throughout China. No matter how inhospitable or steep the terrain, and regardless of how successful, appropriate, or time-tested other uses of the land, terraces were built and grain was planted just as in the hillsides of Dazhai. Tools used in Dazhai were copied and employed everywhere.[11] As the propaganda of the times put it, like the farmers of Dazhai, all the Chinese people would struggle to

> wage a battle against nature to overcome poverty ... transform hills ... prevail over nature... With the simplest tools they had at hand, they cut into the mountains and hewed out rocks to build terraces and retaining walls. With good soil ... they filled in gully-ridden slopes and turned them into good farm land.[12]

A history recently published in China, though not rejecting the use of models, critiques the uncompromising application of the Dazhai ideal:

> In each region, and for each aspect of work, all kinds of advanced models should be discovered and promoted according to practical circumstances. But during the Cultural Revolution, in such a huge socialist country as ours, only Dazhai was considered an "advanced model," and there couldn't be any other advanced models. Only the Dazhai experience could be promoted in the whole country, making Dazhai the absolutistic single model, and then this model was applied to all the country's brigades... This even developed into "whatever Dazhai does, the rural areas of the whole country must do."... Thus the Dazhai production team's specific methods, like moving mountains to create farmland, and neglecting a diversified economy to guarantee the stability and high yield of grain, was imitated even when not practical, and this violated the laws of nature and economics, harmed ecological balance, and wasted human strength and supplies.[13]

In authoritarian and totalitarian societies, the political need for a model usually precedes its creation, as leaders seek to combat unwelcome or noncompliant views and behavior by presenting ideal alternatives. There was thus a clear incentive to fabricate and embellish on Dazhai's success. In later years, Dazhai was exposed as a fraud – the "self-reliant" brigade had received generous external aid, and production figures had been grossly exaggerated.[14] The same was true of other, mini-Dazhai model operations. Sinologist David Zweig drily comments, "Every district in China probably had its own Dazhai model which received the lion's share of state investment, technology, and labor assistance from peasants all over the county."[15] The promulgation of one such model, he writes, was disastrous for Guangdong peasants when a provincial leader forced their brigade to grow grain:

> He sent in a group of cadres who terrified the peasants into leveling the bamboo on the hills. After tearfully obeying, the peasants then terraced the hills, but the soil was too poor, and there was too little water. So the peasants built a reservoir and a culvert to bring the water to the fields. When the rice still did not flourish, Japanese fertilizer was applied. When the fields were finally productive, the district Party secretary made a movie, which was shown county-wide, about how this locality, through self-reliance, mass mobilization, and hard work, was voluntarily growing more grain for the state. After other places emulated this model, the entire county became impoverished.[16]

Positive outcomes did sometimes emerge from application of the Dazhai model, depending on local topography and climate conditions. Contemporary scholars have praised Dazhai-style terracing in the Ordos Plateau as a success,[17] and even sharp critics of Mao-era land reclamation policy have made favorable mention of the construction of more than a thousand kilometers of irrigation canals in Xinjiang.[18] But terracing hillsides to create arable land was often inappropriate. Even where topsoil was thin and slopes were steep, people were made to carve out terraces, thereby causing lasting erosion. In some places, in extreme and slavish emulation of Dazhai's example, hills were even built on flat plains so that they could be terraced. As late as 1976, local leaders told a Western scholar visiting the North China Plain near Zhengzhou that they were embarking on a project to study Dazhai by cutting into the plain to develop terraced fields.[19] The literalistic emphasis on grain could also be damaging: Viable crops were often destroyed because they were not grain; fruit trees, tea bushes, and medicinal plants were cut down, even in places where grain could not grow.[20] Land better suited to grazing or other uses was converted to grain. Blindly following the doctrine of the moment and worshipfully applying Mao's words, local leaders outdid themselves to create land reclamation projects for which they could claim success, regardless of local conditions.

THE DAZHAI SPIRIT AND THE FOOLISH OLD MAN

As we have seen, the notion that ideology had power to remold the physical world was a key element of the Dazhai model. Mao Zedong Thought, used as a tool to unleash enthusiasm for mass labor, was seen as capable, *in and of itself,* of overcoming nature's stubborn unwillingness to produce more grain everywhere. Slogans reflected Maoist voluntarism: "Grasp Revolution, Spur Production." "If people listen to Chairman Mao, the land will listen to them." "When the thought of men changes, the earth yields more grain." As reflected in propaganda materials, the study of Mao Zedong Thought took increasing precedence over the usual practicalities of agriculture, as in this village:

> In the spring of 1966 ... they reversed their usual practice. Instead of first putting aside seeds, fertilizer and other materials, they grasped "ideological preparations" by calling on everybody to concentrate on studying Chairman Mao's works with the idea of solving their problems.[21]

Hard work would conquer nature. The land would be forced to hand over grain, no matter how barren, inhospitable, or better suited to other purposes it might be.[22]

Mao's preeminent statement of his voluntaristic philosophy was a retold legend, one of three short essays familiarly nicknamed the "Three Old Articles" [*Lao San Pian*].[23] These essays became a catechism for revolutionary China; many could recite them from memory. One article was an elegy for Norman Bethune, the Canadian doctor said to represent the spirit of Communist internationalism; another was an exhortation to "Serve the People"; the third was a parable, "The Foolish Old Man Who Removed the Mountains" [*Yugong Yi Shan*], which became strongly identified with the hardscrabble Dazhai spirit. A metaphor for mobilization against feudalism and imperialism, the parable of the Foolish Old Man was Mao's battle cry in the struggle against nature.

The Foolish Old Man decides to level two mountain peaks, bucket by bucket. His dogged faith eventually moves the skeptics, and the joined labor of many hands accomplishes the seemingly impossible, flattening the mountains. While Mao's version describes the mountains as symbols of the twin evils of feudalism and imperialism, the parable was also interpreted quite literally, as the Chinese people labored with simple tools and bare hands to turn mountains into plains and to fill in valleys and gullies. The spirit of the Foolish Old Man, often mentioned in the same breath as the spirit of Dazhai, was credited with transforming Chinese landscapes by inspiring backbreaking physical sacrifices and communal effort.[24] A representative propaganda headline about the Dazhai brigade, for example, praises the peasants as "The Foolish Old Men of Today." The text describes how, "Displaying the revolutionary spirit of the Foolish Old Man ... they have been struggling against nature for over ten years."[25] Promotion of the Dazhai model and Foolish Old Man spirit continued for over a decade; the Dazhai model was officially abandoned only in December 1978, at the path-breaking Third Plenum, when Party Secretary Hua Guofeng, Mao's successor and a great champion of Dazhai, lost power to Deng Xiaoping. Dazhai Party Secretary Chen Yonggui ceded his last central-level position only in 1981.[26] A propaganda poster issued as late as 1977, entitled "Little 'Foolish Old Men' in the Fields of Dazhai," depicts a semicircle of ruddy-cheeked Young Pioneers in red neckerchiefs, flag, shovel, buckets, and megaphone at the ready.[27]

The Dazhai model became a weapon of China's political extremists, and the people of Dazhai were forced to take the lead in leftism. Under the eyes of all China, they had little choice but to suffer. Any hint of capitalism was chased down so fiercely that Dazhai members resorted to barter to exchange goods.[28] Political struggle infused their effort to "reform the heavens and change the earth" [*gai tian huan di*]; in later years, Chen Yonggui was said to have executed numerous people for political "crimes."[29] Official publications such as *China Pictorial* hint at the agonizing physical labor and enormous suffering that the Spirit of the Foolish Old Man brought to the people of Dazhai and their imitators: "Salute to Tsui Chuan-chuan! With swollen shoulders she refuses to leave the site; pledging to learn from the heroic Dazhai girls, she emulates the men in opening up the mountains," reads one photo caption.[30] Peasants went on long midnight treks to fetch baskets of earth for newly carved terraces: "At night, groping their way in the dark, they went to Talaoyu five *li* away for earth. One basketful of soil was piled on another to make up a layer more than one foot in thickness."[31] During my own visit to Dazhai in the early 1980s, after it fell from political grace, conversations with Dazhai peasants confirmed that at least as far as their physical exertions were concerned, propaganda mirrored reality. Model laborer Jia Jincai remembered awaking before dawn to take his corn gruel and giant hammer to break rocks in the hills. By the time he paused to eat, his gruel was often frozen solid.[32]

According to the article entitled "The 'Foolish Old Men' of Today," such hardships were widely imitated:

> With the earth frozen hard, the blow of a pick left only a white mark on the ground. The shock made [the peasants'] hands crack and bleed. But no one complained. During breaks, they nibbled at their cold food while studying "The Foolish Old Man Who Removed the Mountains." The more they studied, the more enthusiastic they became.[33]

As the passage suggests, in an era of extreme leftism, suffering itself was considered a badge of advanced political thought.

Hardship spread to areas near Dazhai, and results were often disastrous. One earth-moving project lay on the border between Xiyang and Pingding counties, where a mountain was to be leveled because it obstructed revolutionary pilgrims' view of Xiyang's northern gateway to Dazhai. When peasants objected, they were told that the project had a good political purpose. But after three months of labor and an investment of 70,000 *yuan,* their labor produced only 50 *mu* of new farmland, for a cost of 1,400 *yuan* per *mu,* half the land that had been projected. In nearby Waqiu commune, peasants were made to spend their reserve funds for a project that resulted in only 3 *mu* of land. In Nieluo commune, construction of "one reservoir, one power station, and three ponds" exacted five years of labor from 280,000 people and an expenditure of more than 300,000 *yuan.* The project failed because the water table was too low.[34]

In imitation of the Foolish Old Man and the people of Dazhai, much of the Chinese peasantry was soon terracing mountainsides, filling ravines, and rewarding laborers' contributions through evaluations of "political showing." "Stirred by a revolutionary spirit which transforms nature, peasant masses all over the country are taking up with a will the large-scale construction of crop land,"[35] proclaimed *China Pictorial.*

A mass movement of learning from, overtaking, and surpassing Dazhai has rapidly spread throughout the country, whether in the plains or the hills, the interior or the border areas, south or north. Wherever the Dazhai spirit spread, there was a change in the mental outlook of the people, in the whole manner of production and in social practices. Now, advanced farming units of the Dazhai type have emerged in every province, every county, and in many people's communes.[36]

The consequences of blind adherence to a single model are attested to not only in numerous altered landscapes, some of which remain denuded to this day, but also, as we shall see, in the memories and recollections of Chinese who spent time in the countryside during the Cultural Revolution.

INTENSIFICATION AND MILITARIZATION
OF THE DAZHAI CAMPAIGN

In 1969, Dazhai Party Secretary Chen Yonggui was named to the Central Committee, and the campaign to imitate the Dazhai Spirit and the Foolish Old Man intensified and imitation became more regimented.[37] Chen's ideas on the forcible submission of nature, echoing Mao's voluntarism, promoted environmental damage. He claimed, for example, that 80 percent of a river bottom could be transformed into fields, leaving only 20 percent of the river: "This is what is called 'getting grain from rivers'" [*xiang he yao liang*]. He also asserted that grain could be grown anywhere, even in ravines and on sandy beaches, and that when China got its grain from mountains and rivers, "even if the population increased to 800 million, people could not finish eating it, and there would be enough left over to supply the needs of other countries." Revolutionary thought and the philosophy of struggle should be the guide, in his view, not the opinions of engineers.[38]

The campaign to grow grain everywhere reached its peak following the 1969 border skirmishes with the Soviet Union and before Nixon's 1972 visit, when China gained confidence that the international balance of power had changed in its favor and war would not break out after all. During those years of heightened tensions, the Chinese people were admonished to prepare for war-induced famine. Regions already self-sufficient in grain were pressured to employ extreme measures to create new arable land, increase grain yields, and turn more over to the state. Complacency was criticized.

As we shall see in greater detail in the next chapter, the slogan, "Prepare for War, Prepare for Famine, for the Sake of the People" [*Bei Zhan, Bei Huang, Wei Renmin*], gained broad currency when it appeared in April 1967 in the widely distributed second edition of the "Little Red Book" of Chairman Mao quotations. Dazhai became linked to the war preparation campaign; leaders of northern provinces were summoned to Dazhai for lessons in growing their own grain in preparation for hostilities.[39] The slogans, "Take Grain as the Key Link" and "In Agriculture, Learn from Dazhai," were key themes in the nationwide effort to stockpile grain. The "Take Grain as the Key Link" policy was thus transformed from a post-famine emphasis on staple crops into a Dazhai-related overemphasis on grain. The policy evolved into a uniformly applied, urgent political campaign to grow grain regardless of natural conditions.

The struggle with nature took on intense military imagery during the "prepare for war" campaign, consistent with the greatly expanded role of the People's Liberation Army in national life. Through Marshal Lin Biao's influence, the People's Liberation Army (PLA) had been made a national model in February 1964 through a *People's Daily* editorial headed, "Learn from the PLA." During the Cultural Revolution, the army was brought in to quell Red Guard factional fighting, and Revolutionary Committees, which included the military, took over the leadership of work units throughout China. The PLA provided Dazhai with significant outside labor and financing for major projects, and was often involved, as we shall see, in Dazhai-inspired land reclamation efforts throughout the country. Metaphorically, this stage of Mao's war against nature was akin to military regimentation in that an attempt was made to standardize the very face of nature.

ENVIRONMENTAL CONSEQUENCES

If the Dazhai model could be destructive even when applied in areas neighboring the brigade, results were often far worse when blindly implemented in ecologically divergent regions. Land reclamation slogans were invented to include a range of geographic possibilities: "Encircle the rivers, build land" [*weihe zaodi*]; "encircle the lakes, build farmland" [*weihu zaotian*]; "destroy the forests, open the wastelands" [*huilin kaihuang*]; "on steep slopes, open the wastelands" [*doupo kai huang*]; "destroy the pasturelands, open the wastelands" [*huimu kaihuang*]; "on flat-lands, construct terraces" [*pingyuan zao titian*]. Other variations included, "plant sprouts in the center of lakes" [*chayang cha dao huxin*] and even this very extreme slogan from Hebei's Pingshan County: "Squeeze land from rock peaks, get grain from rocks" [*cong shitou fengli ji di, xiang shitou yao liang*].[40]

In Shuangfeng County in Hunan province, forests were cut down to create agricultural land without considering the sandy soil; a flood the following year caused sand to erode into rivers and ponds, silting them up and leaving piles of sand in the rice fields. In Ningxia's Yanchi County, conversion of grasslands into croplands started a vicious cycle of creeping desertification and sandstorms.[41] In Hubei province, traditionally known as the land of a thousand lakes (originally more than 1,065), about half that number were filled and the total lake surface area was reduced by three-fourths. Shanxi province's Zhenba County had been without floods or drought until land-reclamation efforts there razed forests that had once covered 60 percent of the land. This led not only to a reduction in forest products, but also to new problems with flood, drought, and hailstorms, and a sharp drop in grain production. In Inner Mongolia's Yikeshaomeng, 18 million *mu* of grasslands became desert because of land-reclamation efforts, and sandstorms advanced south, so that every year agricultural land had to be re-seeded, and more than 1 million *mu* of farmland were destroyed.[42]

As Qu Geping and Li Jinchang state, "Regardless of the topography, grain production became the all-important priority... Large forested areas were either destroyed to produce grain or neglected, aggravating hydrologic cycles and soil erosion."[43] Vaclav Smil describes the destructive loop as follows:

> In most places the vicious circle set in soon after slopes were deforested to make way for grainfields: after a few years, as the accumulated organic matter was sharply reduced and the thin soil rapidly eroded, yields on the newly reclaimed land plummeted

and more land was deforested just to maintain the harvests. The abandoned, barren land then succumbed to erosion, often with the irreparable result of all soil being removed to the bedrock.[44]

In remote labor camps, where Cultural Revolution offenders had been sent to join unredeemed "rightists" and common criminals, enemies of the state toiled to remold the landscape and themselves.[45] Writer Zhang Xianliang barely survived hauling clods in a labor camp in barren Ningxia province. In one of his novels, *Half of Man Is Woman,* he eloquently captures the connection between abuse of people and abuse of nature in the camps:

> The grassy plains had already been destroyed by those who "Learned from Dazhai." On the land before me abandoned fields stretched in all directions. Now covered with a thick layer of salt, they looked like dirty snow-fields, or like orphans dressed in mourning clothes. They had been through numerous storms since being abandoned, but you could still see the scars of plough tracks running across their skin. Man and nature together had been flogged with whips here: the result of "Learn from Dazhai" was to create a barren land, on whose alkaline surface not a blade of grass would grow.[46]

At Lei Da Shi near Chongqing, a woman recalled how her village was ordered to "open the wastelands" in the neighboring mountains:

> They called on us to learn from Dazhai. There was no resistance. At the time, if you said half a sentence, they gave you a "cap" [political label]. So we built terraces on the mountain, and carried up earth and fertilizer. On every spare meter of earth, we tried to grow grain. But the mountain was never suitable for growing grain. It's only good for trees. The whole thing was time-consuming and exhausting.

For animals who depend on forest habitat, the costs of Dazhai were high. A scientist at the Chengdu panda breeding station grew up in Sichuan's Leibo County, where he recalled that as a child he often saw evidence of panda activity in the nearby hills, until "learning from

Dazhai" destroyed much of their habitat. "I remember vividly how we cut bamboo and trees to build Dazhai-style terraces and grow grain wherever possible. There was no awareness of the importance of what was lost." Today, of course, there are only about one thousand pandas remaining in the wild and about one hundred in captivity.

A scholar of traditional Chinese philosophy recalled the Dazhai campaign in his home village of Xiushan, near the Sichuan–Hunan border, where there had once been a rich wildlife population and a sustainable relationship between local people and the land. Originally, the area had been 90 percent forested:

> When I was a child, there were jackals and foxes in the woods, but after the big trees were cut to fuel furnaces during the Leap, there wasn't even a rabbit. New trees grew, but then it was time to "learn from Dazhai." In fact, we didn't need terraces in our area, because the population was sparse. But our per-*mu* production was considered low. So we had to cut the trees. Whoever cut the most got the most political points, and the most grain.
>
> My wife's uncle was the brigade Party secretary. He was taken to Dazhai to have a look. They all walked through the fields single-file, watching people labor. The Dazhai peasants weren't allowed to speak to them, they weren't allowed to answer questions.
>
> We grew grain on the new terraces, but then an inspection team came and said we had it too easy. We had to suffer more to show we were learning from Dazhai. So we had to build more terraces, on steeper, stonier slopes. They weren't suitable for grain, so we tried to grow tea. But of course there was a lot of erosion. There had been a stream in front of our house, and ponds with fish. Later, because there were no trees, the water dried up and the fish disappeared.
>
> In ancient times, the classic texts described harmony among man, society, and nature. It was wrong if you used animals and nature merely to satisfy yourself. Humans and nature were linked, and everything should be done in accordance with natural laws. There was a principle of mutual care. The Daoists thought that the Way imitates nature, and people are part of nature, so not even a blade of grass should be hurt. In the Song dynasty, a woman

philosopher named Zhang Zai said, "All living things are my comrades." In many classics, there are clear prohibitions against hunting while animals are rearing their young. But Chairman Mao never understood these things. All he understood was military strategy.

For at least some knowledgeable Chinese, traditional culture and values pointed toward a very different relationship to nature than the adversarial confrontations practiced under Mao. At the time, however, the more inhospitable the terrain and the more the people suffered, the greater their revolutionary glory and the victory over nature.

In Yunnan province, the White Sheep Production Team of East Wind Commune, Lanping County, carved out terraces on densely wooded, steep slopes. An April 25, 1970 *Yunnan Daily* report conveys the flavor of this local effort. "Learn from the Dazhai People, Go the Dazhai Road, Open the Mountains to Create Farmland for the Revolution," proclaimed the headline.

> [Two local leaders], using Chen Yonggui and [ethnic minority leader] Qilinwangdan as models, and carrying Chairman Mao's Red Book, led more than 140 people to a wild hillside eight *li* from the village. Carrying work tools and pitching a camp, they declared war [*kai zhan*] on the wild hillside... Lacking steel crowbars, they cut wooden crowbars from the mountain; lacking bamboo baskets, they made them from bamboo they cut; when their hoes broke, they repaired them themselves... By mid-April, on a hillside with a 50 degree slope, they had opened up more than 120 *mu* of terraces. Every field had an embankment two meters high, and from the mountains they carried additional earth to improve the soil.[47]

Although the newspaper reported these terraces as a great success, the slope of the hillside was so extreme that they were probably of little lasting value. At least one Yunnan geographer later guessed that they did not endure. "Anything more than 15 or 20 degrees steep shouldn't be terraced," he told me. "In Yunnan, some terraces were built on slopes of 40 degrees or more."

The same article demonstrates how the intensified campaign to learn from Dazhai had been pulled into Mao's battle against Party moderates:

During the day, they opened the mountains. As they worked, they carried out meetings on the "living study, living use" of Chairman Mao Thought. At night, they led the masses to thoroughly criticize the great traitor Liu Shaoqi and his Yunnan representatives ... ceaselessly raising the masses' awareness of the two class, two road, two line struggle... Under the direction of [the slogans], "Prepare for War, Prepare for Famine, For the Sake of the People," "Learn from the Dazhai People, Go the Dazhai Road," "break through the rightist tendency of conservative thought," "display self-reliance and the revolutionary spirit of arduous struggle," "actively open mountains and create farmland for the revolution," and "produce more grain for war preparation," the whole production team's spring production is going full steam ahead.[48]

The article warned against premature satisfaction with the area's achievements in self-reliance and hinted that some people had resisted this latest stage of mobilization to transform nature:

Some say, "in recent years we have already built 44 small canals and one big canal 36 *li* long. We have terraced more than 300 *mu* of fields, raised grain production and changed the situation of relying on the country for grain, so the basic construction of our agricultural fields is already pretty much done."[49]

These people, the article tells us, were placed in "Chairman Mao Thought study class, earnestly to study Chairman Mao's call, 'In Agriculture, Learn from Dazhai,' and study the heroic deeds of [model leader] Qilinwangdan leading the masses to reform the heavens and change the earth" [*gaitian huandi*]. The conflation of ideology and physical transformation is clear: the peasants are praised for "producing more grain to contribute to thoroughly burying imperialism, revisionism, and counterrevolution."

Two scholars from Yunnan recalled the devastation wreaked by the terracing campaign. One remembered,

In the 1970s, there was a strong spirit of "Man Must Conquer Nature." Terraces were built all over China to "Learn from Dazhai." In Yunnan, there was much destruction as a result. Near the Lu River they built terraces, but water flooded down, causing erosion. Of course, in some places terracing is suitable. But in some areas like Xishuangbanna, it is not suitable. People were forced to do it after Dazhai. The forests became grass hillsides, with no trees. They were denuded.

The other Yunnan scholar emphasized the formalistic quality of the terracing:

Every collective, production team, and county had to send a few people to Dazhai to study, and then come back and apply the lessons. None of the terraces built during the Dazhai years were any good. There was no quality at all – it was a political responsibility. Each production team had to complete so many *mu*, within a certain time, and compete with each other. To save time, they cut straight down, below the topsoil, eroding whole hillsides. But they couldn't plant on bedrock.

A former "educated youth" who spent years building terraces commented, "It takes a lot of work to maintain terraces. If there is a leak, the whole thing can collapse."

Efforts to raise agricultural yields sometimes led to brutal violation of local traditions, particularly in areas traditionally proscribed from farming and logging for spiritual and cultural reasons. In Xishuangbanna, for example, along the Laotian and Burmese borders, where the minority Dai culture dominates, local tradition protected "spirit forests" and "burial forests" from extractive use. A slogan was devised explicitly to attack this practice, ordering local people to "Launch a Battle on the Burial Forest, Get Grain from the Spirit Forest" [*Xiang Guishan Kai Zhan, Xiang Shenlin Yao Liang*].[50] A local researcher sadly recalled the damage:

After the famine, the Party put forth the slogan, "Take Grain as the Key Link." They wanted us to grow wheat in the mountains. But most mountain people didn't eat wheat. The Jinuo and Aini people grew tea, which they traded for grain. But now, they had to grow grain for themselves. To carry out orders handed down from above, they cut down their forests. The whole slogan went,

Yi Liang Wei Gang, Ziji Zi Zu, Wancheng Zhengfu de Gongyu Liang Paigou Renwu [Take Grain as the Key Link, Self-Reliance, Fulfill the Government's Grain Supply Surplus Responsibility]. Yunnan had always been dependent on external grain, but now they wanted us to be independent.

In Qinghai province, formerly part of Tibet, 670,000 hectares of grassland were converted to cropland, and nomadic herders were forced to assume an unfamiliar agricultural lifestyle unsuited to local conditions. Desertification ultimately reduced much of this grazing land to the point that it was beyond recovery.[51]

A professor from an agricultural university observed the effects of the grain-first policy in Aba County, in the Aba Mountains, a Tibetan region in western Sichuan:

> In the 1970s, I was sent there to report on land use. The altitude was high, with sharp temperature changes. The land was rich black earth, very flat, with good light. But every year hailstones destroyed the rice shoots. A local leader confided that they shouldn't be growing rice at all. He said they should be growing one-third highland barley, one-third sugar beets, and one-third rapeseed. It was toward the end of the Cultural Revolution, and they were still carrying out the "Take Grain as the Key Link" policy. He hadn't dared to say this before. Also in the Aba Mountains, in Ganze County, at an altitude of more than 3,500 meters, I saw a grassland that had been destroyed because of "Taking Grain as the Key Link." I asked the people what had happened, and they explained, "We are taking grain as the key link." No one dared say it was wrong, no one dared speak the truth.

A Chongqing journalist reflected as follows on the high costs of learning from Dazhai:

> After the Three Hard years, the emphasis was on growing grain for survival. Everyone supported the idea. We sent many people to Dazhai to learn how they "reformed the heavens and changed the earth," turning bad fields into good ones. But it was too absolute. Some land is suitable for commercial crops, not grain. Some places

are good for timber. Sometimes good trees were cut down to plant grain, medicinal plants, or fruit trees. In Sichuan, we have places good for growing tea. Tea needs a high altitude, fog, and acidic soil. It's no good for grain. But after Chen Yonggui was made vice-premier in charge of agriculture, the "Learn from Dazhai" and "Take Grain as the Key Link" campaigns became more intense. In Inner Mongolia, they destroyed the grasslands for wheat. The next year, the desert started coming, and from then on there were sandstorms in Beijing. It spoiled the pastureland and harmed the ecosystem. Later, we could see that some things we did were stupid. The grassland couldn't be turned into grainfields overnight. But at the time, we were all equally stupid.

Some understood that the grain-first policy was a disaster, but dissenters dared not speak out, so dangerous had it become to take a stand against the prevailing political winds. There was resistance to the uprooting of proven cash crops, however. Jean Oi describes how, during the early 1970s, peasants in an herb-growing area of Southwest China refused to plant grain, choosing to satisfy state requirements by purchasing grain on the black market. In another case, she writes, resistance broke out as follows:

> A production team had planted a crop of mandarin orange trees anticipating the big Hong Kong New Year's market for these plants. Although the sale of this popular item would have brought a large cash income for the team, unfortunately for the peasants, these sideline activities were considered capitalist. The work team ordered the peasants to uproot the orange trees, but the peasants refused. At that point the work team itself tried to pull up the trees. In this case, the peasants took violent action and beat the cadres.[52]

If resistance to destruction of viable crops was common, it was far more difficult to oppose projects that reclaimed "wastelands" or created new land from water. However, it was the destruction of forests and wetlands that had the most enduring environmental consequences. While cash crops could often be replanted, much of the erosion and ecological imbalance created during the Cultural Revolution is irreversible.

THE WETLANDS OF DIANCHI

The impact of the Dazhai movement on Chinese waterways is difficult to isolate, for encroachments on rivers and lakes have continued for millennia in China. The effort to create arable land through filling in lakes and ponds was not new to the Mao years; it had been a common practice in a country starved for good farmland, and it was a subject of controversy from at least Song times on.[53] Perhaps the best known encroachments on water have occurred over centuries at the expense of the large lake lying between Hunan and Hubei provinces, Dongting Lake. Once China's second-largest freshwater lake, it was further reduced by the Mao years from an original 565,000 hectares to 282,000 hectares. In eastern Hubei, major lakes disappeared altogether.[54] Chinese officials, journalists, and ordinary people often blame diking and in-filling encroachments on Dongting and other catchment lakes, together with upriver deforestation, for the devastating Yangzi River floods of 1993, 1995, and 1998.[55]

Despite the relative brevity of Mao-era assaults on lakes and rivers, it is difficult to compile a comprehensive picture of their impact. However, the "Take Grain as the Key Link" policy, especially as implemented during the "Learn from Dazhai" campaign, had indisputably severe and concentrated consequences. Zhang and Li express this relationship well:

> Lake Poyang is one of our country's largest freshwater lakes, and in the midst of the *weihu zaotian* [encircle lakes, create farmland] battle, the lake surface was reduced one-fifth, the dikes surrounding the lake reached 800 square kilometers. Another great freshwater lake, Dongting, was also reduced during the *weihu* battle. In the so-called thousand lakes province of Hubei, the total number of lakes was reduced from 1,066 to 326, and the lake area was reduced from 8,330 square kilometers to 2,370. Of course, these destructions did not all occur during the "In Agriculture, Learn from Dazhai" period, but during this movement, *weihu zaotian* certainly was developed to a very severe degree.[56]

Although Cultural Revolution–era encroachments were far from unique, their *yundong*-like quality, vocabulary of nature-conquest, degree of human mobilization, huge scale of land reclamation, and linkage with ongoing political struggles gave them a distinctively Maoist character. Encroachments, often involving extensive military participation, reached into oceans, lakes, rivers, and ponds, including diking projects along the Pacific Coast and intense land reclamation projects on lakes Tai and Poyang. However, of these many projects, the one that most transparently exemplifies the Maoist assault on nature is the filling in of the Haigeng wetlands of Dian Lake [*Dianchi*] near the city of Kunming, a grand-scale campaign that epitomizes the high costs of Mao-era dogmatic formalism.

With an area of about 300 square kilometers (about 115 square miles), Dianchi is China's sixth largest freshwater lake. It lies in far Southwest China just south of Yunnan's provincial capital. Located on a vast plateau rare for its high altitude (1,886 meters above sea level) and proximity to the tropics, Dianchi was created a million years ago when the Yunnan-Guizhou Plateau was uplifted with the Himalayas. The lake current flows north to south, fed by twenty mountain streams but exiting as a single river that eventually joins the mighty Jinsha River.[57] Stretching farther than the eye can see, Dianchi is sheltered on the west by a long mountain range that appears to rise directly from the water. Also called the Sleeping Beauty Hills because of their undulating grace, the Western Mountains are dotted with Buddhist and Daoist temples, pavilions, sculptures, and grottoes, including the famous Dragon's Gate, where, from 1781 to 1835, Daoist monks chiseled corridors and caves into the precipice.[58] These artifacts of traditional Chinese spirituality look out over the lake and beyond it toward the East, where the lake appears to dissolve into vast floodplains receding into distant hills. Poetry and legends concerning the lake's size and beauty abound; most residents can quote from a nineteenth-century poem by Sun Ranweng that is carved into the Western Hills. It begins, "For five hundred *li,* Dianchi rushes before the eyes" [*Wubai li Dianchi benlai yandi*]. So central is the lake to the region's identity that it is said that, without Dianchi, there would be no Kunming.

Kunming's glory is its mild year-round climate. Its average temperature is 14.8 degrees centigrade, varying no more than 12 degrees, the most consistent temperature of any provincial capital in China.[59] The four-character phrase, "four seasons like spring" [*siji ruchun*], expresses the people of Kunming's profound sense of place. Almost every Chinese knows this phrase in reference to the city, and few can resist the temptation to quote it when making small talk about China's geography. The balmy climate is not only the pride of Kunming but of all China; it is mentioned in the same breath as Guilin's Karst mountains, Xi'an's terracotta warriors, and Suzhou's scholar-gardens. In a play on homonyms written with two different characters, it is said that the *ming* (brightness) of Kunming and its *ming* (renown) are equally linked to Dianchi.[60]

But local people say that ever since a section of wetlands was filled during the Cultural Revolution, Kunming's weather is not quite so pleasant. The "four seasons like spring" truism has become unreliable. Local people say that the weather seems hotter in summer and colder in winter. There is more drought. And the lake itself has changed. Where once Dianchi was transparent blue, children went swimming after school, and fishermen caught enormous, delicious fish of great variety, now the water is filthy and the fish are small. A prized fish, the *jinxian* or "golden thread," hasn't been seen in years. An old professor who used to swim every day after work remembered clearly that after the in-filling the *jinxian* disappeared, and within a few more years the whitefish [*baiyu*] were gone as well.

Most Kunming residents to whom I spoke were at a loss to remember an exact date for the in-filling and were unable to be more precise about their feeling of unease. How well-founded is their melancholy? It is true that other factors, including the severe industrial pollution that has accompanied the economic reforms, are to blame for much of Dianchi's filth and the poisoning of its fish; overfishing, eutrophication from detergents and fertilizer, and deforestation have also played roles in the degradation of the lake basin.[61] However, popular perceptions have a basis in fact. In interviews and articles, scientists concur that the lake plays a critical role in regulating the microclimate of the Yunnan Plateau, moderating temperature extremes through evaporation and precipitation. Water retains temperature, and as a lakeside city, Kunming feels cooler during hot weather and warmer during cold. While objective measurements show that Kunming remains mild year-round, it may be true, as is widely believed, that since the in-filling the four seasons no longer feel so consistently "like spring." It is also undeniable, as we shall see, that the ecological consequences of the lake in-filling endure to this day.

Dianchi's boundaries were altered many times before the Cultural Revolution. A local geographer told me that many small lakes and

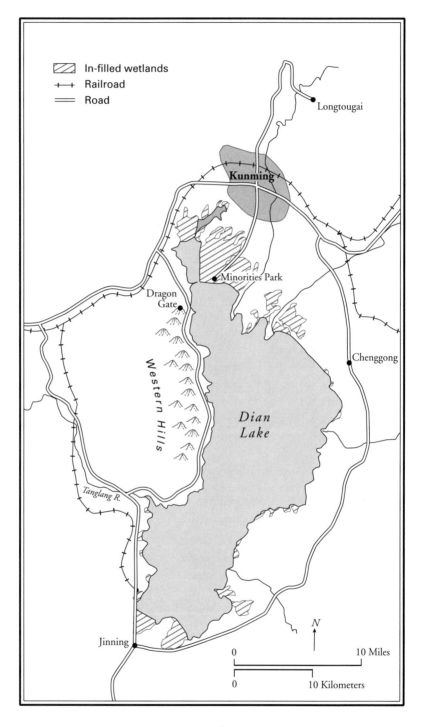

Legend:
- In-filled wetlands
- Railroad
- Road

Longtougai

Kunming

Minorities Park

Dragon
Gate

Chenggong

Western Hills

*Dian
Lake*

Tanglang R.

Jinning

N

0   10 Miles

0   10 Kilometers

ponds in the Kunming area were filled in during the Yuan and Ming dynasties, leaving only a much-reduced Cui Hu [Green Lake] in the city proper. New outlets and reservoirs were gradually constructed, decreasing the volume of water in Dianchi and very gradually transforming what had once been a 1,000-square-kilometer lake to one of less than one-third the size. In 1936, Southwest Associated University scholars measured the lake at 360 square kilometers, and in 1962, Yunnan Normal University Geography Department researchers detected additional decreases due primarily to urban population expansion and increased water use. Today, after the Cultural Revolution infilling, which cut the size of the lake by nearly 25 square kilometers, the lake measures 298.4 square kilometers.[62]

While in the past such land reclamations were not associated with political movements, the filling of the Dianchi wetlands in the spring of 1970, with its environmental and human costs, is a poignant demonstration of the consequences of using the Dazhai model to transform the landscape to grow grain. It also epitomizes the Maoist understanding of nature as a battlefield, a relationship that may conveniently be understood in terms of three central characteristics. First, *urgency to prepare for war against the Soviet Union* created pressure to compress the three stages of the Dianchi project – building the dam, draining the water, and filling in earth for agricultural fields – into a single spring. Great Leap Forward–style urgency reappeared, as work was often done night and day, and as many as 300,000 people at one time were pulled away from other tasks and mobilized for the project. Second, *political struggle in the human world and struggle in the natural world merged;* ideological conflict and the transformation of nature were understood as one and the same battle. Turning Dianchi into farmland was seen as accomplishing the dual goals of attacking Mao's political enemies and conquering nature. Finally, *remolding nature was equated with remolding human nature.* These transformations were ritually melded, so that the external/material and internal/spiritual symbolized and acted as proxies for one another. Victory over Dianchi symbolized spiritual purging and rebuilding for participants in the battle.

The scale and progress of the project, its urgency and ambition, the backdrop of political struggle, and use as a metaphor for human transformation can be gleaned from *Yunnan Daily* articles published in 1970. A short piece that appeared on May 8 announced formation of a new "May 7th Agricultural Farm" (also known as the Haigeng Agricultural Farm) on reclaimed land. The headline story on May 13 proclaimed, *"Weihai Zaotian* Victory News: 10,000 *Mu* of New Farmland Busy with Planting." (In large characters on the top right, the daily slogan read, "Prepare for War, Prepare for Famine, For the Sake of the People.") An extensive article published on August 17 was entitled, "One Thousand *Qing* [160 acres] of Blue Sea Becomes Green Land, Commemorate the Kunming District Army and People's *Weihai Zaotian* Heroic Deeds." A photograph of the lakeside displays the Foolish Old Man slogan. Artists' wood-block renderings of the project depict boats filled with boulders blasted from the mountains, dump trucks loaded with earth, and soldiers laboring strenuously beside peasants in straw hats. In August 1998, I interviewed project participants, former members of the agricultural farm established on the reclaimed land, and scholars and scientists knowledgeable about the history of the lake and the impact of the filling. These conversations recaptured an era in which the study of Mao Zedong Thought alone was believed sufficient to make the earth tremble and in which misgivings about the project were not tolerated.

Wetlands Destruction as Military Campaign

The four-character Chinese expression *weihai zaotian* is usually translated as land reclamation, but its literal meaning, "encircle sea, create farmland," more accurately describes the activity and reflects its origins in coastal areas. When land was reclaimed from lakes and ponds in China's interior, the term, *weihu zaotian,* "encircle lakes, create farmland" was sometimes substituted. *Weihai zaotian* was used to describe the Dianchi campaign in the 1970, perhaps because the lake is so large, while *weihu zaotian* was used in scholarly critiques of the project during the late 1980s. While *weihai zaotian* literally describes a diking-and-filling activity, its implementation in Kunming in 1970 differed from previous gradual, often unorganized encroachment on shallow waters by peasants seeking more territory. Rather, it was a full-blown *yundong,* or political campaign. Typical of such Mao-era bursts of activity, the *weihai zaotian* movement employed intense mass mobilization and political sloganeering designed to unleash energy, build support, convey leaders' expectations, create conformity, and discourage doubt and resistance.

Today, People's Liberation Army commander Tan Puren, a close associate of Lin Biao, is widely blamed for instigating the Dianchi project. Made head of the Yunnan Provincial Revolutionary Committee when the army was installed in leadership roles throughout the country, it seems likely that he was hoping to gain political glory by learning from Dazhai and increasing arable land for grain production to prepare for war. The Dianchi project may even have been a sincere effort to alleviate food shortages. Where terracing was not feasible, leaders often sought to create farmland by other methods; Tan Puren decided to fill in wetlands along the Haigeng (literally "sea wall") Peninsula in the northeastern part of the lake. The work site slogan exhorted, "Establish the Will of the Foolish Old Man, Resolve to Turn Dianchi into Good Farmland" [*Lixia Yugong Yi Shan Zhi, Shi Jiao Dianchi Bian Liangtian*].[63] Tan Puren brought in the army, which was crucial in the dam-building phase. The army's involvement further explains the project's military atmospherics.

Dianchi project slogans reflect a range of typical Maoist attitudes toward nature – conquest of nature as enemy, miraculous transformation of nature by harnessing Mao Zedong Thought, and transformation of nature as a vehicle for human transformation. Although the themes can be distinguished, in practice, slogans were piled one onto the other, often overlapping, with multiple variations. In August, for example, they are listed as: "'Move mountains, change seas, launch an attack on Dianchi, seek grain from Dianchi" [*yishan tianhai, weihai zaotian, xiang Dianchi jinjun, xiang Dianchi yao liang*]. "We want to be the Foolish Old Men of the 1970s," the people are said to have declared. "If the mountain is high, we move it; if the sea is deep, we fill it, bravely turning Dianchi into good fields." Battle imagery permeates the newspaper reports. The project is hailed as a victory for "Mao Zedong's invincible (literally, 'no-battle-is-unwinnable') Thought" [*zhan wu bu sheng de Mao Zedong sixiang*]. Municipal and Provincial Revolutionary Committees are said to have raised the "battle slogan" [*zhandou kouhao*] of "launch an attack [*jinjun*] on Dianchi, turn the wetlands into good fields."[64]

Newspaper reports convey the chronology of the campaign, as well as its military tone and sense of urgency. Beginning on New Year's Day 1970, tens of thousands of people are described as participating in the attack to wrest grain from the lake. A May article declares,

For the past four months, Kunming District's workers, poor and lower-middle peasants, People's Liberation Army soldiers, revolutionary cadres, intellectuals, Red Guards and street residents, armed with red hearts of limitless loyalty to Chairman Mao and iron hands to reform the heavens and change the earth have conducted a people's war against Dianchi... Factories, enterprises, the countryside, organizations, schools, stores, street residents, soldiers stationed in Kunming have all eagerly participated in the *weihai zaotian* struggle.

Project phases are described as "three great military campaigns [*zhanyi*] of building dikes, draining water, and creating earth." War is waged against nature itself:

Under the leadership of the Kunming City Revolutionary Committee, [the broad revolutionary masses] decided to launch a people's war of *weihai zaotian*. Using Dazhai as a model, with the daring of vision to war against the heavens and struggle against the earth [*zhantian doudi*], displaying a spirit of not fearing hardship, not fearing death, self-reliance, and arduous struggle, they moved the mountains and filled the seas [*yishan tianhai*], launched an attack against Dianchi, and sought grain from the blue seas [*xiang canghai yao liang*].[65]

Urgency dominates the project, described in great detail in an August 17 *Yunnan Daily* article. The Great Leap Forward slogan, "Greater, Faster, Better, More Economical" appears often. Rushing to carry out all three phases of the project in a single spring, "They turned the 1,000 years' sleeping blue sea into green land, and attained [the goal of] encircling the lakes, creating the fields, and planting the crops within a year." Military mobilization was required:

"First send in the army." From all sides, they flooded into the work site. Within a circumference of 30 kilometers, one workshed after another was set up. Under the open sky they set up stoves, pitched camp, and opened up the battlefield [*zhanchang*] for the war against the heavens and the struggle against the earth.

The sounds of dynamite, used to clear grass from the lake bed, echoed in the Western mountains: "Look, one mountain after another collapses, one boat after another full of boulders and earth catches the wind and breaks the waves, one big rock after another is thrown into the sea."[66]

Unloading rocks by night, forgoing Spring Festival celebrations, many tens of thousands of soldiers worked to complete the dike. Although rocks vanished into the mud, the soldiers sensed success; but on February 15, the northern part of the dike was breeched. A "Red Maidens' Boat Team," working hardest of all the teams, became heroines. As waves rushed toward the breech, the news article relates, a girl named Li Muying shouted, "Comrades, we must use our blood and lives to protect the dam." With all her strength, she sank a boatload of sand and earth into the gap. Two more boats followed, and the breech was closed. According to a *Yunnan Daily* editorial, the lesson to be learned by this is that capitalist fortunetellers may try to predict the future according to their data, "but one can never predict the strength of the revolutionary masses, armed with the weapon of Chairman Mao Thought, to move the mountains and fill the seas, and to create miracles that astonish the heavens and move the earth [*jingtian dongdi*]." Clearly, the voluntaristic notion that Mao's ideas had the power to alter the material world was in full force.

With planting only two months away, and a vast expanse of water still within the dam, time was of the essence. An "even greater scale people's war" was launched. While "reactionaries" suggested that a pump should be purchased from another province, several hundred "self-reliant" factories and communes instead contributed more than 200 pieces of drainage equipment. Power lines were raised, and the great battle [*da huizhan*] to drain the water began. In the cold winter weather, water was pumped through hundreds of pipes to the lake beyond the dam. At last, the wet black earth of the lake floor lay revealed.

A "great army" [*dajun*] of 300,000 members of the revolutionary classes, including workers, poor and lower-middle peasants, PLA soldiers, cadres, revolutionary teachers and students, and neighborhood residents was dispatched to the reclamation area. "On the great battlefield of 1,000 armies and 10,000 horses, the muddy sea was to be made into good farmland." Each morning at daybreak, this "army" walked more than 10 kilometers from city to lake. There were "tens of thousands of people, [including] Red Guards and Young Pioneers. The person was small, but the heart was Red and the will was strong." This army dug ditches, piled dirt, carried earth, and built fields, their bodies entirely covered with mud and their hands blistering. In places, the mud was fine as soup, and it ran out through their woven baskets. So they brought metal washbasins from home, which they filled and emptied with their bare hands. Where horses and tractors were useless, they pulled the earth-leveling equipment themselves. To pile on 500,000 *fang* [cubic meters] of red earth, the *"weihai zaotian* soldiers launched a 'storm the fortifications' [*gongjian zhan*] battle to gather earth, and transport earth." Pits were dug at Hui Wan and Su Family Village, and tens of thousands of carts were assembled to bring loads of earth to the dock. To accelerate the project, Sheng County Brigade's poor and lower-middle peasants and Panlong Team's revolutionary masses also launched an attack [*huizhan*] and, working day and night, in twenty days built a 1,500-meter road across the sea. Led by a driver named Hu Jialin, who worked more than ten hours a day without leaving the site, the workers from some ninety Kunming District work units brought hundreds of vehicles, working through the night to transport the earth. The war preparation mentality of urgency and mind-over-matter is evident in this passage:

> They used the war preparation viewpoint to see everything, carry out everything. They saw creating fields as a necessary part of war preparation. It was [a means] to wrest time and speed from imperialism, revisionism, and counterrevolution. They used 33 days to turn 10,000 *mu* of silt into good earth and break through the superstition that you cannot build fields out of silt.

From behind the 3-kilometer dike, the "great army" drained 1,000 *qing* of water and created 30,000 *mu* of land, of which 10,000 *mu* was said to be good farmland. "Half a mountain of the Western Mountains was moved, creating 10,000 *mu* of fields in Dianchi," boasted the news articles, a literal application of the "move the mountains, fill the seas" slogan. Blue seas were said to have turned into green land, and the people to have shouted, "Long Live Chairman Mao! Long, Long Live Chairman Mao!" Credit for the transformation of nature thus went to the ideas and slogans of a man who apparently never visited the lake and may not even have known that the project was under way.

Virtually all adults then living in the Kunming area to whom I spoke recalled participating in the project. One young man told me that his aunt, a 4-year-old at the time, was taken to the site to help. School-age children devoted full-time labor. Workers came from factories and shops on weekends. A man who was then 12 recalled the long hike to the lake as exhausting in itself, with only two *jiao* for daily compensation. A middle school history teacher, then a student, remembered the workers' enthusiasm and the sense of urgency concerning the grain supply:

> Everything was rationed, and grain was very tight. We all thought it was a good thing, to create more land to resolve the grain problem. We were in high spirits, often singing as we worked. There were informal competitions among groups to move more earth. Only later did we understand that the wetlands purify water and provide a haven for migrating birds.

A reform-era study, *Yunnan Plateau 'Four Lakes' Ecological Problems and Ecological Consequences* confirms figures cited in the 1970 newspaper articles. A total of 32,700 *mu* of land were created from 21.8 square kilometers of Dianchi surface area.[67] But the Haigeng Peninsula was not the only place where land was claimed from Dianchi. The Haigeng area was filled in during four months, but reclamation work in other counties and districts, such as Guandu, Xishan, Puning, and Sheng County, lasted two years, employing hundreds of thousands of additional laborers and countless transport vehicles.[68] Together with smaller-scale in-fillings, reclaimed land is said to have reached 23.8 square kilometers. Later research comparing military maps from 1962 and 1978 detected an even greater decrease in lake surface area, amounting to 24.25 square kilometers.[69]

Political Struggle

If urgency to transform the lake and force it to relinquish grain was a major theme of the Dianchi story, political struggle was another vital component. The *weihai zaotian* campaign was celebrated as a victory in the "two-line struggle" and as a triumph over American imperialism, Soviet revisionism, and counterrevolution. On a symbolic level, the local war against nature served as a metaphor for the national-level political struggle between Maoist radicalism and the political revisionism associated with President Liu Shaoqi. Dianchi in-filling skeptics were accused, for example, of *paxingzhuyi* or "reptilianism," an epithet applied to the allegedly crawling pace of Liu Shaoqi's more cautious approach to China's development. Scientists who had previously warned that the dike could not be built or that the resultant land would not be arable were criticized, and traditional engineering methods were abandoned for on-the-spot improvisation by revolutionary technicians and the masses. Liu Shaoqi and his alleged Yunnan cronies were said to have quashed plans to fill in part of Dianchi on the north bank prior to the Cultural Revolution:

> Traitor/ secret agent/ scab Liu Shaoqi and his Yunnan representatives Yan Hongyan and Zhao Jianmin ferociously opposed the Three Red Banners, strongly blew the black wind of capitalism, and killed the *weihai zaotian* movement of the masses… They killed the creativity of the revolutionary masses in its cradle.[70]

By contrast,

> The people cannot forget that last year, under the leadership of the newborn Revolutionary Committee, the broad masses of poor and lower-middle peasants of Sheng County's Dragon Road Commune, Wulong Production Team, acting according to Chairman Mao's directive concerning "self reliance, arduous struggle," [carried out] *weihai zaotian* on Dianchi's eastern bank. They constructed a stone dike and earthen dam a kilometer long, built more than 300 *mu* of fields, and in the same year reaped a great harvest.

Targets of attack were not only individuals but also methods that relied on established scientific practice or capital outlay. The August 17 *Yunnan Daily* scornfully declares, "to build a dike six *li* long, according to the specifications of foreign capitalist technical 'authorities,' the Dianchi grass was [too] thick, and its mud was [too] deep, so it was a 'forbidden territory' for dam construction." "Authorities" were said to have argued that silt would have to be dredged and reinforced concrete pillars would have to be brought in. But "if this foreign method were used, it would require more than 10,000 cubic meters of reinforced concrete, and just to produce and transport those materials would require several months' time." This was not an option on an urgent timetable. Instead,

> The broad revolutionary masses and revolutionary technicians, using the workplace as a battlefield, strongly criticized the traitor/ secret agent/ scab Liu Shaoqi's foreign slave philosophy, reptilianism, and other such things in his counterrevolutionary-revisionist black bag, and established Chairman Mao's proletarian revolutionary line, ... designing as they worked... They didn't use steel, didn't use concrete, but relying on their own hard-working two hands, they used rock and mud to build a dike.[71]

The article clearly identifies political struggle with nature-conquest as in this description of how workers threw rocks into the water to build the dam:

> Each of these great boulders is a heavy bomb launched [*she*] at the traitor/ secret agent/ scab Liu Shaoqi's "foreign slave philosophy" and reptilianism, it is a sword that cuts at the heart of American imperialism, Soviet revisionism, and the counterrevolutionary faction of each country.

The Dianchi project operated on multiple levels, then, with symbolic activity seemingly as real to those involved as actual behavior, and political struggle metaphorically waged, as nature was transformed through the physical effort of thousands.

Spiritual Transformation

If building fields was understood as a strike at Mao's enemies and an act of political struggle, filling in the lake was also a metaphor for the spiritual or internal transformation of individual participants. This symbolic meaning was derived directly from the words of Mao Zedong:

> Chairman Mao said in a great directive, "To reform [*gaizao*] the objective world is also to reform your own subjective world"... To

struggle with the heavens, struggle with the earth, struggle with the waters, struggle with class enemies, and struggle with all kinds of wrong ideas is [also] powerfully to promote a revolution of thought.

Purging and rebuilding the lake was seen as a ritual enactment of purging and rebuilding the mind:

> In 150 days of struggle, the mountain changed, the water changed, and the people's thought also changed. [People said], "We not only pulled 1,000 *qing* of lake water from the reclamation area, we also took out the muddy wastewater of capitalism from the deep parts of our souls. We not only constructed a great dam to encircle the waters at Dianchi, we also constructed a Great Wall against revisionism in our minds; we not only built 10,000 *mu* of farmland, we also built a brand new proletarian world in ourselves."[72]

For Maoists, the implications of this transformation were far-reaching, for the attack on nature and the revolution in thought propelled production:

> This great revolution of launching an attack on nature subjected each Revolutionary Committee and the broad revolutionary masses to tempering [*duanlian*]. It both created land and tempered people, and greatly promoted the revolution in people's thought. In launching an attack on nature, this great revolution promoted a new leap in each line of revolutionary production. In all Kunming District there occurred a leap like that of 10,000 horses rushing forward, its greatest lesson being: if you do everything according to Chairman Mao Thought, then "mountains can be moved, seas can be filled in, [and] any miracle among men can be created."[73]

By constructing 10,000 *mu* of farmland, it was said, 300,000 people were tempered. Their internal transformation lasted beyond the Dianchi work experience. When the participants returned to their factories and fields, they reportedly remained charged with revolutionary spirit. Heroes were said to include the "East is Red" Machine Bed Factory's 240 workers, the Provincial Transport Bureau's Mechanized Road Construction Department, and peasants from the counties and districts of Xishan, Guandu, Puning, and Sheng, who threw themselves enthusiastically into planting as soon as they returned home.[74]

In sum, the battlefield of the lake was an arena for urgent struggle: against nature, against political enemies, and against the limits of human will. Filling in the lake symbolized tempering and re-creating the human mind, while the power of Mao Zedong Thought was held to be capable of accomplishing an enormous public works project. The conquest of nature by military-style action was a crucible for political revolution and the transformation of the masses. In the heat of the moment, it was believed that these battles had been won.

Consequences

The May 7th Agricultural Farm (or Haigeng Agricultural Farm) was established with great fanfare. "This is the glorious result of the whole city of 1,300,000 people carrying out Chairman Mao's May 7th proclamation," a city Revolutionary Committee leader declared.[75] In interviews, peasants from outlying counties recalled their excitement at being given the opportunity to shed their peasant status and draw government salaries for the first time. By volunteering to join the state farm, they became classified as workers.

But the "superstition" that "you can't build farmland on sludge,"[76] derided as the project was being implemented, proved no superstition at all. The new land, soft, moist, and cool, proved all but useless for growing grain. A woman who works in Haigeng Park as a refreshment-seller told me that water in the fields rose to her waist when she tried to harvest the rice. Peasants had to use boats to cut the grain, and then it sprouted or rotted because there was nowhere to spread it out to dry.

A 1987 scientific report, *The Yunnan Plateau 'Four Lakes' Ecological Problems and Ecological Consequences,* written after it became politically safer to criticize some aspects of the Mao years, provides a devastating critique of the economic and environmental impact of the project. In May 1970, the 3,637 workers of the new Haigeng Farm attempted to grow rice, but the earth was too soft and soggy for planting. More earth was added. In all, 7,500 *mu* of rice were planted, with a total harvest of 2,947,000 *jin,* for an average yield of 392.9 *jin* per *mu* and a total income of 334,000 *yuan* on an investment of 1,388,000 *yuan.* The debt of 1,054,000 *yuan* was covered by the state. In 1971, 717 additional workers were brought in, for a total of 4,354 workers, but again the state had to support the farm, to the tune of 900,000 *yuan.* To make up the loss, the farm started a lakeside quarry, producing 32,000 tons of rock, with an income of 403,000 *yuan,* or 55.6 percent of total farm income. But the land only got worse, and after two years, the farm tried growing wheat instead of rice, with continued poor results. Another production shift, to raising mulberry trees for silkworms, met with failure because of processing and transport problems. Arable land decreased yearly, from 8,236 *mu* at the farm's inception to 1,500 *mu* by 1981. From 1970 to 1979, total income was 12,312,000 *yuan,* of which only 15.4 percent (or 1,896,058 *yuan*) came from agriculture; the rest derived from industrial sidelines, 78.2 percent of that from quarrying. The report concludes, "The Haigeng State Farm, from inception, had an extremely low land and labor yield: not only could the farm not produce products for society but it also returned losses year after year." Between 1970 and 1980, the project is estimated to have cost the state 10,750,000 *yuan.*[77]

Authors of a similar study, a 1988 monograph entitled *Dianchi District,* conducted a more rigorous economic analysis using statistics from the Kunming City Agricultural Management Bureau and the Haigeng Agriculture Farm. They calculate that from January to August 1970, more than 100,000 workers participated daily in the project, for a total of 24 million labor days. Although this was "duty" labor – meaning that no cost was officially incurred by the state – and although vehicles and food were contributed, expenditures for other categories of materials and services amounted to an initial state investment of more than 13 million *yuan.* Food consumption in the first year would have totaled 16,800,000 kilograms of raw grain. Considering that from the farm's inception until it was disbanded in 1982 the workforce averaged 37,475, more than 9,368,500 kilograms of raw grain would have been required for food. During twelve years of operation, the state had to pay compensation of 10,750,000 *yuan* over and above the initial investment of 13 million, yielding a total loss of 23,750,000 *yuan.* Moreover, the authors calculate, although it was claimed that 7,500 *mu* of new farmland were created, in fact only 6,300 were new. Each *mu* thus required an average investment of 3,809 workers and 20,630,000 *yuan*. Given a total harvest of 40,715,000 kilograms, less investment for seed, each *mu* produced only about 45 kilograms of grain per year, or 540 kilograms per *mu* over the life of the project, a dismal performance.[78]

There were economic failures on other in-filled sections of the lake as well. In some counties, reclamation efforts yielded no land at all, since lake depths and currents were prohibitive:

> In Sheng County, for more than a year beginning at the end of 1969, each day 2,000 people, 35 big boats, 200 horse carts, 5 trucks, 40 hand tractors, and 10 rubber-wheeled tractors transported earth and rock. They destroyed 5,030 meters of willow groves that people had planted along the Dianchi banks and consumed the country's investment of 15,000,000 *yuan,* planning to build 20,000 *mu* of fields. But the result was that one person was killed, more than ten were injured, and not even one *mu* of earth was created, the only "benefit" being that "cheap" stones became available to peasants for building houses along the lake... Puning County consumed 35,000,000 *yuan* in order to develop 40,000 *mu* of fields, but the result was that ten people were killed and not one *mu* of arable land was created.[79]

According to an elderly former worker interviewed in Haigeng Park, a military officer surnamed Liang ordered local people to encircle a bay between Chengong and Kunyang counties to try to fill it in. County Revolutionary Committees invested 4 million *yuan* in materials and wages and set villagers to carting earth. "It was a bottomless abyss," recalled the old man angrily. "It was too deep. Everything disappeared into endless mud. It was impossible to encircle it."

No matter how the economic and human costs are calculated, it is clear that they were huge. More damaging, and more difficult to remedy still, are the environmental costs still being tabulated. Both monographs argue that filling in the lake in 1970 affected Kunming's legendary microclimate, although they are unsure to what degree. The *Dianchi District* authors explain that "the reason Kunming's climate is not too hot in summer or severely cold in winter, and the four seasons are more or less the same, is that Dianchi regulates evaporation by storing [energy] in the water."[80] The *Yunnan Plateau* authors state unequivocally that *"weihai zaotian* is a major reason for the ecological deterioration of Dianchi," causing an "astonishing" [*jingren*] decrease in water volume due both to a shrinkage of surface area and to a shallower lake basin. They write that the lake shrank from 330 to 305 square kilometers and decreased in average depth from 6 meters to 5.7 meters, changes attributed to two years of relentless *weihu zaotian* activity, with millions of people daily moving stones, earth, and gravel onto embankments, thus causing siltation of the river bottom and a gradual rise in the riverbed. When the authors consider the additional factor of erosion from 1957 to 1982 due to deforestation of surrounding hillsides and mountains, they estimate that between 37,160,000 and 63,500,000 tons of silt entered the lake.[81] With the decrease in area and depth of the lake, and the concomitant decrease in water evaporation and energy retention, they argue, temperatures have become more like those in the rest of the Yunnan-Guizhou Plateau, hotter in summer and colder in winter.[82] Although other scholars told me that they believe the evidence of microclimate change is inconclusive, it is undeniable that the in-filling holds a powerful place in people's imaginations as the starting point for the region's environmental ills.

If environmental impacts on microclimate are difficult to evaluate, that is less the case with impacts on avian and aquatic life. Disruption of Dianchi's ecological balance severely damaged its biodiversity. Soon after the in-filling, it became apparent that the wetlands had provided valuable habitat for birds and fish. A large percentage of native fish had spawned in the lake's gravel areas and wetlands, but these natural features were destroyed, forcing fish to seek other spawning grounds in areas that later became heavily polluted. "The harm brought to aquatic organisms by *weihu zaotian* was such that it caused those fish that spawn in grasses to lose their spawning and rearing grounds," write the authors of *Yunnan Plateau.*[83] Even ordinary people noticed that particular damage was done to oilfish, whitefish, and the gold thread fish unique to Dianchi. The 1969 catch of fish was 6,160,000 tons; by 1981, it was only 109,000 tons, an astonishing drop, although there was a modest recovery the following year, when 795,000 tons, mostly of *yin yu* or whitebait, were caught.[84] Birds that had used wetland grass for shelter, nesting, and fishing were also adversely affected.

The highly critical monographs also detail aesthetic harms to the area. Among the concerns cited by the authors of *Yunnan Plateau* is the transformation of the Haigeng area into a swampy wasteland. Zoomorphic rock formations were destroyed in Puning. Beaches and clear blue waters on the eastern bank, once lined with willow trees, were lost when the trees were cut and burned for cooking fires during the campaign. Moreover, when the wetlands were filled in, legendary scenic views from the Western Mountains, from Daguan Tower to Dragon Gate, were irrevocably altered.[85] As we have noted, factors other than the 1970 project have contributed to the lake's degradation, including post-1978 reform-era industrial pollution, overfishing, introduction of exotic species like ornamental water hyacinth and farmed fish, eutrophication, and loss of forest cover in the lake region.[86] However, blame for microclimate change, shrinkage of the lake's area and depth, change of aquatic plant structure and amount, alteration of fish ecological structure and numbers, and aesthetic loss must be linked primarily to the *weihu zaotian* movement.[87] The *Dianchi District* authors render the following harsh verdict:

> The results of *weihu zaotian* were to reduce the volume of Dianchi, weaken its water collection capabilities, harm the ecological balance of the natural world, limit the development of water products, and destroy the original lake scenery. Its long-term results, of course, are not something that can be seen in just a few decades; they are not something that this generation can calculate. But at the very least, one can say that *weihu zaotian* ... went against the objective rules of nature and economy. A plateau lake basin is very rare, and not to protect it, but instead to add earth to grow grain ... not only did this not have positive effects, but instead it did endless harm. Exactly how much, future generations must judge.[88]

A geography professor told me that the scholarly world foresaw the consequences and would have opposed the project if they had been able to do so. She was a student at the university when her professors worried aloud that Kunming's spring-like year-round climate depended on Dianchi.

But who dared to oppose efforts to resolve the food problem? So the Western Hills were used to fill in the lake. With the best intentions, good people did stupid things. They didn't respect objective scientific laws. The water table was too high, and the land was no good for grain. But at the time, people didn't consider that. Later, after the Cultural Revolution, I told this to my own students. There were many good conditions for agriculture, but the water table was the real problem. People used the "Three Old Articles" to create an attitude of determination. But to use the spirit of the Foolish Old Man to fill in lakes, this was definitely wrong.

A researcher at a Minorities Museum now located on the in-filled land expressed resigned sadness about the project, attributing the in-filling to the effort to learn from Dazhai without respect for local conditions, "planting grain in the middle of lakes" if necessary:

> Originally, this place was wetland. There were many fish. Dianchi was clear and blue. The *weihai zaotian* practice originated in coastal areas, in imitation of the Netherlands. But then Revolutionary Committee leader Tan Puren got the idea of filling the lake. At the time, China was "learning from Dazhai," creating arable land by terracing hillsides. Where that wouldn't work, the leaders tried to find other ways.

The problem, in his view, lay in Mao's notion that the same techniques used to win military successes could be used in national development. "How did he make this mistake? It was a lack of practical knowledge. He had political and military experience. But he didn't know how to build China."

Another professor recalled, "They hoped to resolve the problem of meeting people's basic needs. But some of their methods created conflict with nature. They thought, if there isn't enough land, then just create it." Before the project began, the professor had been sent with the rest of the university faculty to Luyuan County for reeducation through manual labor. Returning in February 1970, they were put to work on the lake. He remembered how rocks were transported from the Western Mountains and old construction materials were added for fill, which helped explain the subsequent poor quality of the earth.

In the first year, it was clear that the result wasn't what had been imagined. Some of us said so in meetings, but we couldn't publish our views. After three or four years, everyone knew the project had been a failure. But as far as public acknowledgment goes, that didn't come until the 1980s. There seemed to be a change in Kunming's microclimate. The temperature seemed more extreme, colder in winter and warmer in summer. It seemed as if there were more droughts. Of course, the in-filling was only one of many factors in the degradation of the lake. But other factors, like global climate change, deforestation, and pollution, are more difficult for people to understand. So they remember the *weihu zaotian* campaign.

He blamed Revolutionary Committee leader Tan Puren for not understanding nature and ruining a beautiful lake. Tan Puren met his fate soon after the lake was filled in, leading some to say that the lake was having its revenge. He was murdered in his home the following year in one of those murky Cultural Revolution–era intrigues, perhaps because he was a close associate of Lin Biao. There were also rumors that Lin had him killed because he failed to obey orders to shoot down a plane carrying Premier Zhou Enlai to a meeting in Southeast Asia. A military leader was later arrested for Tan's murder and then released. The circumstances surrounding his death remain unclear.

Eventually, in a new era, commercial rather than political considerations reigned. Too soft to farm or to support buildings of much weight, another use was found for the soggy land created through the sweat and sacrifices of so many. A "Minority Village" tourist attraction, constructed of indigenous peoples' light wooden houses, was erected where the old wetland had been. Essentially a large walled theme park evocative of a human zoo, the village allows the time-pressed tourist to experience all Yunnan's ethnotourism in a single afternoon, visiting "villages" peopled by members of the province's many minority groups. (Eventually, all twenty-six nationalities are to be represented.) The tourist can buy native crafts, taste native food, and take in song and dance performances. Minorities who live in the villages, mostly attractive young women, sign two-year contracts to stand around decoratively in ethnic costume, sing and dance on schedule, and make conversation about their culture. But life as displayed is far from authentic. Except for the Naxi women, who told me that they sleep in their traditional stilted house according to matriarchal custom, residents of the other minority villages are housed in a dormitory. After a few years they move on, often to Shenzhen and the other coastal cities where they can make even more money.

At the gates of the Minority Village, a 27-year-old tour-wagon driver waited for customers. He told me that his parents had been among 1,000 middle school graduates deployed to the project from the Kunming area. "Each work unit sent people. Everyone participated. They made dikes with rocks and sandbags, then they drained the area and filled it with dirt." His parents were then assigned to the May 7th Agricultural Farm, where he was born and raised. "But they couldn't grow enough to live on. Later, the government didn't even bother to divide up the land [under the reforms]. So they turned it into a tourist attraction." A tour group from Thailand climbed into his wagon and he drove off, providing an ironic coda to a tale of misplaced enthusiasm, waste, and destruction.

Under the economic reforms, Dianchi's waters suffered deeply from increased industrial chemical discharge, sewage and detergents from a burgeoning urban population, and agricultural fertilizer runoff. The lake became one of the most polluted in China, choked with trash and the water hyacinth and algae that often indicate eutrophication. Today, together with Lake Tai and Lake Chao, the Chinese government has identified Dianchi as one of three lakes targeted for major environmental cleanup. With major funding from the World Bank and Kunming's "twin city" of Zurich, Dianchi has been made a symbol for China's seriousness about its pollution problems. Attempts are being made to contain and treat wastewater, and many of the most polluting factories have been shut down. Clearly, the story of Dianchi is not over.

In sum, the 1970 reclamation of Lake Dian's Haigeng wetland was a grave mistake. A uniquely Maoist admixture of public works project, political struggle, and spiritual transformation, it was a true *yundong* in its mass mobilization, urgency, suppression of dissent, and excessively literal application of slogans and directives handed down from above. The project typifies the Maoist tendency toward dogmatic formalism and uniform use of a single model, and represents an unusually distorted and inappropriate permutation of the Dazhai campaign. With its multiple slogans and layers of symbols, the Dianchi in-filling also exemplifies the Mao-era war against nature in one of its most militarized, extreme, and ideologically charged expressions. Its disastrous legacy provides an enduring example of the foolishness, waste, and misguided enthusiasm of similar projects of the era.[89]

Years later, Dazhai was discredited. The Dazhai "miracle" was exposed as having been achieved only through much outside help. Before he was attacked in the Cultural Revolution, President Liu Shaoqi had sent work teams to investigate the situation, but it was not until 1980 that the *People's Daily* revealed that Dazhai had accepted huge amounts of aid and PLA help. Premier Zhou Enlai, usually credited with moderating the worst Cultural Revolution excesses, is said to have cautioned early on against universalizing the Dazhai experience, while Lin Biao, who is often named as the chief Cultural Revolution villain in place of Mao, was accused in post-1971 denunciations of precisely that sin. But it was not until after Mao's death that China's leaders finally turned away from the idea of planting grain wherever possible.

On a visit to Dazhai in 1975, a group of foreign publishers commented that in the West such land would not have been considered suitable for farming to begin with.[90] As elsewhere in the world, population pressures explain much about China's efforts to expand their arable lands, yet rarely has there been such a complete merger of revolutionary political agenda and development project as during the "Take Grain as the Key Link" and "In Agriculture, Learn from Dazhai" phase of the Cultural Revolution. Rarely has there been a historical moment in which political repression, misguided ideals, and an absolutistic vision of priorities and correct methods coincided to achieve such concentrated attacks on nature, environmental destruction, and human suffering. As such, this episode provides a cautionary tale concerning the dangers of dogmatic thinking.

"Prepare for War, Prepare for Famine,
for the Sake of the People"
Bei Zhan, Bei Huang, Wei Renmin

"In Mountains, Dispersed, in Caves"
Shan, San, Dong

4

WAR PREPARATIONS AND FORCIBLE RELOCATIONS

How Factories Polluted the Mountains and Youths "Opened" the Frontiers

In previous chapters, we examined the impact of political repression, utopian urgency, and dogmatic formalism on China's environment. State-sponsored resettlement of Han Chinese into remote and rural areas provides a final defining them: The Chinese Communist Party's willingness to reorder society by administrative fiat, and the comparative powerlessness of Chinese people to resist these measures, were hallmarks of the Mao era.[1] The state sometimes enticed people to volunteer to relocate with the promise of higher salaries, better future work assignments, or better living conditions. More frequently, it exacted cooperation by manipulating fears that a lack of political enthusiasm would have adverse consequences or by employing blatant coercion. Such relocations almost always had the dual purpose of transforming the landscape and accomplishing political goals.

State-induced migrations began almost immediately after the 1949 victory, when politically progressive Chinese were asked to volunteer to settle ethnic minority areas along the frontiers [zhibian]. The newcomers helped to dilute local populations, suppress opposition to Han Chinese and/or Communist rule, and provide labor to build an infrastructure for extracting and transporting rich natural resources from border regions to more developed coastal lowlands.[2] Migrants also helped to secure and reinforce the territorial boundaries of a nation long subject to foreign incursions.

For urban Chinese, relocation was often a form of political punishment. In 1957, many of the more than half a million intellectuals and Party leaders labeled "rightists" were sent to remote labor camps, where they quarried rocks, felled trees, dug irrigation canals, and otherwise struggled to change the land. Some remained in exile for as long as twenty years, until their political labels, or "caps," were removed after Mao's death. Journalist Liu Binyan, for example, spent his long political ostracism laboring in rural Shaanxi, Shandong, and Henan; English professor Wu Ningkun and fellow labor camp inmates built diversion dikes to reclaim land from lakes in the Great Northern Wilderness in Heilongjiang.[3]

"Socialist education" campaigns, such as that of the early 1960s, induced less punitive migrations. Urban residents were expected to go voluntarily to the countryside to uncover Party corruption, participate in farmwork and public works projects, and receive ideological tempering. They, too, had a role in transforming nature's face. As we have seen, large dam projects of the sort Huang Wanli warned against, perhaps the paramount examples of profound human manipulation of the natural environment, also involved large-scale forcible resettlements – in this case, away from the affected areas.

During the Cultural Revolution, the Chinese state displaced millions of people and relocated them to the hinterlands. Heavy industry was transplanted to the interior in an effort to prepare China for war; hundreds of factories and entire workforces were picked up and placed in regions inhospitable for human habitation. These relocations not only disrupted the lives of hundreds of thousands of urban workers but also brought intense extractive and manufacturing activity into remote areas. In another sort of mass transfer of human beings, 20 million "educated youths" were sent to the countryside for land reclamation. They "opened up" a total of 19,670,000 *mu* of land, transforming it by clearing, dredging, or irrigating. Of this land, 13,540,000 *mu* were proclaimed arable [one *mu* equals one-sixth of an acre]. In Inner Mongolia, a million *mu* were cleared, bringing arable land to a total of 1,530,000 *mu*. In Heilongjiang, from 1969 to 1972, 4 million *mu* of arable land were expanded to 17 million. In Xinjiang's Taklamakan Desert, after the conversion of desert to arable land by youths relocated from Shanghai, Zhejiang, and Jiangsu, grain yields were said to soar from more than 3 million *jin* in 1966 to 13 million *jin* a few years later. In all of Xinjiang, a total of 30,330,000 *mu* of arable land were "reclaimed."[4] Despite these apparent successes, the long-term environmental impact of all this activity was, as we shall see, often devastating.[5]

Relocations launched for political, economic, or security reasons often disrupted strong bonds to region, hometown, and family. From the Maoist point of view, these disruptions were a useful means of breaking through the strictures of traditional culture so as to build a new society and "new socialist man." Residence permits [*hukou*] and grain ration coupons [*liangpiao*] restricted freedom of movement. Once a residence permit had been transferred, it was difficult to return home even if a labor camp sentence had been served or a political "cap" removed. There were numerous bureaucratic obstacles to moving from a lower administrative unit (like a rural village) to a higher one (like a county seat or provincial capital), but without a local residence permit, a person could not receive ration coupons for food staples. Only after Mao's death were many transplanted individuals able to return to their native cities. Those who had established new families in the countryside were often not permitted to leave, or they were forced to leave behind new family members because of residence permit problems. While economic reforms have weakened the power of the residence permit and removed the need for ration coupons, many who were uprooted during the Mao years remain far from home to this day.

Despite such separations from native place, relationship to family and identification with region of origin have remained powerful, and the connection between family and place continues to be strongly linked – in Chinese, the word *jia* denotes both family and home. Many people feel deeply tied to ancestral homelands, landscapes, and customs, even if they and their families have lived elsewhere for generations. Decades after moving south of the Yangzi River, where rice is the staple food, for example, a person may identify as a Northerner, with a Northerner's preference for wheat, and vice versa. A person may call himself a Shanghainese, while admitting in the next breath that he has never visited the city. Mao-era relocations thus had a particularly punitive quality for many Chinese, as traditional culture imparted an intense sense of connection to ancestral home.

A powerful connection to native place may have positive implications for land stewardship. Generations of farmers learn how to tend the land so that it nurtures and sustains them, passing down local knowledge from generation to generation. Conversely, when connection to place is absent, there are negative implications for the environment. When migrants are transported abruptly into regions where they have no personal history or understanding of local geographic conditions, and little or no say in how to use the land, they may disrupt and destroy the very resources they intend to rely on for survival.

Land-reclamation projects present a more general environmental issue: conversion of wilderness to agricultural use may transform highly specialized ecosystems. Habitat suitable for wild animals yields to that suitable for humans and, in Alfred Crosby's elegant formulation, for their "portmanteau biota" of domestic animals.[6] Such conversions then promote the survival of species adapted to human habitat, but they often destroy the complex natural systems on which humans ultimately depend. In particular, mono-culture or single-cropping (such as the rubber plantations that will be discussed later in this section) is inimical to the support of a diversity of life forms.

The War Preparation Campaign

The war preparation campaign of the late 1960s and early 1970s is the best Mao-era example of the unintended negative environmental consequences of human migrations. Millions were sent to hinterlands and frontiers in response to China's heightened international security concerns. Coercive and semivoluntary relocations of people to inhospitable regions and pristine wilderness areas damaged or destroyed ecosystems even as they created enormous human hardships. War preparations brought new intensity to the effort to conquer nature, as the "battlefront" shifted to the mountains of Guizhou and Sichuan, the rainforests of Yunnan, the forests and wetlands of Heilongjiang's Great Northern Wilderness, the grasslands of Inner Mongolia, and the forests and deserts of Xinjiang. Nature and people alike were victims of these relocations. Young urban Chinese had to scrape out a harsh existence far from home, workers and entire factories were uprooted and sent inland, while indigenous ethnic minorities faced an influx of people and policies that threatened and destroyed traditional ways of life. The intimate link between the suffering of people and the abuse of the land because of forcible, state-sponsored relocations is the focus of this section.

War preparation relocations involved two major campaigns. One campaign was to create a "Third Front" [*sanxian*], or inland industrial and military base. (The First and Second Fronts were the vulnerable coastal regions and the midcountry regions that would be at risk during a long conflict.)[7] The other was the "educated youth movement" [*zhiqing yundong*], in which 20 million urban young people were sent to the countryside and frontiers. Third Front construction began in 1964, with the Third Five-year Plan, which called for building a base for rearguard defense in the event of war. The educated youth, or "up to the mountains, down to the countryside" movement [*shangshan xiaxiang yundong*] (often awkwardly translated as the rustification campaign), intensified in late 1968 after the worst of the Red Guard violence. Among millions of youths "sent down" to the countryside, more than two million were deployed to border areas to join the Production-Construction Army Corps [*Shengchan Jianshe Bingtuan*] under People's Liberation Army leadership.[8] Both movements peaked in 1969 following border skirmishes with the Soviet Union, when the war preparation campaign reached its height.

From an environmental perspective, the Third Front primarily affected mountainous interior areas of West and Southwest China. The new strategic base required roads and railroads to open up the hinterlands. The relocated industries engaged in mining for minerals with defense applications and logging for fuel and timber. They sent air pollution into narrow mountain valleys and chemical wastes into river headwaters. In contrast, the rustification campaign's impact was felt along the frontiers, particularly in Southwest China near Vietnam, Laos, and Burma and along the long northern and northwestern border with the Soviet Union. The influx of Production-Construction Army Corps youths represented a major wave of resettlement of Han Chinese into ethnic minority areas, introduced alien agricultural practices, and provided massive labor power for reclamation projects that degraded ecosystems.[9] The "war preparation" campaign epitomizes Mao's war against nature in its most explicit incarnation, for the Chinese people were called on to make war against the country's external and internal enemies and conquer nature at one and the same time.

The Security Environment

China's international isolation became profound after the 1960 Sino-Soviet split. War waged in Vietnam by American "imperialists" and border skirmishes with Soviet "revisionists" soon led Mao to see war as imminent in a world hostile to China. China lacked allies and feared attack from either or both superpowers. Mao's view that an apocalyptic struggle between the forces of revolution and reaction was imminent helps to explain why he intervened to put the country on a war footing just as consumption-oriented policies were bringing China's economy greater stability after the Great Famine.[10]

After the United States bombed North Vietnam on August 4, 1964, Mao called for accelerated inland development in preparation for war, sounding his favored themes of urgency, decentralization, and self-reliance.[11] Relations with the Soviet Union worsened as Khrushchev's reforms and territorial disputes exacerbated differences with the former "elder brother." From October 15, 1964 to March 5, 1969, there were 4,189 border incidents on the Soviet border, half again as many as in the period from 1960 to 1964. After Soviet troops marched into Czechoslovakia in August 1968, a large-scale invasion of China seemed increasingly plausible. In February 1969, Chinese troops were put on alert on the Far East border, and on March 2 and 15, there were armed clashes with the Soviets on Zhenbao Island in Heilongjiang province. Mutual displays of aggression continued throughout the year. In the summer, clashes erupted in Xinjiang and Heilongjiang; a July 30, 1969 *People's Daily* editorial called on the Chinese people to expect war through surprise attack at any time. Premier Alexei Kosygin visited China on September 11, 1969, meeting Zhou Enlai at the airport in a failed attempt to defuse tensions, and in the latter half of 1969, the Soviets used even stronger anti-Chinese language. By mid-October 1969, China was at a fever pitch of war preparation; tensions decreased somewhat only when talks resumed on October 20.[12] These talks failed, and on January 31, 1970, Mao called on the people to "use the war preparation viewpoint to see everything, examine everything, carry out everything."[13] In his famous May 20 speech, "People of the World Unite, Defeat American Invaders and their Running Dogs," he declared, "the danger of a new world war still exists, the people of each country should prepare."

The army's participation in the Revolutionary Committees formed in 1967–68, as mentioned, had brought military governance to civilian institutions. The country's increasingly militarized stance now colored the domestic struggle against internal counterrevolutionary "enemies" that had been launched with the Cultural Revolution. As war preparation increased, the whole country came to resemble an army on alert. Mao maintained that "all people are soldiers" [*quan min jie bing*]. Green military clothing and red-starred PLA caps became the fashion. Party directives propounded such war preparation slogans as "Raise Vigilance, Protect the Motherland" [*Tigao Jingti, Baowei Zuguo*] and "Deeply Dig Tunnels, Broadly Gather Grain, Never Seek Hegemony" [*Shen Wadong, Guang Jiliang, Bu Chengba*]. Military expenditures rose. In 1969, defense military preparations were 34 percent greater than the previous year, and in 1970 and 1971, they continued to increase by 15 and 16 percent, respectively.[14] Strategic considerations dominated, to the exclusion of other values.

THE THIRD FRONT

"Prepare for War, Prepare for Famine, For the Sake of the People" [*Bei Zhan, Bei Huang, Wei Renmin*] became the defining slogan for the war preparation phase of Mao-era environmental degradation. The formulation emerged during preparatory discussions for the Third Five-year Plan (1966-70), which specified that China's straitened economic circumstances should be confronted through austerity and arduous struggle.[15] Commenting on a draft document, Mao remarked on June 16, 1965 that the focus of the next period should be on the people, war preparation, and the possibility of famine. An August version of the plan stated that China should prepare for a big, early war, place national defense first, speed up Third Front construction, and slowly improve people's lives. Zhou Enlai is credited with creating the slogan and Mao with repeating it in March 1966. As has been noted, it was propagated nationwide with the April 1967 edition of Chairman Mao's Little Red Book.[16]

The Third Front strategy originated during the same period. In a June 6, 1964 talk on the Third Five-year Plan, Mao commented, in his earthy fashion:

> As long as imperialism exists, there is always the danger of war. We must build up the strategic rear... This does not mean that we no longer care about the seacoast, which must also be well guarded so that it can play the role of supporting the construction of new bases. Two fists and one rear-end. Agriculture is one fist, and national defense is another fist. To make the fists strong, the rear-end must be seated securely. The rear-end is basic industry.[17]

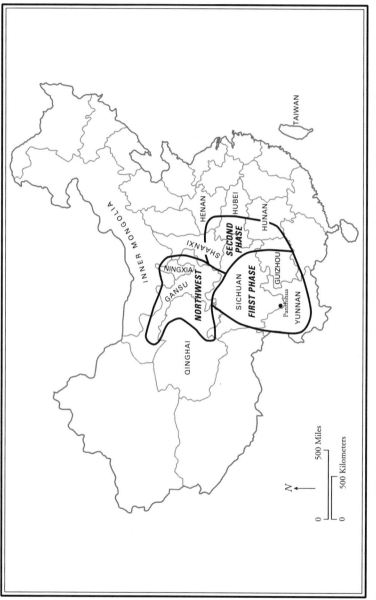

Based on a map created by Barry Naughton. Naughton describes first phase construction as beginning in 1964 and the second phase around 1969. In the Northwest, Third Front construction dates to the 1950s, but accelerated during the major phases. (Adapted, with permission, from "The Third Front: Defence Industrialization in the Chinese Interior," *China Quarterly* No. 115 [September 1988], pgs. 354, 356–361.)

The Third Front would be built in the mountainous interior, where rugged terrain would provide protection in the event of a military attack. Urban factories, particularly strategic industries, would be relocated to remote areas for shelter and concealment.

The Third Front comprised two sections, corresponding approximately to interior mountainous regions above 500 meters in altitude.[18] The southerly part included most of Yunnan, Guizhou, and Sichuan and the southwest parts of West Hunan and West Hubei; the northerly one included all or parts of Shaanxi, Gansu, and Ningxia, and Qinghai and the northwest parts of West Henan and West Shanxi. Each province was ordered to develop its own military industries and to manufacture rifles, bayonets, light and heavy machine guns, mortar, grenades, and dynamite.[19]

Hundreds of inland sites were surveyed as possible Third Front locations in September 1964. The ideal site was said to be "in the mountains, dispersed, and hidden" [*kaoshan, fensan, yinbi*]. A report on Guizhou province, home of the minority Zhuang people and one of China's most barren and sparsely populated regions, identified forty-eight suitable sites.[20] The slogan, *Shan, San, Dong,* or "In Mountains, Dispersed, In Caves," (which at least one source attributes to Lin Biao[21]) came to describe the ideal location.

Barry Naughton, who has studied the Third Front's huge economic losses, describes the Third Front as the largest investment in military development ever pursued by any country:

> The intention was to create an entire industrial base – not just an armaments industry – that could survive a prolonged war. The program was so huge that it can fairly be said that, with the exception of petroleum development, the central government's industrialization policy from 1965 through 1971 *was* the Third Front.[22]

Some industries were rebuilt from scratch, but, especially in the machinery and chemical industries, relocations were common. Whole plants were moved, or split up and partially relocated. From 1964 to mid-1971, 380 factories were moved inland, representing one-fifth of all large Third Front plants. Machine-building and arms factories in northern Guizhou, the Number Two Automobile Factory in Hubei, and nuclear and aerospace industries in the Northwest were all part of Third Front policy, along with the Gezhou Dam on the upper Yangzi River.[23] In 1970, construction investment in the interior totaled 197.98 billion *yuan,* of which Third Front expenditures comprised 163.13 billion, or almost all.[24]

The high costs were due not only to difficult terrain but also to the urgency with which Mao's directives were implemented. Site selection, design, and construction were to be implemented simultaneously, with revisions conducted as needed; construction had the ad hoc character of a guerrilla war. Naughton writes:

> The great haste with which Third Front projects were initiated meant that in most cases design and preparatory work were inadequate or nonexistent. Nearly every project about which we have information ran into substantial additional costs and delays because of inadequate preparatory work.[25]

Thus, with the Third Front, Mao again sounded the same theme of urgency which had devastated the environment during the Leap. Apparently, Mao had not learned that political will alone could not force time to collapse.

The Panzhihua steel mill in Southwest Sichuan, which ultimately cost the state 3.74 billion *yuan,* was the centerpiece of the Third Front and the primary reason for the construction of the Chengdu-Kunming railroad, which was to bring Guizhou coal to the mill and carry Panzhihua steel to Chongqing. Today, Panzhihua is trumpeted as a Third Front success story that validates Mao's strategic genius. An English-language investment brochure boasts, for example, "Looking back into the past and forward into the future, we cannot help marveling at the profound foresight of our great leader." The brochure continues, "Standing on the very spot where the construction of Panzhihua started, we can see a picture unfolding before us, a picture of man conquering nature."[26] The story of Panzhihua, as detailed in books and annals about the city and as reflected in interviews with ordinary people and officials, is a microcosm of Third Front relocations in many parts of the interior, a tale of arduous struggle by thousands of resettled individuals who had little say in their activities.[27] There were extraordinary engineering achievements in carving a complex mining and manufacturing operation out of an inhospitable landscape and building a railroad with so many tunnels that much of it is underground. There were also enormous environmental and economic costs to placing strategic considerations above all else. Within the broader scope of this book, the story of Panzhihua reveals a different aspect of Mao-era environmental problems than we have discussed thus far, and it shifts our focus from misuse and overexploitation of resources to industrial pollution.

Panzhihua: A Steel Mill Like a "Miniature Carving in Ivory"

Because of the extraordinary difficulty involved in siting an enormous steel mill on only 2.5 square kilometers of land, official mythology compares the Panzhihua Iron and Steel Mill (*Pangang*) to a carved ivory miniature. Panzhihua city is named for the flower that is the region's botanical marvel, a rare and ancient fern-like plant called a cycad. The cycad is often described as a "living fossil" and listed together with pandas and dinosaurs as one of the three jewels of Sichuan. Until the late

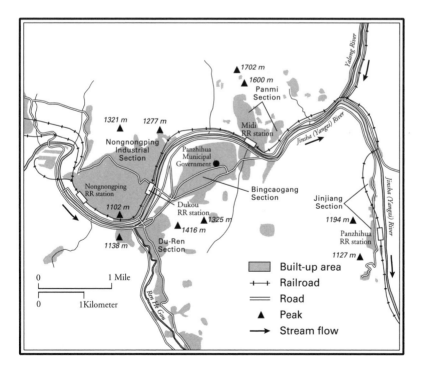

1980s, the city was also known by its original name, Dukou, which means ford.[28]

Created out of a tiny village in 1965, Panzhihua is located at the confluence of the Jinsha and Yalong rivers 749 kilometers south of Chengdu and 351 kilometers north of Kunming. It shares a rift valley with Xichang, today's satellite-launching city. In the 1930s, beneath a seemingly barren landscape, geologists discovered tremendous mineral resources, which were confirmed through additional surveys in the early 1950s.[29] Chairman Mao dreamed of tapping these resources, and by the mid-1960s, when war looked increasingly likely, he became determined to do so. The rich deposits included plentiful iron and coal – forty-seven minerals in all, including rare metals. Coal deposits included coking coal and anthracite, and iron ores included hematite and titanium-bearing titano-magnetite, all of which are highly suitable for the manufacture of steel. Panzhihua has 69 percent of China's vanadium and 93 percent of its titanium, both are metals with defense applications. Its proven titanium reserves are first in the world.[30]

Chairman Mao raised the question of exploiting Panzhihua's rich mineral resources for steel-manufacture as early as a March 1958 meeting in Chengdu, but he put aside his ambition in the aftermath of the Leap. He revived the plan at the earliest opportunity. The official Panzhihua myth thus begins with "a wise decision" of March 4, 1965, when Mao scrawled, "good proposal" on a Ministry of Mining and Industry report recommending construction of Panzhihua. In May, Mao criticized overly cautious leaders for abandoning plans for Panzhihua and the Kunming-Chengdu railroad, declaring, "The decision to build Panzhihua City is not an issue concerning only one particular steel plant, but a strategic consideration." He then made a dramatic offer: "I cannot sleep until we build the Panzhihua Iron and Steel Mill... If capital is lacking, I will donate the royalties from my own writing."[31] From this meeting until 1967, Mao is estimated to have mentioned the Third Front twenty-one times in writings and speeches and to have explicitly linked it to Panzhihua more than six times. He is said to have been obsessed with Panzhihua.[32] In conversation about this history, a Panzhihua resident sighed and shrugged. "What could we have done? Chairman Mao couldn't sleep, so we had no choice." During the initial drafting of the Third Five-year Plan, when other leaders sought to emphasize living standards, agricultural development, and production of consumer goods, Mao intervened, rejected their plan, and prevailed in his war preparation strategy.[33] Responsibility for implementing the plan was retained at the highest level, with Premier Zhou Enlai placed in charge of opening Panzhihua. In 1965, then-Communist Party General Secretary Deng Xiaoping also reviewed the plans, as evidenced by a photo reproduced in many public settings in the city.

When the first 50,000 workers arrived from ten Sichuan and Kunming work units in 1965, only seven Han Chinese households consisting of about seventy individuals were living in the area.[34] The surrounding mountains were Yi minority territory, an ethnic group famous for its aggressive resistance to the Han. Today, the newcomers' early hardships are presented in museum dioramas illustrating Panzhihua's glorious origins. Pioneers built huts of thatch and rammed-earth in the barren and dusty land. "The pot on three stones is our kitchen, the tent in the open is our bedroom," boasts the legend.[35] Young men in mining hats stand below a slogan, "Don't Think of Father, Don't Think of Mother, Until You Produce Iron, Don't Go Home" [*Bu Xiang Die, Bu Xiang Ma, Bu Chu Tie, Bu Hui Jia*]. In an odd bit of arcana, the museum also displays Premier Zhou Enlai's 1969 U.S.-made Belair automobile.

If not for war preparation considerations, the place selected for the steel plant, a hillside called Nongnongping, would hardly have been a logical site for a factory. In designing previous steel plants, the Chinese had used a Soviet model that specified "three greats, one person" [*san da yi ren*] – a great plain, a great factory district, and a great railroad, all laid out in the shape of the character for "person" [人]. Nongnongping was a cramped, 2.5-square-kilometer area surrounded on three sides by high mountains and on the fourth by the Jinsha River. The slope of the land varied from 10 to 20 degrees and in some places was as steep as 50 degrees, with cliffs, boulders, and other geographic challenges.[36] There was as yet, of course, no railroad. But at the end of 1965 a design team of 1,300 specialists drawn from throughout the country arrived, and, by the beginning of 1966, they had come up with a plan.

This plan was immediately thrown into disarray with the onslaught of the Cultural Revolution. Radicals propagated the notion that "the workers are the masters of design, technicians can only be consultants" [*gongren shi sheji de zhuren, jishu renyuan zhi neng dang canmou*]. They claimed that the plan's costs were too high and that there was no need for a roof on the sintering plant, since, "if peasants can farm under the open sky, why can't workers make steel under the open sky?" Because of the "dispersed" element of the "in mountains, dispersed, in caves" slogan, they recommended that the stages of the steel-making process should be separated out and the various components concealed in valleys throughout the region. Presumably, this greatly complicated production. Ultimately, through clever reporting, the technicians were able to minimize the most damaging of these proposals. However, many design flaws remained because of this interference.[37]

Meanwhile, 20,000 road-builders and mine-diggers assembled from around the country were hard at work. Eighty percent of these workers were completely inexperienced. In addition to their dangerous and difficult work, they were also required to conduct political study, criticizing Liu Shaoqi even as they struggled to open roads to the mines. They are said to have "demonstrated a spirit of arduous struggle, a spirit [like that expressed in Mao's youthful poem] of 'boundless joy at struggling against the heavens.'" When ventilation was inadequate for using dynamite, they persisted, using wet cloths pressed against their faces. Their heroic efforts soon produced martyrs and model workers, like one Tang Dahei who is said to have emerged from his work cut and bleeding, his pants in shreds.[38] Strategic considerations made hard work even harder: in accordance with the mandate to hide critical installations in caves, for example, a tunnel was burrowed into the mountains to house an electric generator, its coal chimneys poking out just above ground-level where no bomber would notice them.[39] The death rate in 1965 was 13 percent of the work force, an extraordinary figure. For the period between 1965 and 1975, the death rate averaged 5.42 percent, still exceedingly high.[40]

As various "battles" of design and road-building were declared, planners turned urgently to sintering, coking, and smelting in Nongnongping itself. Steel workers arrived from Angang and Wugang, the huge steel mills of the city of Anshan in Liaoning province in the Northeast and the city of Wuhan in central China. Large numbers of workers from Hunan had been sent first to Angang for training. In all, 700 factories were mobilized to help build Panzhihua.[41] The goal was to "speedily construct the Number One furnace system and make the Number One furnace quickly produce iron, so as to let Mao Zedong rest easy, let the Central Committee rest easy!"[42] A woman whose steelworker parents came from Liaoning told me:

A huge group of steelworkers came from Angang in 1969. Of course, no one wanted to come. But in those days it was impossible to say how you really felt. Of course, there may have been a few motivated by idealism. But if Chairman Mao said he couldn't sleep at night, that was because of the international situation, with the Soviet Union, India, the U.S., even Japan. He felt surrounded by enemies. In fact, building the railroad or producing steel in Panzhihua wasn't going to give him any sleep. It was all for political considerations, nothing else. The wishes of the people were never part of it.

The official *Panzhihua Record* notes that this "immigrant city" was characterized by "mechanical" population changes (due to policy fiat), uneven distribution, many more males than females, lots of ethnic minorities, and a small population.[43] In 1965, Panzhihua (then Dukou) administratively assimilated several great people's communes from Yunnan and Sichuan, comprising 80,836 people. In the first year, 41,407 immigrants arrived, for a total of 122,243. From 1965 to 1971, 373,639 more people arrived, for an average of 53,337 immigrants per year, or an average annual increase of 263.84 percent. In the same period, 158,840 people left, reflecting the short-term nature of certain assignments, for an average of 22,691 people per year. When the influx and outflow of people are considered together, from 1965 to 1971, the total increase in the city's population was 214,799 people, an average of 30,686 people per year, and the mechanical increase, or increase due to administrative relocations, was as high as 151.68 percent. Not surprisingly, the *Panzhihua Record* tells us that the majority of immigrants were young men. In 1965, 62 percent of the population was male; by 1970, the figure was almost 70 percent.[44] This must have been the source of another kind of suffering beyond the harsh struggle with the land, as these young laborers would have been unable to find wives and establish families.

Premier Zhou Enlai set a target date of July 1, 1970 for Panzhihua to produce iron and for the railroad to be completed. This date is said to have been a powerful motivating goal that focused everyone's energy and attention.[45] Meanwhile, as the Cultural Revolution raged on, some experienced technicians spent their daylight hours submitting to political criticism while continuing to oversee steel plant construction by night.[46] The goal was met: in July, Panzhihua turned out its first furnace of molten iron. The following year, it turned out its first furnace of molten steel.[47]

The Chengdu-Kunming railroad, built to transport Pangang's steel and primarily constructed by People's Liberation Army Unit 7659, was also completed, with great fanfare, in 1970. An extraordinary engineering feat of bridge and tunnel-building, the railroad has played a huge role in opening up China's Southwest to development. Some 300,000 laborers built 427 tunnels, with an accumulated length of 340 kilometers; the tunnels cover about one-third of a rail-line that totals just over 1,000 kilometers. In all, 999 bridges were built.[48] Rail links through the difficult terrain of the Third Front averaged double the cost of normal construction: the Chengdu-Kunming railroad cost 3.3 billion *yuan*.[49] Testaments to the great loss of life during construction accidents can be glimpsed today in the form of memorial markers near tunnels and ravines.

Environmental Costs

Siting Panzhihua at the foot of high surrounding mountains, where emissions from the plant were trapped, caused severe pollution problems. Prevailing winds blew polluted air out of the valley during the day and back in at night. To exacerbate matters, temperature inversions often trapped pollution beneath warmer air masses, so that not even the tallest chimney could carry emissions out of the area. Moreover, for economic and political reasons, the 274 pollution and wastewater control devices that the plans originally called for were never installed. In 1975, after environmental monitoring began, the steel mill's particulate emissions were 2,197.5 milligrams per cubic meter, more than 218 times above the national recommendation, and those of the sintering plant were more than 320 times above it. A 1984 medical investigation showed that nearly 3 percent of workers had lung diseases.[50]

Water pollution was also severe. Because human health was not considered during the design phase, the steel plant was situated upriver from human settlements, and toxic wastes spewed directly into the river and contaminated household water supplies. Eventually, more than 400 factories, 51 of them with heavy industrial output, were sited on the Jinsha River. In the 1970s, when water pollution was largely uncontrolled and sanitary conditions poor, infectious diseases were rampant; the official *Panzhihua Record* states that dysentery and hepatitis were common.[51] One man who lived in the city in 1973 recalled that the Jinsha River had been yellow with pollution.

There were other environmental issues as well. Panzhihua's enduring soil pollution by toxic metals is not surprising in an environment in which chemicals and metals were so heavily and carelessly used. Moreover, the extent of deforestation increased steadily, leaving the area surrounding Panzhihua almost completely barren. Under the influence of the Leap and "learning from Dazhai," according to the official *Panzhihua Record*, deforestation climbed from lands at 1,300 meters to those at 1,500 meters above sea level. After Panzhihua was founded in 1965, three unnamed foreign countries were permitted to log heavily, extending deforestation to 1,700 meters above sea level and reducing overall forest cover in the region to 24.22 percent. "From dense, to sparse, to barren," comments the *Record*. The result was terrible erosion.[52]

A high-ranking planning official acknowledged past mistakes:

In 1965, everything was in the service of producing steel. There was no environmental bureau in Panzhihua until 1979. In the early years, we were surrounded on all sides by enemies. War preparation was the only consideration.

A local Environmental Protection Bureau employee spoke more specifically about Panzhihua's location as the source of a host of problems:

The main plant should have been in a more open place, a less densely concentrated place. At the time, transport and politics were the only considerations. The main problems come from the siting of the plant. Now, the coking factory is the main polluter. We had two benzene spills in 1995.[53] The water tasted strange for a week or so each time, and we put out an alert that the people should not drink it. This year, the oldest electricity generating station [the one built in a tunnel] was shut down for pollution. Now we have a new one. The biggest problem is our reliance on coal. Panzhihua is fourth in the nation in steel production after Shanghai, Wuhan, and Anshan. It is so rich in resources.

Everything we need to produce steel is right here in the mountains. But it wasn't necessary to place it in a mountain valley.

It is extremely unlikely that the Panzhihua Steel Mill will be able to meet new pollution remediation requirements, mandatory since the millennium. It is equally unlikely that a major industrial operation of such national importance, employing tens of thousands of workers, will be shut down. As it is, the city has been sharply affected by the mill's layoffs of several thousand steelworkers. However, a second steel production base, with a projected output of three to four million tons of steel per year (as compared with Panzhihua's current one million tons), is being built in Dechang in Liangshan Prefecture to Panzhihua's north.[54] More attention is being given to siting and pollution issues, and some of Panzhihua's operations could shift there in the future.

Panzhihua's pollution problems were typical of those caused by other Third Front industries; industrial pollution in excess of what might have been expected with better planning and more suitable locations was a major consequence of policy. Qu and Li describe the "In Mountains, Dispersed, In Caves" formulation as "direct[ing] many factories to remote mountains and gorges where they subsequently discharged large amounts of pollution. If conditions for diffusion and dilution were poor, serious air and water pollution resulted."[55] They characterize the Third Front as an example of irrational distribution of industry, with serious environmental consequences. Mountain gorges often trapped industrial air pollution, while mountain streams frequently could not assimilate and dilute the influx of large quantities of chemicals.

Today, the Panzhihua Steel Mill and other factories remain sources of serious pollution of the Jinsha and Yalong rivers, which are among the headwaters of the Yangzi River. Deforestation has contributed to serious soil erosion and water siltation, and siting problems and inadequate investment in pollution remediation have created ongoing health problems for local residents. Panzhihua hopes to become a major tourist destination and economic powerhouse for the region. If these goals are to be realized, environmental concerns must be a major priority.

The human and cultural tolls remain. Even today, Panzhihua's residents often retain a deep sense of affiliation with others from their home provinces. A journalist told me, "After all these years, we Wuhan people still have a special connection. We spend the holidays together, more than thirty years after our arrival. We eat together and commemorate those who died because of the heavy work." However, the younger generation may be losing this sense of connection to their parents' homes. A young woman whose parents came from another part of Sichuan province told me that the people of Panzhihua have blended into something that is not quite Sichuanese, not quite anything else. She seemed to take her connection to Panzhihua for granted in a way that her elders did not, indicating that for a new generation, the deep Chinese sense of place may be tending to dissipate. Interestingly, she and other young people to whom I spoke complained vocally about Panzhihua's environmental problems and seemed deeply concerned about resolving them.

As the Panzhihua story demonstrates, locating heavy industry in remote mountainous valleys is obviously unwise from an environmental perspective. Air pollution is trapped in mountain basins and valleys; chemical effluents all too often seriously pollute river headwaters and streams. Ecosystems can be harmed when roads and railroads are built through rugged territory to facilitate transport of supplies and workers, as they can when land ill suited to agriculture is converted to farmland to feed relocated workers. Creating transportation routes through wilderness areas can extensively degrade ecosystems, as the heated controversy over the International Development Bank's funding of a highway through the Amazonian rainforest suggests. Similar debate rages over the propriety of United States Forestry Service road-building activities in government-owned wilderness areas. In China, the Third Front policy opened up formerly inaccessible areas through construction of railroads and roads. The propaganda of the time boasts that the effort resulted in human footprints left everywhere.

Today, Panzhihua is a city with great ambitions. An airport is under construction, and the enormous Ertan Dam on the Yalong River, a few hours' drive from the steel mill, was completed in 1998 with a huge World Bank loan of 1.2 billion U.S. dollars. Two hundred forty meters tall, it is the highest dam in China (pending completion of the Three Gorges Dam) and the third highest in Asia. Despite the enormous human and environmental costs, some may see Panzhihua as one of the few Third Front success stories in that it did indeed give China access to a wealth of mineral resources, while the Chengdu-Kunming railroad associated with the project opened up a great section of the country. Mobilization of so many to realize such difficult goals may seem to speak for the strengths of Maoism. Yet these achievements were won through the involuntary participation of thousands, through great suffering and loss of human life, and through the diversion of precious resources that other areas of China needed for development.[56]

Most of the hundreds of Third Front factories were impractical and inefficient. Out of four large steel mills built as part of the Third Front, only Panzhihua ever approached its intended capacity, and several others were complete failures. In 1985, well into the economic reforms, China adopted a plan for dealing with these problematic Third Front dinosaurs of another era. Some were closed down or merged into other units, and 121 were moved back to medium-sized cities or whence they came, including 24 slated for removal to Chongqing. Even so, as many as half of Third Front projects are still in place,[57] the most famous of which, in addition to Panzhihua, are the Mianyang Television Factory and the Shiyan Number Two Automobile Factory. Many people relocated to the interior with the Third Front have not gone home. In Guizhou, as in Panzhihua, for example, such resettlements have left a diverse population unusual in an insulated inland province, and, for such a poor area, the region has unusual capacity in such high-tech products as optical instruments and precision bearings.[58] These industries and their employees, struggling with a legacy of poor siting and irrational investment, and having endured great hardships for many years because of Third Front demands, are now under great pressure to become profitable against great odds.

As Third Front architects boasted in the 1970s, there are now human traces in almost all of China, and few ecosystems have been left unaltered. The legacy of the Third Front can be seen in oddly situated factories and in railroads through mountain regions that under other circumstances would have been bypassed. While any country might eventually have wished to open up interior regions and exploit the mineral resources of places like Panzhihua, the strategically driven Third Front development was premature and came at an unnecessarily high economic and environmental price, much of which is still being paid today. During the Cultural Revolution, China was not ready to develop and industrialize its interior in a responsible and sustainable fashion. However, at the time, the incursions into inland China must have

In 1952, Mao ponders the Yellow River at the site of the Sanmenxia Dam. A legend predicted, "When a Great Leader Emerges, the Yellow River Will Run Clear."

Demographer Mao Yinchu in the early 1950s, while president of Beijing University.

Hydroengineer Huang Wanli being honored in old age. His "rightist" label was removed after Mao's death.

Huang Wanli, his wife Ding Yujun, and a granddaughter in 1967 during the Cultural Revolution.

In 1958, Mao admires "big character posters" denouncing "rightists."

The Sanmenxia Dam under construction on the Yellow River in 1958.

The Sanmenxia Dam, two years into contruction. The People's Pictorial caption claims
that the dam is already helping to control floods downstream.

Mao inspects crops in Henan province in 1958, during the summer of the Great Leap Forward.

During the Great Leap Forward, peasants in Hebei province, Xushui County, combine "deep plowing" with militia exercises.

In October 1958, an Anhui province girl sits on rice boasted to be so thick that it can support her weight. A 1.03 *mu* experimental field in Rongchang County is said to have yielded 43,075 *jin* of rice.

In Hebei province, Wei County, children display giant vegetables. China's country-side was engaged in elaborate genetic experiments during the first summer of the Leap.

Backyard furnaces in Hebei province, Xushui County (autumn 1958).

In October 1958, in Henan province, Xinyang City, housewives stoke backyard furnaces.

Smelting "steel" by night (October 1958).

Smelting "steel" in Yunnan province (October 1958).

After the Great Leap Forward led to history's severest human-created famine, Mao let go temporarily of his urgency to achieve socialism. Here, in 1961, he "rests" at the Communist Party mountain retreat in Lushan.

Dazhai People's Commune Party Secretary Chen Yonggui and other leaders work in the fields with ordinary peasants.

Dazhai leaders are said to demonstrate an "iron maiden spirit" and throw themselves into the "struggle to transform the mountains and rivers."

A panoramic view of a transformed ravine in Longfengpo Brigade, Xiyang County, near Dazhai. In a little more than a year, local peasants are said to have built a tunnel longer than 700 meters and constructed more than 300 mu of arable land above it. The slogan reads, "The Foolish Old Man Removed the Mountains - Reform China."

Dazhai-style terraces, 1975. The caption reads, "Barren mountains become terraced fields."

Mao prepares to swim in the Yangzi River near Wuhan. The caption accompanying this photo mentions his poem, "The High Gorges Yield Calm Lakes" [*gao xia chu pinghu*], about Mao's dream of building the Three Gorges Dam. On July 16, 1966, Mao swam in the Yangzi to signal his vigor and his command of the Cultural Revolution.

The People's Liberation Army builds a dike with their bare hands to "reclaim" farmland from the West Lake.

Fighting waves to build a dike for "land reclamation" in West Lake. Note the floodlight for use at night.

Woodblock print from Yunnan Daily of the in-filling of Lake Dianchi near Kunming. The slogan reads, "Prepare for War, Prepare for Famine, for the Sake of the People."

Panzhihua in 1965, before the railroad was built, the mines dug, and the steel mill constructed. The mill was situated "in the mountains, spread out, and in caves" to protect it from possible air attack. Pollution was trapped in the mountains and the steel mill's effluents polluted the river near upstream residences.

Railroad soldiers constructing a road for the Chengdu-Kunming Railroad. The slogan reads, "Quotation from Chairman Mao. We applaud this slogan: 'First, do not fear hardship. Second, do not fear death."

Yi minority women from the Liang Mountains bring wood to aid construction of the Chengdu-Kunming Railroad. The photo caption from a 1971 book commemorating the railroad reads, "Under Chairman Mao's great strategic directive to speed up Third Front construction, all minority people from Yunnan and Sichuan provinces must regard assisting in railroad construction as a political responsibility."

Yi minorities carry dynamite to blast railroad tunnels near Panzhihua. In their hands are copies of Mao's Little Red Book of quotations.

Railway soldiers at work on the Chengdu-Kunming Railroad.

Panzhihua mineworkers break from labor to criticize Liu Shaoqi's "reptilian, technology is Number One reactionary viewpoint."

The first train from Chengdu to Kunming passes through a tunnel. On the train is written: "Warmly celebrate successful completion of the entire line of the Chengdu-Kunming Railroad by July 1." July 1, 1970 was the target date set by Zhou Enlai both for the railroad and for smelting Panzhihua's first steel.

A booklet of propaganda prints depicts the glorious life of educated youths. To great fanfare, the youth depart the cities for the countryside to "open up the wastelands."

"Educated youth" help construct reservoirs.

In 1973, "educated youth" prepare to cut trees in the Great Northern Wilderness of Heilongjiang province.

In rubber plantations carved out of the rain forests, Xishuangbanna "educated youth" learn to tap rubber in 1974.

Mao in Beijing in 1972, the year of the Nixon visit and the end of the war preparation campaign. Mao died in 1976.

seemed to Mao the very definition of national transformation, since the Western countries he sought to equal had been engaged in unfettered development as well.

THE EDUCATED YOUTH MOVEMENT

When the war preparation campaign resumed after an interruption during the chaos of the early Cultural Revolution, it changed the destinies of millions of urban educated youth whose lives had already been turned upside down through their participation in Red Guard rebellion, factional struggle, and revolutionary pilgrimages.[59] Now they were swept up in yet another campaign, one that in many cases would cast them to the far reaches of China for as long as a decade.

The campaign to send China's young people to rural areas had originated long before the Cultural Revolution. In 1955, for example, Mao said, "All the educated young people ought to be very happy to work in the countryside if they are able to go there. There is plenty of room in the vast rural areas for them to do something truly worthwhile." In 1964 alone, it is said that 300,000 young people "went down" [*xia fang*].[60] Many stepped forward on their own, motivated by political activism and patriotism. But in the winter of 1968–69 the campaign affected unprecedented numbers, and soon few were exempt from the duty to "volunteer."[61] Eventually, 20 million young people were organized to "go down to the countryside and up to the mountains."[62] Of this group, more than two million prepared for war in quasimilitary encampments known as Production-Construction Army Corps.[63]

The movement served many purposes. Babies born during the postrevolution population explosion had grown up, but socialist China, which claimed to guarantee employment for everyone, had no work to offer the restive urban youth, whose role as rebels in the Cultural Revolution now made them difficult to rein in. Packing them off to the countryside would resolve the unemployment problem, help to quell the chaos of the Cultural Revolution, and discipline the country. It also facilitated Mao's control by changing the national focus from domestic matters to mobilization for defense.[64]

By exploiting young people's adulation, Mao was able to induce compliance with a policy that, in classic Confucian terms, violated basic tenets of filial piety by tearing youths as young as 14 away from their parents. During the campaign, a slogan exhorted, "The Farther from Father and Mother, the Nearer to Chairman Mao's Heart." As flags and drumbeats honored them for revolutionary loyalty, young people departed the cities by bus and train for the countryside and frontiers. Although "volunteers," they often left home with tears in their eyes, not knowing when they might see their families again.[65] Far from home, China's urban revolutionary generation saw their dreams of family and education vanish in the upheavals of revolution.

Officially, the government painted the educated youth movement as a grass-roots initiative, generating enthusiasm by portraying the countryside as a socialist paradise where the youths would have an important role to play in building New China and serving Mao. Cultural Revolution activists and youths exhausted from political battles and factional struggles were among the first to volunteer. The official press constructed a legend: seeing the country's economic plight, some unemployed young women were said to have written a letter to Chairman Mao containing the famous phrase, *Women ye you liangzhi shou, bu zai chengli chi xianfan* [We also have two hands, we don't need to stay home living off idleness]. Mao himself was said to have read the letter and given them permission to "go down."

Young people had two avenues to the countryside. Some were sent in small groups to rural villages to "join production teams and establish residence" [*chadui luohu*], whether through Party assignment or family connections. These young people had relatively little environmental impact, although they often lived in bitter circumstances without government help, stretched local resources thin, and experienced resentment from impoverished peasants. Others were sent to China's frontiers to join the Production-Construction Army Corps, where they were given the tasks of "opening the wastelands" [*kai huang*] and transforming virgin land for agriculture. These teenagers, many of them accustomed to relatively privileged lives before the Cultural Revolution, also suffered enormous physical hardship as they tried to sustain themselves in hitherto sparsely populated regions, carry out land reclamation under extremely harsh conditions, and conduct endless military drills to prepare for war. Their impact on the environment was enormous.

The twenty-fifth anniversary of the educated youth movement was marked in 1994 by self-organized reunions where memories were shared and group photos taken.[66] Participants describe these get-togethers as evoking mixed feelings; they felt renewed anger at their betrayal by a revolution in which they had too much faith, but also a sweet nostalgia for lost youth and idealism. The struggle to come to terms with their years in the countryside is far from over. Many credit their hardships with teaching them independence, social skills, self-reliance, and values that extend beyond material things. At the same time, they feel resentment and sorrow that their educations were interrupted. This loss has become especially damaging for those living in a reform-era society that values diplomas and skills. Many have not recovered the social status and jobs that they would have enjoyed had they not been sent down. Some say that the next generation is now becoming a secondary victim of the educated youth movement, as tuition costs rise and the former youths are unable to pay for their children to go to school.

Hundreds of memoirs and fictional accounts about the educated youth experience have been published in recent years, among them works by the well-known writers Kong Jiesheng, Zhang Kangkang, Ma Bo (Lao Gui), Liang Xiaosheng, and Zhang Chengzhi. Although it is not their main focus, such accounts often describe grasslands, wetlands, and rainforests damaged beyond repair through the sudden influx of thousands of youths conducting land-reclamation activities. Sociological studies by Shi Weimin and He Gang, Liu Wenjie, and others are also rich sources of information on the movement and its legacy.

The Production-Construction Army Corps

The Production-Construction Army Corps [*Shengchan Jianshe Bingtuan*] was a quasimilitary network under the leadership of the People's Liberation Army or its demobilized officers. It was structured like a full-fledged military unit, and military terminology described its operations. At its largest, it consisted of twelve armies [*jun*] based in Xinjiang, Heilongjiang, Inner Mongolia, Lanzhou, Yunnan, Anhui, Jiangsu, Fujian, Zhejiang, Shandong, Hubei, and Guangdong. These armies were subdivided into divisions [*shi*], regiments [*tuan*], battalions [*ying*], and companies [*liandui*]. In addition, three divisions in Tibet, Jiangxi, and Guangxi were labeled agricultural construction divisions [*nongjian shi*].[67] The Army Corps had diverse responsibilities to "open the wasteland" [*kai huang*], defend border areas, and contribute to production. A bulletin issued at an August 1970 meeting of Corps representatives described its duty "to militarize the frontier, oppose imperialism/oppose revisionism, protect the frontier, and build up the frontier" [*tunken rongbian, fandi fanxiu, baowei bianjiang, jianshe bianjiang*].[68] Thus, educated youth encampments were by turns agricultural production units, military defense units, thought-remolding camps, and "shock troops" to create new arable land. The youths were at once soldiers, farmers, workers, and objects for revolutionary tempering. The work meeting bulletin proclaimed the link between the Corps and national security: "To establish the Production-Construction Army Corps … is to carry out Chairman Mao's great strategic directive, 'Prepare for War, Prepare for Famine, for the Sake of the People.'"[69] At this stage in Mao's war against nature, the military metaphor and the real world were indistinguishable.

Military exercises became constant when tensions with the Soviet Union mounted during the bitterly cold winter of 1969–70. More than a million auxiliaries were deployed along the Soviet border in the expectation that fighting could break out at any minute. When not occupied with land-clearing and cropping, the youths prepared for war, and the pace of life was pressured. News about enemy troop movements kept them in a state of constant anxiety. In Heilongjiang, lightly armed youths were backups for front-line PLA soldiers.[70] In Xinjiang, where the PLA had been heavily armed since 1962 when many local Kazakhs fled to the Soviet Union, educated youth joined the border patrol.[71] Marches and drills were grueling, sleep was inadequate, and accidents during training were common. Emergency assemblies were called in the middle of the night, with Soviet attacks announced suddenly, often with sirens. But when no fighting broke out after numerous false alarms, passive resistance developed even among student leaders. Even as they shouted that war was breaking out, they deliberately wore their pants inside out, or shoes that didn't match, to signal to their bunkmates that it was only another drill. Eventually, few believed the alarms and they stayed in bed.[72]

Unlike the educated youths who moved into existing rural villages and had to feed themselves by working land that had already been converted to agricultural use, the youths of the Production-Construction Army Corps had to sustain themselves in regions with little cultivated land and with little support beyond meager salaries provided by the state. They created farmland by clearing trees, plowing grasslands, and filling in marshes; these activities were intended eventually to contribute grain to the state. The work was often brutal. In Inner Mongolia, an activity called "manage the sand and create farmland" [*zhisha zaotian*] entailed basin-by-basin removal of endless sand dunes, after which the soil had to be reworked.[73] Military imagery of battle and conquest was similar to that used to inspire Dianchi wetlands laborers. A typical slogan was, "We army reclamation soldiers must conquer the desert to open up ten thousand *qing* of arable land."[74]

Although some reclamation created arable land, in other cases it caused widespread environmental damage. Wetlands were destroyed, but land remained unsuitable for farming. Deforested hillsides were too steep to plant, and erosion and changes in moisture level dried up streams. Scarce water supplies could not support increased irrigation needs, and water tables fell, leading to serious water shortages. Intensified animal husbandry yielded apparent success at first but poor long-term results. In Inner Mongolia, for example, each live-stock regiment "opened up" 310,000 *mu* of water-poor grasslands and increased herds from 431,600 to more than a million. Overgrazing was often the result.[75] In Yunnan, as we shall see in detail later in this chapter, ecologically rich rainforests and evergreen forests were cleared to grow rubber, only to have the rubber fail in areas inappropriate for its cultivation.

Memoirs and "reportage fiction" set against a background of historical events are among the most revealing expressions of the link between the suffering of these educated youths and their unwitting abuse of nature. Perhaps the most famous tale of Army Corps life is that by Ma Bo (also known as Lao Gui), whose *Xuese huanghun,* a fictionalized memoir of the rough-and-tumble lives of educated youths in the Inner Mongolia Army Corps, has been beautifully translated by Howard Goldblatt as *Blood Red Sunset.* On the youths' arrival, the beauty of the grasslands is striking: "In the valleys peonies, chrysanthemums, and Chinese roses grew in profusion, and the stillness was unimaginable; the absence of any sign of human activity accentuated a feel of the ancient."[76] When the narrator's bad class background and penchant for fighting soon earn him a label as a counterrevolutionary, he is ostracized to the mountains to break rocks and cut trees among the wolves. There, the landscape continues to astonish him:

The valley was lush and green, with tall, pristine peonies creating an explosion of color amid the shrubbery... I loved this gorgeous valley, where the melodic chatting of birds floated on air redolent with nature's perfume. It was free of the arrogance of the civilized world. Violence existed only as a by-product of the law of the jungle, but all creatures received equal treatment; there were no class distinctions here.[77]

In the service of land reclamation, the youths suffer extreme physical hardship, political struggle, and senseless deaths during a mishandled forest fire. But after years of sacrifice, Party leaders announce that the youths' labor has not only failed to contribute to the country but has been actively harmful: "reclamation activities had destroyed the ecology of the steppes, with a loss of water and topsoil, virtually turning them into a desert."[78] With this realization, the Army Corps abandons the grain silos, built with hundreds of thousands of adobe bricks, and the 35,000-square-foot concrete threshing ground underlaid with tons of rock smashed and carted by hand. The narrator cries out in anger:

> For eight years we had labored for this. And it was worse, for we had wreaked unprecedented havoc on the grasslands, working like fucking beasts of burden, only to commit unpardonable crimes against the land...
>
> A huge international joke. The depletion of resources was staggering; the waste of manpower, mind-boggling; the financial losses, incalculable.[79]

Upon departure, the narrator reflects on the enormous physical toll exacted by the stones the educated youths were forced to break and transport while their youth slipped away. He asks the steppes of Huolin Gol for forgiveness, linking human suffering to the suffering of the land:

> The vast, silent steppe, how bleak and hideous you became: your glossy skin gouged by coarse, blistery sand; your broad chest crushed by thudding hoes; your lovely face pocked and scarred by rat holes, stove pits, wagon-wheel ruts, electric poles, firebreaks.

Huolin Gol, forgive us our ignorance, our fanaticism, and our cruelty. There's consolation in the knowledge that we too suffered and that we made horrible sacrifices, even the ultimate sacrifice for some. Tens of thousands of lovely flowers bloomed and died here, silent and unnoticed.[80]

Scholars corroborate Ma Bo's melodramatic account. Qu Geping and Li Jinchang write that youths mobilized under the slogan, "win the fight between man and grass," degraded fragile grasslands that could not withstand the population influx.[81] Sociologists Shi and He write:

Blindly opening wastelands and planting on the grasslands harmed the ecological balance. Not only did agriculture fail to develop, but [this activity] caused large-scale grassland degradation, increased grassland desertification, and destroyed herd production to different degrees.[82]

Ironically, although attempts were later made to convert some reclaimed lands to their original state in an effort to halt and reverse desertification, much has been degraded to the point that restoration is impossible.

The Sanjiang (Three Rivers) Plain in Heilongjiang, widely known as the Great Northern Wilderness, is a well-known instance of a place where educated youths caused great ecological destruction.[83] With its harsh terrain of wetlands, marsh grasses, and dense forests, and its frigid six-month winters, the region is strategically critical for China, reaching like a finger into the Soviet Far East at the confluence of the Amur, Songhua, and Ussuri rivers. Before 1949, there were almost 5 million hectares of wetlands in the 108,900-square-kilometer territory, about half the area. Today, there are almost 2 million, sharply reduced through land reclamations but still the largest such expanse in East Asia. Rare migratory birds such as the red-crowned crane, hooded crane, white stork, black stork, white-tailed eagle, and steller's eagle nest in the wetlands, and salmon and sturgeon still swim the rivers. The Siberian tiger roamed the area as recently as the 1950s. The Great Northern Wilderness became home to some 1,250,000 educated youths sent to prepare for war with the Soviet Union during the late 1960s and early 1970s.[84] Among them was a conservation activist now working on environmental economics at a Beijing university. He credits his environmental awakening to the years he spent in the wetlands and to a realization that he unwittingly participated in a great destruction of nature.

On September 2, 1969, I was sent from my home in Beijing to Fuyuan County in easternmost Heilongjiang. I lived there until 1974. We were charged with "opening the wilderness" to convert the land to farmland and with making preparations for war with the Soviet Union. The county was 6,000 square kilometers, with 4,000 indigenous people, mostly fishermen of the *Hezhe* minority. I was part of the Heilongjiang Production-Construction Army Corps, Division Six. There were five divisions already there when we arrived. [These included soldiers demobilized after the Korean War and earlier waves of young urban "volunteers" sent to reclaim land in state agricultural farms.] The other educated youth came from Beijing, Shanghai, Tianjin, and Harbin. There were more than 10,000 of us. Our battalion [*ying*] of about 400 people was called "Oppose Revisionism Battalion" [*fanxiu ying*]. To this day, the place is still called *fanxiu ying.*

Heilongjiang was the earliest province to form a Revolutionary Committee, and the provincial party boss, Pan Fusheng, was very leftist. We were to carry out revolution and increase crop production. The place I was sent was mostly marshland, with some forests on higher ground that we called "island forests." It was virtually uninhabited until we arrived. To prepare for war, the People's Liberation Army built a road using tractors.[85] There was little to eat, and it was too cold to plant. By October, it was snowing. That year, they issued us only leftover corn flour from the warehouses. No vegetables, little soy sauce, just dried hot pepper and salt. We made corn cakes without oil. There were deer, but in the beginning we didn't know how to hunt. We saw rabbits, but didn't know how to catch them. Later, we learned to fish and hunt. I was the youngest, only fifteen.

In spring, it was time to plant. There were a hundred of us, like a village, with five tractors. But after we ploughed the wetlands, we found it impossible to grow anything. In three years, we moved many times, but found only ten *mu* that could be farmed. It was our only success.

From the first, we cut many trees, mostly poplar. We formed wood-cutting teams to look for the biggest trees, going by tractor as far as twenty kilometers away. We formed a logging camp during the second winter for about three months. I was the cook. While the others went to cut trees, I stayed in camp to prepare meals and watch our things. I spent a lot of time alone in nature then. I saw lots of animals – foxes, rabbits, a snow hare, wild pigs, black bear, roe deer. Nature seemed vast, the snow deep, the trees straight and tall. There was a fragrant medicinal plant called wintergreen. The camp looked over a river, and in winter, the wind blew strong. My feelings for nature date from that time. It was a feeling I cannot put words to. Sometimes I was afraid, because of the war atmosphere. We were told that the enemy could attack at any time, and we all had rifles. But there was also a fear of the power of nature.

Later, after we learned to fish, I spent a lot of time alone on the water. My feelings about nature changed. In the evening, in my boat, setting out the nets, I could hear the calls of hundreds of birds. Collecting the nets in the morning, at sunrise, in spring, the warming came fast and there was mist on the water. A kind of long-legged crane nested in a tree. The whole tree was full of their nests, and we took their eggs to eat every day.

During my five years in the county, beginning in 1969 when I arrived, the old forest was almost completely cut down and some animals were wiped out. One was an amphibious muskrat. During my second year, two hunters and a dog stayed with us. Every day they came back with a huge bag of animals that they were going to sell for two or three *yuan* each. The Army Corps only gave us 36 *yuan* a month, so that was a lot of money to us. So we all went out to hunt the muskrats, and after a few years, they were pretty much all gone. They were easy to hunt because they would stand up and cry out. I caught three. The disappearance of the muskrats affected the whole ecosystem. They eat fish; foxes eat them. It was a change in the whole food chain. Serious harm was done. But their fur is good.

At the time, I didn't understand the destruction. It was only when I went back in 1988 [and even more environmental destruction had occurred] that I understood what we had done. Before, there were so many trees that you couldn't see the river from the road. But in 1988, the whole forest was gone. There was nothing to eat but farmed fish – the wild fish were gone. Today, there is a tiny bit of forest left in the Great Northern Wilderness, there's a little wetland in the northeastern counties. I'm working to protect it, but some people still talk about "opening the wasteland."

From 1969 to 1979, he recalled, the educated youths "reclaimed" 310,000 hectares of wetlands in the Great Northern Wilderness. By 1975, 14.6 percent of the region was under cultivation, up from only 3 percent in 1949. This isolated story was multiplied across the frontier regions of China, to the steppes of Inner Mongolia and Gansu, the deserts and forests of Xinjiang, and, as we shall see, to the tropical rainforests of Hainan Island and Yunnan. While even the economic and security benefits of so much activity were questionable, the environmental harm was extreme.

In the Great Northern Wilderness today, salmon harvest has dropped from 10 percent to 1 percent of previous levels, and soil erosion is serious. Bird populations have been negatively affected by the conversion of so much forest and wetland to grassland. There are signs of hope, however: China has signed the Ramsar Convention to protect wetlands and the Convention on Biological Diversity, and international organizations such as the United Nations Development Programme and the International Crane Foundation are active in the area, working to support China's efforts to expand and manage the Great Northern Wilderness's eighteen nature reserves and to connect them by restoring wetlands. Agriculture and land-reclamation officials looking for ways to feed China's still-growing population often undercut the conservation activities of the environmental protection bureaucracy, and other problems are created through the ongoing willingness of international lending institutions such as the World Bank and Japanese aid agencies to fund reclamation projects in the area.[86] One official position, articulated in rebuttal of Lester Brown's controversial 1995 book, *Who Will Feed China?*, was that China still had lots of wetlands that could be converted to grain.[87]

"The Last Green Place on the Tropic of Cancer"

As the above examples suggest, thousands of tales could be told about the environmental impact of state-sponsored relocations of China's young people to the frontiers. We now turn to a more detailed examination of involuntary ecological destruction by educated youths in tropical Southwest China, at the opposite frontier from the Great Northern Wilderness. While this case is remarkable for the precious ecological setting in which the youths found themselves, the basic dynamics of the situation – the youths' lack of say in their relocations and in their activities in their new surroundings, the hardships of their lives, their longing to go home, and the profound impact of so many hands set to transforming the "wastelands" – is typical.

China has the greatest biodiversity in the Northern Hemisphere, and half this plentitude of living beings can be found in Yunnan province. Within Yunnan, the greatest number of species is concentrated in Xishuangbanna, a Dai Autonomous Region prefecture abutting Laos and Burma.[88] Sheltered to the northeast by the high Ailao and Wuliang mountains and by the Hengduan mountains against which it nestles, Xishuangbanna is protected from cold northern winds while it lies open to warm and humid southern monsoons. Multiple branches of the upper Mekong River, known in China as the Lancang, carve deep valleys through the area. There are such sharp variations in altitude that Xishuangbanna's "vertical climate" can range from northern tropical to deciduous broad-leafed forest within a small area.[89] A veil of fog wraps the region until mid-day most of the year. Although its land area covers only .02 percent of China, it is widely recognized as the richest biological sanctuary of the country.[90] Xishuangbanna is also culturally rich, home to twelve ethnic minority groups who have practiced sustainable relationships to nature for centuries. Chinese environmentalists study and admire polytheistic "Longshan forest culture" for the home gardens that mirror rainforest canopy layers and the "spirit" and "burial" forests, or sacred groves, that are *de facto* nature preserves.

The most often-heard boast about Xishuangbanna from those who would protect its remaining virgin rainforest is that it is the only place on the Tropic of Cancer that is not desert. Although this is an exaggeration (especially since technically Xishuangbanna lies quite a bit south of the Tropic of Cancer), a glance at the globe reveals the Tropic of Cancer running through the Sahara, Saudi Arabia, and the Central

Mexican Desert.[91] Xishuangbanna's ecosystems have evolved over thousands of years, and some parts of the region are thought not to have experienced the Ice Age, so some species may date to millions of years ago. Certain trees are particularly ancient; an iron tree [*tieshu*] is thought to predate human existence. Others are so tall that it is said you cannot see their tops. The interdependent canopy layers form an elaborate system that promotes highly specialized roles; some seeds, for example, can sprout only when eaten and excreted by certain birds.[92] Among numerous unusual plant species are huge fig trees remarkable for their dangling aerial roots, some of which penetrate the earth and thicken until it appears that dozens of trunks support a single crown. A tangle of lianas and epiphytes, including colorful orchids, contribute to a "hanging garden" effect. In all, there are 153 endemic species of plants, 30 ancient "relic" plant species, and 130 rare plant species.[93]

The spirit groves have helped support an abundance of wildlife in the region, including elephants, gibbons, slow lorises, the rare Indian wild ox (gaur), leopards, chevrotain, deer, macaques, and leaf monkeys, many of which survive despite the assaults on nature of the Mao years. Twenty wild tigers remain in the region. The 102 species of mammals found here comprise 21.79 percent of the total number of species in China. There are 179 wild Indian elephants, out of a total of 193 remaining in the country.[94] Birds include hornbills and the fairy bluebird; about 40 percent of the 1,073 species of birds in Yunnan can be found here, and reptiles, amphibians, and insects are equally diverse.[95] An estimated 10 percent of Xishuangbanna's species have not yet been described scientifically. Once such a rainforest is destroyed, it is virtually impossible to re-create. The system is too complex and diverse, coevolution has taken too long, and climatic conditions now are different from those in which biological niches and mutual dependencies evolved. During the war preparation movement, it was precisely into this biological miracle that 200,000 educated youths were relocated with the mandate to "open the wasteland" and plant rubber trees.[96]

Rubber: The Early Years

After a failed attempt by the Nationalist government to grow rubber in Xishuangbanna with Thai saplings in 1947, the effort to grow rubber started again soon after the Communist revolution. In the early 1950s, People's Liberation Army troops were assigned to state reclamation farms in Xishuangbanna and tropical Hainan Island, as were some cadres with questionable political backgrounds who were permitted to "volunteer" as a way of demonstrating their loyalty to the new regime. In 1952 and 1953, Yunnan University students and teachers from the Forestry and Biology Departments conducted studies on where to grow rubber. According to a local scientist to whom I spoke about the history of rubber in the region, the researchers were concerned that the environmental impact on the tropical rainforest would be enduring, while rubber trees need seven or eight years before they produce and then have a useful life of only a few decades before they must be replanted. However, the State Farm and Reclamation Bureau exerted pressure, and once again political expediency won out over scientific expertise. In 1953, experimental small-scale rubber plantations, started with seeds from Malaysia, were established in Xishuangbanna's capital, Jinghong. A longtime Han resident of the area recalled the Soviet influence: "The USSR wanted rubber from us when relations were good. Later, it became a question of national defense, since rubber was a war material."

Premier Zhou Enlai visited Xishuangbanna several times after the revolution and spoke, with his typical ability to see two sides of a question, both of China's pride at producing rubber and of the need to protect Xishuangbanna. In 1961, when visiting the region to conduct negotiations with Burma's U Nu, he saw the rubber plantations and proudly declared, "We finally have our own rubber" [*Women zhongyu youle ziji de xiangjiao*]. But he is also said to have commented, somewhat presciently, "If we destroy the forest, [Xishuangbanna] will become desert. Our Communist Party of China will become criminals in history, and future generations will curse us."[97]

I spoke to several Han Chinese who were sent to the frontier soon after the revolution. Like other interviewees, they wished to remain anonymous. One of them, a museum director who has spent most of his professional life studying and trying to preserve minority cultures, recalled the early period:

> When we Han arrived in the 1950s, the local people knew how to use the forests in a sustainable way. The minorities cut trees according to the decision of a chief. Spirits were believed to live in the forests and water. If they were harmed, people would be punished. Slash-and-burn agriculture, as practiced by the mountain people, was carried out sequentially. They would let the land lie fallow until it recovered. In some places, the "spirit forests" were completely off limits to people. At the time, we thought these people were backward. Our leaders said we had to "break through" their superstitions. So first we conducted "socialist reformation" to make the local people settle down. We tried mechanistically to make them change. We removed the old

chiefs and put in new leaders. We carried out propaganda to per-
suade the people that there were no spirits. They had to listen to
the new cadres. Before, they hadn't dared to go into the spirit
forest or the burial forest, but now, they cut trees freely. The
rejection of traditional animist beliefs created chaos. And what
did we give them instead? We gave them the "Take Grain as the
Key" policy. The new leaders didn't understand how to respect
indigenous ecological knowledge. Our political movements
caused problems. The relationship with nature was destroyed,
and people felt confused. Then more and more people came in –
too many people – they built houses, burned fuel, planted rubber. Yes, they built roads, schools, reservoirs, and clinics. But
they also brought an outside culture that created conflict. The
Han are now one-third of the population.

Another early migrant, now an environmentally minded researcher
at the Yunnan Minorities Institute, was sent to Xishuangbanna in 1949
after he graduated from middle school. He joined a campaign to mobilize the masses against defeated Guomindang soldiers still hiding in
Burma. He commented:

We didn't learn from the local people. Instead, we thought they
were backward, and we destroyed many good things. Now I know
that many of their practices are very advanced. The things they
emphasized are what we [environmentalists] are emphasizing now
about the man and nature relationship. The Dai, Aini, Hani,
Miao, Bulang, Wa, Yao, Jinuo – they all have experience with
protecting nature. They separated the forest into sections. Because
the sections rotated, they could be cut only every thirteen years.
When there are few people, slash-and-burn agriculture can protect the environment.

But then the educated youth arrived, from Beijing, Shanghai,
Kunming, and Sichuan, many tens of thousands of them. All
these people had to eat. They couldn't take over the Dai lowlands,
so they asked the Aini and Lahu to teach them to slash and burn
to open up space in the mountains. They didn't known when to
cut. In this way the "advanced" educated youths became the back-

ward slash-and-burners. But the forest destruction was too great to recover.

Of course, there was deforestation throughout China. But tropical virgin rainforest is especially precious, and it can never be replaced. In my opinion, the Party should repay its debt to the forests.

By the 1960s, the Yunnan Army Corps had a special mandate because of the war in nearby Vietnam. The reinforced border was intended to support North Vietnam's war effort, protect China, and produce rubber for defense. While the rubber production of the early Han migrants increased steadily, it was dwarfed by that of the hundreds of thousands of educated youth who arrived after the start of the Cultural Revolution and by their vastly greater impact on the environment.

Official figures on the number of educated youths sent to Yunnan province (breakdowns are not available for Xishuangbanna) do not include those sent to the countryside from cities within the province. In 1968, 1,779 were sent "down"; in 1969, 26,321; in 1970, 23,568; and in 1971, 54,874, for a total of 106,561. Of these, 47,575 were from Shanghai, 41,068 from Sichuan (mostly Chengdu and Chongqing), and 8,385 from Beijing. In addition, from 1966 to 1968, 60,000 were sent from Kunming.[98] According to a researcher in the provincial records department, who was himself an educated youth, the figure should actually be closer to 200,000 or 300,000, if Kunming youth and rural youths sent home from their studies are included for the war preparation years. Of these, he estimated that about 50,000, not including Kunming youths, were sent to Xishuangbanna, the majority to join the Army Corps.

Official statistics on rubber production in Yunnan (including Dehong, Hekou, and other rubber-growing areas outside Xishuangbanna) reflect the waves of migration. In 1953, there were only 4,000 *mu* planted in rubber. In 1960, when the first rural Hunan migrants were brought in to alleviate their own poverty and "settle the frontier" [*zhibian*], there was an increase of 103,300 *mu* and 3.08 million rubber trees. Steady increases are recorded thereafter, with another spike in 1971, when the largest influx of youths arrived, an increase of 116,600 *mu* and 3.076 million trees.[99]

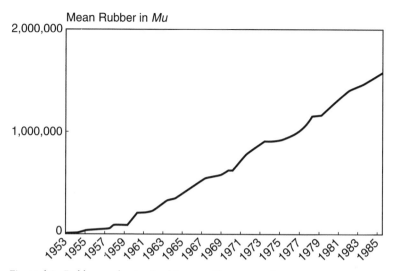

Figure 4.1. Rubber production land increase, Yunnan province.

"Everything Must Yield to Rubber" {Yiqie Wei Xiangjiao Rang Lu}

Few educated youths had any idea what they were getting into. A woman from Chengdu now living in Kunming told me that she volunteered early, in 1965, out of what she now sees as naïve patriotism, when there was still a choice about going to the countryside. The Cultural Revolution had not yet begun, and normal opportunities for young people were still in place. "I could have taken the college exams or gotten a good job assignment," she said regretfully. "But I was full of ideals. I imagined a lush paradise." When her group arrived in Kunming, they were feted and banqueted, and newspaper articles appeared lauding their revolutionary spirit. It took five days to get to the Laotian border, and she wept the whole way. By 1969, after the Red Guard violence, rustification had become compulsory. As another Sichuan youth put it,

Before the Cultural Revolution, it was voluntary or semivoluntary. Mao took advantage of our idealism. But later, there was no choice. They tricked us. They told us if we didn't go we would never get work assignments. If we agreed to transfer our residence

175

permits to the countryside, maybe later we would have a chance. Many of us were from "bad" family backgrounds – our parents were intellectuals, rightists, and capitalists. So we had no way out.

At first, the youths approached their work with enthusiasm. "We were China's second rubber base, after Hainan Island," recalled a young woman. "China needed rubber, and we saw a chance to use our own hands and sweat to help the country. According to the propaganda of the times, we were opposing revisionism and capitalism. We felt we were engaged in something meaningful." Another youth who has written about the educated youth experience recalled the difficult work:

> We were only 16 or 17, and full of energy. We were awakened at 3 AM to clear the forest. Every day, we cut a great swath of forest. We had a target of a *mu* per day apiece. After we clear-cut the trees, we let everything dry out. Later, we burned what was left. Every day we cut until 7 or 8 AM, then ate a breakfast of rice gruel sent by the Corps kitchen. We recited and studied Chairman Mao's "Three Articles" and struggled against capitalism and revisionism. Then it was back to work until lunch break, then more work until 6. After we washed and ate, there were two more hours of study and criticism meetings. We each had 40 *jin* of rice a month [about 53 pounds]. It wasn't enough. Some families sent ration coupons, but it still wasn't enough.

After the land was cleared, the youths built terraces, "learning from Dazhai." Then rubber seedlings were planted. A woman recalled:

> There were clear standards about how many holes had to be dug each day, and competitions to outdo each other. Holes had to be 80 square centimeters and about a meter deep, spaced 3 to 5 meters apart. Between the rows of rubber, we planted pineapple. There were so many new people coming in, we were always expanding the rubber-growing areas.

After their initial revolutionary enthusiasm, the emotions of many grew more complex. Another woman explained:

We were thrown from one style of big city life to another life, a hard life. Xishuangbanna had good natural conditions for fruit and crops, but at the time the country was "cutting off the tail of capitalism," and no private crops could be grown. So life was very difficult, and sometimes all we had to eat was rice. I suffered for many reasons. First, I hadn't even graduated from middle school [because of the disruptions of the Cultural Revolution], so I could never hope to go to college. This was a great suffering that remains with me even now. Second, the work itself was very hard. Third, I had never been away from home. I missed my family terribly, and I worried about my parents, who had political troubles of their own. Fourth, it was hard to adjust to peasant life – my parents had been government officials, and I had lived comfortably in Shanghai.

As the war preparation campaign accelerated, the youths' lives became more regimented, and rubber-growing for national defense became an intense political movement that lost touch with nature's limits. To fulfill a national mandate to increase production radically, Yunnan rubber-growers were asked to ignore scientific convention and grow rubber beyond the accepted limitations of latitude, altitude, and average temperature. Although Xishuangbanna is at the northernmost edge of the tropics, youths in parts of the province even farther north were ordered to plant rubber. In his work of reportage literature (a genre of fact-based fiction), "Dream of China's Educated Youth" [*Zhongguo Zhiqing Meng*], Deng Xian recalls how scientific wisdom was cast aside in the heat of the rubber campaign:

> International experts believed rubber couldn't be grown north of a latitude of 20° N; above that it was impossible. But relying on imports meant allowing the imperialist revisionist counterrevolutionaries to strangle us. ... The heavy responsibility to answer the call to struggle for rubber fell on the Yunnan Production-Construction Army Corps' 200,000 cadres and workers and educated youths.[100]

Responding to a May 19, 1970 directive to expand rubber-growing areas,[101] the Army Corps Party Committee established a plan to "break through" the "three forbidden areas" and ignore conventional geographical limitations regarding latitude, altitude, and temperature. Deng writes:

The youths had to throw themselves into this great battle of reforming the heavens and changing the earth [*gaitian huandi*] to grow rubber. The 15th Company of the 3rd Division was assigned to the foot of the snowy mountains of Gaoligong [in Eastern Yunnan], at a latitude of 25°N. They "opened the wilderness" and cut down the forest, and with their own sweat refuted the legendary world saying that you cannot grow rubber north of the 20 degree latitude.[102]

Rubber-growing was seen not as a question of agricultural production but of line, stance, point of view, and attitude. Armed with Maoism's "spiritual atomic bomb," the young people are said to have overcome all difficulties posed by nature.

It was announced that a rubber "base" had been established in Yunnan ranging from 21 to 25 degrees latitude and 97 to 106 degrees longitude. But the winter of 1974–75 saw many rubber trees die in a great freeze. Deng writes, "Again they made a vow, using the 'Man Must Conquer Nature' spirit. When the trees died, they replanted them; when they replanted them, the trees died; they replanted them again and the trees died again."[103] Seventy-one percent of the tapped trees were lost, as were 190,000 *mu* of young trees. Although the Corps retreated to lower altitudes, they continued to expand rubber-growing areas.

Those who knew the value of the rainforest were in no position to voice their opposition. A retired Kunming botany professor told me that he had helped to establish a nature reserve in Xishuangbanna after the revolution, but a military commander ordered the trees cut down, saying that the reserve was worthless.[104] "The army controlled everything," he recalled. "We intellectuals were the 'stinking ninth category' [the lowest political classification, during the Cultural Revolution] and our ideas didn't count." By this point, scientists had had caution drilled into them, and they dared not appear unpatriotic. A researcher who has worked all his career in Yunnan's Forestry Department felt similarly helpless:

We had no power to stop it. Most of us were opposed to what was going on. But the State Farm and Reclamation Bureau was in charge, not the Forestry Department. In fact, I was being "reeducated" in a May 7th Cadre school [an agricultural work camp for intellectuals and cadres] during the early 1970s. When I read about the new rubber plantations in the newspaper, I felt very sad. But we ourselves were being attacked. We were being struggled against, just like the earth.

As in the case of the Dianchi in-filling, "opening wasteland" military imagery was that of an endless attack. There were great battles, decisive battles, storm the fortifications battles, and shock attacks [*dazhan, huizhan, gongjianzhan, tujizhan*]. Deng Xian recalls numerous exhausting campaigns, their significance a blur: "great battle for a week, fight bravely for twenty days, decisive battle for forty days, great red battle of May, July, August, October." The youths had to work more than ten hours a day to cut trees and burn the brush.[105] Another youth told me how they had to meet targets, digging holes for ten rubber trees in a single day. Like the youths on the Soviet border, they participated in military drills; but in Xishuangbanna the enemies were different – sometimes the Guomindang troops who were said still to be hiding in Burma, sometimes the United States imperialists:

We had to get up at 1 AM and run to combat the interlopers, whom we never saw. We were told that if the Americans invaded Vietnam, China was the next step. Those who had "good" political backgrounds were given rifles. The rest of us only had them during military drills.

Eventually, the educated youths came into sharp conflict with their team leaders, who were often army officers or the uneducated peasants who had come from the Hunan countryside in the early wave of migration in the 1950s and 1960s. One woman told me that she is still angry at the leaders:

With the military in charge, there were a lot of problems. There was tight control. During weapons training, there were accidents. There were beatings. Some military leaders raped girls. They were despots. They could do whatever they liked. Our team leader raped an educated youth from Chengdu, and she became pregnant. My best friend, a girl from Beijing, tried to seek justice, and was politically persecuted for protesting. They ostracized her, and I was the only one who dared speak to her for a year. Eventually, she ended up going insane. She was like a teacher to me because her parents were

Beijing University professors, and she knew a lot. I still hate the Hunanese for what they did to her.

Frequent accidents plagued the campaign, as when there was a fire in Linjiang County (near Vietnam, east of Xishuangbanna), during which ten young girls who had been "sent down" only a month earlier burned to death in their dormitory.

Restlessness increased after the Lin Biao Incident in September 1971, during which Mao's chosen successor Lin is said to have crashed in a Trident Jet in Outer Mongolia after conspiring to assassinate Mao.[106] The Incident was a turning point for many Chinese from adulation of Mao to deep disillusionment with the revolution and its promises, and it was no different for the educated youths of Xishuangbanna. For young people, especially, who had sacrificed their educations and family lives in the name of left-wing ideals, the Incident was experienced as a revelation that they had been manipulated. The exposure of the man responsible for inflaming the cult of Mao worship as Mao's would-be assassin convinced them they had been used as pawns in a high-stakes power struggle. For many whose arduous rural experiences had also exposed the hollowness of Party promises about the blessings of socialism, the incident profoundly challenged their Maoist faith. A youth recalled, "The rubber-growing campaign was closely linked to Lin Biao and the war preparations. After the Lin Biao Incident, I didn't believe anything anymore. People began to fake illnesses, then we just stayed in bed."

Problems and pressures created numerous emotional problems, including high rates of depression and suicide. The director of a psychiatric hospital in Kunming told me that he treated more than one hundred educated youths with problems linked to the pressures of their dislocations. He noted that since those who were sent to the capital had been screened locally, they must have represented only a fraction of those with psychological problems:

I always felt sorry for them. Usually, after they felt better, I signed papers to allow them to go home to the cities. There was a lot of schizophrenia, with delusions of grandeur and hallucinations. The most common delusion was that Mao was talking directly to them. They were convinced that they belonged to Mao's inner circle but local leaders were obstructing them. One young man thought he had direct links to the Gang of Four. The suicidal ones rarely made it to Kunming. They succeeded in killing themselves.

One time, a youth wrote a letter to Mao saying that Lin Biao was planning to blow him up. Provincial Revolutionary Committee leader Tan Puren's people contacted me urgently in the middle of the night to look into the case. I spoke to the fellow and certified that he was simply mentally ill. Later, when his prediction turned out to be true, he was released from the hospital.[107] Of course, not all were so lucky. Some who cursed Mao out of mental illness ended up in prisons and labor camps.

At a time when it was tantamount to mortal sin to criticize Mao or impugn his name in any way, people who were literally insane and cursed Mao were often punished as if they had all their faculties.

There were so many problems and appeals for help in Xishuangbanna that the government finally sent work teams to find out what was going on. A *Chongqing Daily* journalist was among those who visited Xishuangbanna as part of a "solicitude team" [*weiwen tuan*]. "We were sent to investigate their concerns and we found many problems," the man recalled. "The work was too heavy, and it was a kind of forced, military-style labor. There were many conflicts with the local leaders." He vividly remembered the devastated landscape. "Dazhai terracing had turned the earth into a sponge. Mud, fertilizer, and water were running down the mountainsides."

In 1973, several military leaders, including three from Xishuangbanna, were executed for rape and extortion. After that, the leaders' behavior improved. War preparation exercises had fallen off after the Nixon visit, and land-reclamation campaigns lost their intensity. Educated youths began, with uneven success, to find their way back to the cities, often "going through the back door" of bribery and connections, the only available avenue through which residence permits could be transferred home.

Environmental Consequences

The environmental consequences of the clear-cutting and rubber planting became clear soon after the influx of so many young people. A youth recalled:

By 1972, there was not supposed to be any more cutting of virgin rainforest in Xishuangbanna. But it was too late. All the forest near towns had been cut down. Starting around 1973, there were frequent directives ordering an end to the cutting and announcing that whoever set fires would be arrested. But the directives were ignored. Dazhai-style terracing led to erosion, which led to loss of topsoil. I saw for myself how the springs dried up after the big trees were cut down. In 1971, in Jinuo, more than forty small springs disappeared. And some of the animals disappeared. There had been a tiger in the area when I arrived, and muntjac [barking deer]. The production team killed six or seven deer a day until they were gone. I heard the tiger die. It was shot with a poison arrow, and it roared all night, and then it died.

Statistics merely hint at the devastation that habitat loss, overhunting, and other human-induced disturbances wreaked on wild animal species. According to a 1983 survey of rare animals in Xishuangbanna, the population of endangered white-checked gibbons was reduced 86.2 to 88 percent in the twenty-three years after 1960, for an average loss of 20 to 23.5 individuals per year. Eighteen groups remained, comprised of only 74 individuals.[108] Another kind of loss was the damage to plants which the local people relied on for cash. A former educated youth, now a computer scientist in the United States, was taken from rubber-planting duty and assigned to teach elementary school. She recalled that her students came from seven different ethnic minorities, including Miao, Zhuang, and Yao:

> My students were very poor, and their parents sometimes didn't have money for books and shoes. For their cash income, they depended on medicinal bark from the eucommia tree, which they could sell for a high price. They gathered this, and bamboo shoots, from the mountains in the spring; in the fall, they went to cut rattan, which they sold for chairs and other furniture. I learned this when a child came to school without book money; he told me his parents would go cut rattan. But as the years went by, even the trees on the steep hillsides were cut down. The eucommia bark, bamboo shoots, and rattan became harder and harder for the local people to find. Rubber has shallow roots, and the erosion

was bad. And the monkeys, which were so common when I arrived, disappeared, as did the pheasant [*shanji*] with their beautiful long tails. I used to see them flying, and once or twice my students' parents brought me one to eat. Gradually, I understood that we had destroyed the local people's livelihoods. And eventually there was no way for us educated youths to work hard anyway, since there was no forest left to clear for rubber.

A Chinese doctoral dissertation on the causes and impact of deforestation in Xishuangbanna, based on site surveys and statistical data, provides valuable information about the environmental consequences of forest destruction. Yang Rungao describes how, in comparison with Hainan Island, China's other major tropical rainforest, Xishuangbanna was settled late, in 1941. At the time, 69.4 percent of the region was forested. By 1981, forest cover was 26 percent, with most of the loss virgin forest.[109] In all, there was a loss of 3,820,000 *mu* of forest from 1959 to 1979. The reasons Yang enumerates for the deforestation include rubber plantations (the primary cause), slash-and-burn agriculture (which, he mentions, is a favorite explanation of the government because it shifts responsibility to local people), forest fires, tea and sugarcane plantations, and logging. In the 1950s, there was almost no rubber grown; by 1983, there were 753,000 *mu* of rubber, or 2.62 percent of the land. By 1996, there were 1,620,900 *mu,* or 5.65 percent of the land, more than double.[110] Among the impacts Yang analyzes are changes in number of fog days and duration of fog, mean annual relative humidity, rainfall, temperature, river silt content, soil fertility, and water and soil loss. In Jinghong, the capital, for example, fog days dropped from an average of 166 from 1954 to 1959 to an average of only 118 from 1970 to 1979. The length of fog time in winter dropped from a total of 858 hours in the 1950s to about 509 in the 1970s. Mean annual relative humidity dropped from 84 degrees in 1959 to 82 degrees in the 1970s. The mean annual silt content of the Lancang (Mekong) River in Jinghong increased from an average of 0.988 cubic meters in the 1960s to 1.74 cubic meters in 1979. These trends only worsened during the post-reform 1980s and 1990s.

Numerous conversations with local Chinese professionals bore out Yang's findings and provided rich reflections on the environmental degradation of Xishuangbanna. A Chinese geographer who has spent his life conducting research in Yunnan provided these observations on the enduring impact of the educated youths on the province's forests:

> The educated youth had a severe impact on nature. After 20 years of leftist thought and policies, only 25 percent of the original forest was left. Sixty thousand square miles of forest have disappeared. In the 1950s, when I came to Yunnan, the rivers were clear. Now the rivers are yellow and red with sediment. The erosion is continuous. It is very difficult to reforest because the topsoil is gone and there is only bedrock left. Aside from some well-terraced places, you can't grow things in the mountains. Some groundwater has gone dry. In April and May, water is scarce.

A retired botany professor offered similar observations:

> During the 1950s, 60 percent of the land was forested. But after the 1970s, it was reduced to 30 percent. Half the forest was gone. Our research told us there was much less moisture in the air. There were greater temperature extremes, the wind was stronger, and there was less rainfall. People didn't understand the relationship between forests and climate. After 1985 or 1986, they paid more attention and tried to stop the cutting. But they have to police the natural areas better. Buddhism says we shouldn't kill living things. This is also part of the Dai people's Longshan culture, and the spirit forest. The Chinese characters for tree, grove, and forest provide a visual illustration of the danger of simplification, of mono-culture [木 林 森]. The plantation has only one kind of tree.

The director of a renowned Xishuangbanna tropical plant institute made a comment in English, as if to underline his disdain: "Rubber is forestry, not forest." A less adamant position was taken by a Kunming geographer, who argued that the real problem was not rubber per se but the way in which it is grown. He pointed out that Yunnan is geographically complex, and there are few absolutes. There are basins where growing rubber makes sense. The mistake is to use the standards of flat lands in hilly areas, and not to recognize the area's complexity.

A Chinese anthropologist who has studied Yunnan's ethnic minority cultures and written about Han migration as a factor in destabilizing systems that worked well listed his own reasons for the deforestation:

> Why was there so much deforestation? The first reason is population pressure. In 1950, there were less than 200,000 people. Now there are 800,000, four times as many. The second is land use. What was originally forest was turned into plantations, as many outsiders came to plant rubber. There was much deforestation. Third is policy. The "Take Grain as the Key" policy, the People's Communes, the Cultural Revolution, and the responsibility system all had their impact on the forests. Fourth is our destruction of local people's customs of forest use. There was a great change in only forty years. By the early 1980s, there were many denuded mountains. Although there has been some restoration, the rainforest can't be brought back.

Ironically, as in the Dianchi case, the economic costs of this Mao-era development project were great. According to Shi and He, educated youths opened up a total of 250,000 *mu* of land in Yunnan and produced 17,700 tons of rubber. But losses mounted from 5,810,000 *yuan* in 1970 to 9,120,000 *yuan* in 1971, 5,430,000 *yuan* in 1972, and 16,070,000 in 1974, for a total loss of 34,530,000 *yuan,* even if a 1973 profit of 1,900,000 is included in the calculations.[111]

Even today, Yunnan's rubber plantations are the world's highest and northernmost.[112] Because the temperature tends to be too low, much sunlight is required, and rubber trees must be spaced far apart. As a result, production costs of Chinese rubber tend to be higher than those of places in Southeast Asia with long rubber-growing traditions and better natural growing conditions. These high production costs make it difficult for China to compete in the international rubber market.

The Movement to Return to the Cities

Mao died in September 1976 at the age of 83. In the summer of 1977, Deng Xiaoping returned from political exile, supplanting Mao's hand-picked successor Hua Guofeng at the Third Plenum of the Eleventh Central Committee in December 1978. Deng had been in political disgrace, broken by a brief comeback, since the start of the Cultural Revolution, when his pragmatic emphasis on economic results rather than ideology had put him at cross-purposes with Mao. One of the pressing tasks of the new regime was to correct some of the injustices of the Mao years. In October 1978, a national-level decision was made to deal with the educated youth question, and the last of those who had joined rural villages [*chadui luohu*] were permitted to return to the cities. However, the road home was harder for the 2 million youths in the Army Corps because their meager state salaries placed them in the category of employed workers.

Thus began a national protest movement to return to the cities [*fancheng yundong*], initiated in Xishuangbanna, where several thousand Beijing youth, including some high-ranking cadres' children, served as links with the capital.[113] On October 18, 1978, a Shanghai youth named Ding Huimin posted a petition on a Jinghong street, where nearly 1,000 educated youths signed it. In mid-November, forty youths representing thirty-seven battalions held a secret meeting among the trees of a rubber plantation. On December 10, the Xishuangbanna youths went on strike. On December 16 and 18, two groups of petitioners [*qingyuan tuan*] set out for Beijing to present their case. When the first group was prevented from boarding a train in Kunming, they obstructed trains to Beijing for three days. On December 27, the second group of petitioners made it to Beijing, led by Ding Huimin, and on January 4, 1979, in an extraordinary event, they were received by Vice-premier Wang Zhen. Although Wang Zhen urged them to go back to Xishuangbanna and work hard to develop the region, he agreed to send a work team to Yunnan to look into their situation.[114]

When the work team arrived in Ruili (a rubber-producing town west of Xishuangbanna), more than one thousand youths knelt weeping in front of the work team, asking to come home. Legend has it that the old cadres on the team were so moved that they wept as well. In mid-January, the team arrived in Xishuangbanna, where they discovered severe problems. The food was watery soup; oil, meat, and vegetables were scarce; there was a high incidence of gynecological infections among the women due to lack of basic sanitation, for toilet paper and sanitary napkins were unavailable. Suicide rates were so high that they were the leading cause of unnatural death.

As the youths awaited the team's report and the disposition of their case, Ding Huimin wrote again to Wang Zhen. Others, impatient, resumed their hunger strikes and work shutdowns. In the town of Mengla, near the Laotian border, they protested by cutting down nearly 100 rubber trees that were already two or three years old. By this time, Army Corps youths in other provinces were joining the protests.

The "returning home wind" [*fancheng feng*] became a gale that could not be stilled. Despite centrally issued documents and exhortations, the movement was unstoppable. In Yunnan, the youths were finally allowed to claim sickness to go home [*bingtui hui cheng*]. Lines for permission grew so long that local leaders gave up and left official seals out on office window ledges so the youth could stamp their own papers. By the end of spring 1979, the work farms in Yunnan were nearly empty. According to statistics from the State Farm and Reclamation Bureau, thirteen teams in Mengla evacuated completely. Province-wide, 61,515 people went home, or one-third of the workforce. Seventy-one percent of the drivers disappeared, as did 71 percent of the teachers, 67.5 percent of hospital workers, and 78.6 percent of rubber tappers.[115] Within a few short weeks, the educated youths had abandoned the frontier and gone home.

Reflections from a "Sacrificed Generation" {Xisheng de Yidai}

According to a scholar of the educated youth movement, the campaign has never been officially negated, despite the Party's repudiation of the Cultural Revolution itself. "There is a silence around it," he said. "Twenty million youths were treated as playthings. Even now, they say our spirit of self-sacrifice is worth imitating. If they publicly negated the movement, it would be a great validation and consolation for us."

Despite their suffering, many find good things to say about being sent "down," and some even have nostalgia for the rural hardships of their youth. Especially during the mid-1990s, during the twenty-fifth anniversary reunions, large numbers of "educated youth restaurants" and cafes opened up to provide meeting places for "old educated youths" [*lao zhiqing*]. These were often decorated to evoke the rainforests, grasslands, or deserts where the owners lived out their service.

One educated youth, still struggling to find a place for herself and her family in post-reform society, spoke for many in her generation with these reflections:

> Our government never considered whether it would be better to import rubber. They said China should be self-reliant. They didn't understand what we were wasting. So they sent us "down" to get us out of the cities and solve their economic crisis. Asking us to plant rubber was what they came up with. Chairman Mao was a poet, so sometimes his thinking wasn't so logical. He could be impulsive, imaginative, creative. He sent everyone off to do the opposite of what they were trained to do.
>
> Our generation were victims. There was no preparation for our experience. The government saw us as a burden and didn't think about the future. We are a sacrificed generation, caught in a twist in their planned economy. We were some of the country's best minds, from five regions, mere teenagers. But we lost our chance for an education.
>
> When we went home, by 1979, few could get their old social positions back. Our parents had also been sent down. It was hard to find work, and we were too old to take the college examinations. Many ended up doing menial work. Now, since the reforms, promotions are tied to education, and we don't have degrees. With the market economy, we don't have the money to buy apartments. And it's hurting the next generation, too. It's a cycle. We can't get our children into good schools because they cost more.
>
> Still, I feel I learned a lot about independent life and independent thinking, things that would not have been possible if I had stayed home with my parents. We matured. Although it was not systematic, we learned from many different sources, from each other and from the local minorities. There was a lot of social interaction, much time to debate each other and discuss philosophy. It was a time to reflect. I don't care about material things now because I have learned how to live with what I have, to make it up with spiritual things. I feel all difficulties can be overcome, since I've already survived the worst.

Others, particularly when reflecting on the environmental costs of their experience, are less sanguine. *Da lin mang* [The Vast Forest], a well-regarded novel by Kong Jiesheng, thoroughly "negates" the rubber-planting life. It tells of a group of five youths who enter the rainforest to clear it, knowing full well that what they are doing is wrong. They have no choice but to obey their politically fervent leader. Eventually, all but the leader die senselessly and tragically in the jungle.[116]

One educated youth who was one of the few to remain in Xishuangbanna, caught by its beauty and rich biodiversity, now produces environmental television programs. She had these reflections on the rubber campaign:

> At the beginning of the 1950s, China was isolated, so it was understandable that we would try to grow our own rubber for survival. By the 1960s, China could buy rubber from Malaysia and Singapore, but still China wanted to develop its own rubber. Then there was the enormous expansion of rubber-planting in the 1970s. After U.S.-China relations warmed up, China could easily have imported rubber. At that point, China should definitely have stopped planting rubber in Xishuangbanna. There was too much harm to the rainforest, and it is very precious, the only remaining rainforest on the Tropic of Cancer. It has the tree fern and the sky-looking tree [*wangtian shu*], which is very tall, and extremely rare even within the rainforest. In Mengla, there is still a swath of it. So many species haven't even been discovered yet. If they can't restore the rainforest, then at least they should permit the broad-leafed evergreen forest to return.

Another educated youth who saw rubber trees die in the great frost of the mid-1970s observed how the mountain that he helped to clear remained denuded and how the streams had disappeared. He had this to say: "At this altitude and latitude rubber shouldn't be grown. The forest is gone, it will be dry and frozen ... only now do we understand."[117] Shi and He comment, "Blindly increasing the rubber reclamation area and destroying virgin forest at the same time, the people only realized their guilt many years later. At the time they only used all their energy to declare an insane war on the forest."[118]

If the educated youth have not healed from their experiences on the frontier, neither has the natural world recovered from their incursions. Throughout the frontiers, the scars remain in the form of lost and threatened species, destroyed rainforests, desertified grass-lands, in-filled wetlands, and steep hillsides eroded to bedrock. While some of this damage might have been reversed if nature had been left to recover, another powerful motivating force took over from political coercion. With post-Mao economic reforms, market forces began to drive both modernization and environmental degradation.

Today, the population of Xishuangbanna has continued to grow despite the departure of the educated youths. Notwithstanding much more government attention to environmental protection and better management of the Xishuangbanna Nature Reserve, more rubber is being produced than ever, as Yang Rungao's research indicates. The market has replaced political mobilization as the primary motivation. In the 1980s, small landholders, eager for income from inflated world markets, chose rubber over other crops. The ratio of rubber grown on state farms to that grown privately has gone from about 95/5 in 1979 to about 60/40 in 1996, and the total rubber-growing area has increased from 460,000 to 1,620,000 *mu*, as more and more land is placed in private hands and those landholders choose to plant rubber.[119] Other researchers concur: a geographer at a prominent Kunming university studied the ratio between rubber and virgin rainforest by comparing satellite photos taken in 1984 and 1997; he informed me that now there is at least twice as much rubber, despite national directives and prohibitions.[120] Except for nature reserves and collective forests, most private lands have already been cut in the search for profit. Once again, the geographer noted, rubber is being grown in freeze-vulnerable zones. "And now world rubber prices have dropped, and the small landholders are vulnerable. With rubber from Southeast Asia flooding the market, local people are in a panic. We have to find another way." Since there is no longer a powerful economic justification for growing so much rubber, and given that the environmental consequences are so severe, he argued, Xishuangbanna should effect a major shift toward less destructive land use.

Reflections

Forcible relocation of people into alien territory has provided the final ingredient in Mao's war on nature. The Third Front brought human activity into rugged terrain and left deep scars on remote landscapes in

China's interior. The transfer of educated youth into the Production-Construction Army Corps was responsible for much environmental destruction in Xishuangbanna, the Great Northern Wilderness, Inner Mongolia, Xinjiang, Hainan Island, Gansu, and other frontier regions. Few of these dislocated people chose their fates, and many longed for home and a different life. The activities that degraded nature were neither of their design nor volition, yet they could not dissent, refuse to participate, or depart, even as the onslaught of their activities disrupted ecological systems too deeply and rapidly for nature to adapt. During Mao's war preparation campaign, lack of scientific and practical knowledge and ill-considered top-down policies victimized both people and nature.

The environmental destruction wrought by people forced into unfamiliar areas in which they had no say about their activities indicates the importance of local governance and sustained connection to the land. The iron and steel workers of the Third Front and the educated youths of the frontiers did not understand their new lands and had little incentive to care for them – to paraphrase the words of Aldo Leopold, those who have no "vital relation" to the land cannot protect what they do not love.[121] By contrast, the indigenous people whose traditions the Han attacked and disrupted often lived comparatively harmoniously in the natural world. Their ways of life serve as a reproach to the Maoist war on nature and offer alternative modes of living on the earth that may be fruitful for China to consider as it seeks to resolve its current environmental crisis. To the woman who chose to remain in Xishuangbanna, the traditional Dai way of life seems to harken back to simpler times, when another model of human–environmental relations dominated:

Their homes mirror the rainforest canopy, in levels. The upper [roof] level provides shade. The middle level [even with human living quarters] is fruit trees. The bush level [at stairway height] is medicinal shrubs, and the ground level is herbs and vegetables. In the courtyard below the house are chickens and pigs. There's a pond for fish. Each home is its own ecosystem, with insects for pollination. It is all self-sustainable.

As her appreciation for local customs demonstrates, for many youths a sense of environmental responsibility to and for the land came only after the destruction they had wrought was apparent. By then, in many cases, it was too late.

With the easing of military tensions after the 1972 Nixon visit, the "prepare for war" slogan was replaced with a milder formulation, "seize revolution, promote production, promote work, promote war preparation."[122] Mao grew increasingly infirm with heart and respiratory ailments and the early stages of Lou Gehrig's disease,[123] and his war against nature went into retreat. Motivated in part by several cases of severe industrial pollution, in 1972 China participated in the United Nations Conference on the Human Environment in Stockholm. This marked a turning point in China's attention to environmental issues and a departure from the official position that environmental problems could occur only in capitalist countries. Environmental institutions were established and gradually strengthened, regulations were issued, and principles such as "polluter pays" and reuse of the "three wastes" (liquid, gas, and residue), briefly propounded in the early 1950s, were revived and publicized.[124] However, the Party did not relinquish Mao's voluntaristic notion that, with the power of will, all difficulties could be overcome. In 1974, the Environmental Protection Leading Group under the State Council set targets to control pollution within five years and eliminate it within ten.[125] Of course, such problems only got worse.

Under the reforms, despite the high priority assigned to environmental issues, the impressive promulgation of environmental laws and regulations, and the integration of "sustainable development" goals into national planning, China's environmental difficulties have increased severely. Environmental measures have not kept pace with rapid economic growth, continuing population pressures, and rising consumer expectations. Even as deforestation continues, local cultural traditions such as those practiced in Xishuangbanna and elsewhere are being bulldozed over by modernization and globalization. External influences, rising material expectations, and population expansion have complicated local situations, so that a sense of long-term connection may no longer be enough to guide people to care for the land. Without responsible government regulation, decollectivization has not in itself proved to be the answer. However, as we shall see in the conclusion, devastating floods and some of the world's worst urban pollution have strongly focused the nation's energy on environmental issues. China has made enormous investments in pollution remediation, phasing in international environmental standards and shutting down substandard factories; new nature reserves are being created and existing ones are being more seriously respected; anti-logging laws are not only being enacted but being enforced; farmers are being required to move away from steep slopes and floodplains; and environmental science is becoming mandatory in school curricula. Whether these efforts will turn China's environmental situation around remains to be seen.

"Battling with Nature is Boundless Joy"
Yu Tian Dou, Qile Wu Qiong

5

THE LEGACY

As we have seen, political repression, utopian urgency, dogmatic formalism, and state-sponsored relocations affected and distorted Chinese relationships with nature during the Mao years. Maoist controls interfered with deep cultural traditions such as the intellectual's duty to speak out in order to help top leaders become better governors, while Mao's disrespect for scientific principles and ambition to transform the country in a great leap led China on a self-destructive rush toward ecosystem collapse and famine. Local leaders and farmers were forced to implement inappropriate models and were forbidden to continue traditional sustainable practices like planting suitable crops and building terraces judiciously on gentle hillsides. Overemphasis on strategic concerns led to destructive and premature development of the interior, connections to ancestral homelands were ruptured when the state ordered massive population shifts, and military values came to dominate all others. As military discipline, mobilization, regimentation, redeployments, and campaigns moved the Maoist war against nature from the realm of metaphor and propaganda into reality, millions down the chain of command were pressed to obey orders in the service of Maoist goals. The lack of freedom to behave responsibly toward the natural world was a hallmark of the Mao years. However, as I have also indicated, responsibility for these missteps lies with others in addition to the top leadership.

External influences, as well as Chinese traditions, enabled Maoist social control. Environmental problems were profoundly influenced by China's links to Soviet mentors with appetites for grandiose projects and state-led social engineering. Moreover, many adversarial aspects of Chinese relations with nature can be traced back to imperial China, when the state also played a major role in shaping the traditions and practices on which its authority rested, conditioning human conduct toward nature through sponsorship of major agricultural and public works projects. Imperial China also saw intense periods of deforestation and erosion, encroachments on waterways through wetlands drainage, and land reclamations that degraded ecosystems, destroyed wildlife habitat, and threatened indigenous people. As discussed in the section on the Sanmenxia Dam, Chinese debates over whether to dam rivers or let them take their natural course have a long history, and grandiose plans to harness great rivers were set forth in the early years of the Republic.

Although Mao Zedong played a pivotal role in the degradation of the environment by failing to fulfill the ruler's Confucian obligation to create harmony between humans and nature, what occurred was not due solely to the tyranny and aberrations of one man, or even to the Chinese Communist system per se. However, post-revolution efforts to master nature represented an unprecedented role for the state, which under Mao became a powerful driving force behind environmental degradation. Maoism constructed a world that pitted humans against nature, and inculcated this world view among the people through repression, indoctrination, utopian promises, and censorship. Mao and the Party launched a series of economic and social polices and large development projects that transformed and degraded the environment. Mass mobilization and political rewards for extreme sacrifice and physical labor undermined traditional ideals of harmony, accommodation, and moderation. Maoist values also laid the groundwork for intensified exploitation and despoliation after Mao's death. The Maoist example suggests that the IPAT equation that describes the impact of human beings on the natural world (Impact = Population × Affluence × Technology) inadequately accounts for the role of the state, which may powerfully shape the elements on the right side of the equation and govern their interaction.

In Chapter 1, we saw that soon after the Communist revolution political repression thoroughly chilled debate on issues affecting the natural environment. Influenced by the Soviet emphasis on "mother heroes," his own experience with the military value of human capital, and the Marxist anti-Malthusian tenet that population could only be a problem in capitalist societies, Mao Zedong purged preeminent demographer Ma Yinchu, silencing a powerful voice of caution about a population explosion which may have done more to distort the human–nature relationship than any other policy error of the period. Persecution of intellectuals thus contributed indirectly to a dramatic decrease in the amount of arable land per person, increasing pressure to convert China's limited remaining uninhabited land to human purposes, extract resources, and deposit industrial waste and pollutants. Despite concerted, state-sponsored efforts to increase arable land, population pressures on the carrying capacity of land suitable for human habitation have remained acute. Today, China has one-tenth the per capita land resources of the United States.

We also saw how the labeling of hydro-engineer Huang Wanli as a rightist for his opposition to the Soviet-designed Sanmenxia Dam heralded an era of development projects in which human will was considered more powerful than objective scientific law. The notion that the face of the earth could be miraculously transformed through ideologically motivated determination was repeatedly translated into policy and action during the Mao years, and the natural environment was devastated through the efforts of millions of laborers.

As we saw in Chapter 2, the war on nature reached an early peak during the 1958–60 Great Leap Forward, when Mao called on China to industrialize and catch up with Britain in an ever-condensing span of time. Collectives and villages were reorganized along military lines into "Great People's Communes," and peasants, enticed by dreams and promises of a better life, or cowed by persecution of those who opposed wrong-headed policies, were mobilized as foot-soldiers for vast earth-moving projects. "Backyard furnaces," fueled by timber from forests which have yet to recover, smelted metal utensils, tools, and gateways into useless agglomerations of scrap. An effort to control grain predation by birds was launched as a political movement, and schoolchildren and adults were mobilized to bang pots and pans until exhausted sparrows dropped dead, leaving crops vulnerable to insects. The Leap's utopian urgency, its focus on fantastic industrial output at all costs, and the 1960 withdrawal of Soviet aid and advisors contributed to the collapse of agriculture-based ecosystems on which people depended for food. China experienced the greatest human-created famine in history.

Chapter 3 examined how dogmatic formalism dominated agriculture during the Cultural Revolution, when central dictates and mass campaigns imposed a uniform agricultural model on the entire country regardless of local conditions. Zealous misapplication of the slogan, "Take Grain as the Key Link" forced farmers to fell productive fruit trees, forests, and tea bushes and to fill in parts of lakes and rivers to plant grain where no grain would grow. At the height of Mao-worship, dissent was stilled; millions became obliged to respond literally to Mao's most casual utterance. When peasants from Dazhai, the model agricultural brigade, terraced rocky hillsides, filled in gullies, and brought irrigation water from distant rivers through superhuman, highly coordinated labor, the rest of the country was forced to imitate the "Dazhai miracle," no matter what the local climate and geography. Such formalism supplanted local practices and wisdom, damaged the natural world, and inflicted enormous hardship on the Chinese people.

Finally, in Chapter 4, we saw how state-sponsored relocations transferred heavy industries into remote areas and dispatched educated urban youths to faraway "wastelands." Efforts to form a defensive Third Front against anticipated air attack opened fragile hinterlands to pollution; orders to create arable land while preparing for war initiated the collapse of rainforest and grassland ecosystems that had once supported a range of precious life forms. Air and water pollution became legacies of strategic industrial sitings that made little economic sense, while deforestation, erosion, desertification, habitat destruction, and falling water tables followed in the wake of a program that wrested young "volunteers" from family and home and forced them to implement policies they did not understand, on lands to which they had no prior connection.

ENVIRONMENTAL DEGRADATION IN OTHER LANDS

While Maoist relations with nature were often unique in their extremity and in their blatantly adversarial stance, we can readily find parallels to their themes and environmental mistakes in other societies and periods. In the West, for example, the attempt to tame nature and reshape it to fit human needs has been a central part of the modernist project since the Enlightenment. This ethos is only now being reconsidered and rejected in developed countries, as it becomes apparent that excessive success in remolding the face of the earth may actually threaten our survival. Adopting a comparative historical perspective may lead us to soften harsh judgments about Maoist China's foolhardy and destructive behavior and lack of environmental consciousness.

Overexploitation of the North American frontier was sparked by conviction concerning the benefits of harnessing and conquering nature for the human good. Economic incentives, not political coercion, were used to settle the frontiers; land grants and railroad-building, financed by government subsidies, enticed Easterners westward and promoted the genocide of indigenous peoples and the extinction of native species such as the passenger pigeon, whose migrations once darkened the skies for days, and the South Carolina parakeet, North America's only indigenous psittacine. Military campaigns for land acquisition and subjugation of minorities had parallels in China's conquest of its own frontiers. Like the Great Leap Forward in its urgency, the Gold Rush's headlong incursions into wilderness exacted a heavy toll, as efforts to get rich scarred the Western landscape and polluted the waters. Federal agencies such as the Bureau of Reclamation and the Army Corps of Engineers (like the Production-Construction Army Corps, a military institution) saw watershed management as nature-conquest. Their mandate was to correct the "irrationality" of wild rivers, and they undertook to tame great waterways through mighty dams such as the Glen Canyon above Lake Powell, now the target of criticism and of a Sierra Club campaign to have the dam removed. The use of language to manipulate public consciousness also invites comparison: If the Chinese Communist Party used slogans to perpetuate power and projects regardless of human or environmental cost, American business often used advertising to perpetuate itself and foster consumption, creating markets for the products of increased exploitation of natural resources. Those who settled the American West were often heedless of the earth's limitations, much as the Chinese sought to tap the wealth of their frontiers without understanding the consequences of their actions; Donald Worster has explored the destructive power of the myth of America as earthly Eden of unlimited resources, identifying this fallacy as underlying much of the degradation of the West.[1] Chinese effort to "open the wastelands" and American effort to tame the "wild West" thus shared a common impetus. But where Mao's socialist vision was promoted by fiat and appeal to utopian urgency, the pursuit of quick profit and material ambition tended to propel the unsustainable exploitation of nature in North America.

The environmental history of the former Soviet Union, the "elder brother" who inspired so many early Maoist errors, also provides a valuable analogue. Like China, the USSR was an authoritarian rural society with ambitions to modernize, whose Marxist doctrine held that "socialism itself, by its very essence, guarantees harmony between man and nature."[2] But the dissolution of the Soviet Union has exposed a landscape laid waste through central planning and Stalinist overemphasis on heavy industry and defense.[3] As in China, political repression and environmental destruction were linked: like environmentally aware Chinese intellectuals, Russian conservationists strove loyally for inclusion in Soviet policy-making in a last-ditch effort to retain influence before their liquidation under Stalin. Also as in China, Stalinism constructed nature "as an enemy to be conquered in the course of the creation of the totally man-made socialist environment."[4] Boris Komarov's *samizdat* manuscript, eventually published under the title, *The Destruction of Nature in the Soviet Union,* captured an atmosphere of secrecy, suppression of information, and economic irrationality also characteristic of China under Mao. Komarov wrote, "the State Planning Committee is paying for its economic and social losses with chunks of its former patrimony: with lakes, rivers, lands, and whole seas."[5] From the Soviet Union, China imported misguided theories on deep-planting and inheritableness of acquired characteristics, as well as a predisposition toward grandiose engineering projects intended to humble nature. As in China, forcible relocations into the Soviet labor camp system were essential to creating a vast network of workers tasked with exploiting the Soviet empire's natural resources, as was location of strategic defense industries in remote locations, many of them inhabited by indigenous minorities. Given the Soviet Union's enormous influence on Maoist China, the countries' structural similarities, and common ideology, it is no coincidence that the environmental histories of the two societies share so many themes. Similar themes emerge in another Soviet-influenced socialist dictatorship halfway around the world, Cuba. In their book, *Conquering Nature: The Environmental Legacy of Socialism in Cuba,* Sergio Diaz-Briquets and Jorge Pérez-López argue that core elements in Cuba's environmental degradation included the Cuban government's efforts to "conquer nature" and a central planning approach that led it to ignore local circumstances. They also argue, as I do for China, that

Cuban socialism's environmental legacy presents serious challenges for future generations.[6]

Elsewhere in the Third World, roads built in the name of progress and development have opened and damaged wilderness areas as they did in China during construction of the Third Front. Just as "socialist" agriculture replaced time-tested practices in the service of Maoist China's utopian schemes, so has "modernization" supplanted indigenous knowledge in many of today's developing countries, often with concomitant environmental harm. The ideology of modernization has often disregarded local custom and practice just as the Dazhai model ignored local differences. Replacing a diversified agricultural economy with mono-cropping usually has hidden costs in terms of biodiversity loss and increased vulnerability to disease; the structural adjustment policies of multilateral lending institutions can be coercive, forcing farmers to switch from traditional produce to cash crops that do not sustain their communities. Rapid, human-induced change too drastic to permit ecosystems to recover, is yet another environmental misstep common to both Maoist China and the Third World.

Such comparisons, however brief and preliminary, suggest that the Mao era is both unique, with a specific set of underlying dynamics, and an extreme and revealing example of a general pattern. Elements of this pattern have created similar problems in other situations. The heuristic usefulness of the Maoist case derives from the blatancy of Maoism's coercive aspects, the ambition of its utopian idealism, and the transparency of the link between human political repression and the effort to conquer nature by portraying and treating it as an enemy. Maoist China reveals the connection between humanity's suffering and nature's suffering, as well as the unfortunate role of the developmental state in launching and implementing nature-conquest schemes, more clearly than do many other cases where these fundamental relationships also play a role. The Maoist war on nature thus provides insights into China's recent history and serves as a starting point for reflection on the degradation of nature in other situations.

The Mao era's starkly revealed environmental dynamics may perhaps be understood as warning flags for other scenarios. If so, it may be that solutions to the problem of environmental degradation lie in reversing Mao-era behavioral hallmarks. The inverse of the drive to conquer nature, for example, is humility and accommodation; that of political repression is promotion of political and legal accountability, and fostering creativity and individuality; that of urgency is moderation and allowing sufficient time for debate and feedback; that of dogmatic formalism is respect for difference and willingness to make mid-course corrections; that of state-sponsored relocations is localism and sustained connection to place. While humility, accommodation, creativity, individuality, rule of law, moderation, measure, respect for difference, flexibility, and localism are surely not sufficient in themselves to point humans toward a better-integrated relationship with the organic and inorganic "other," surely they are worth emphasizing. Thus, the environmental mistakes of the Mao era strongly indicate the importance of free speech, democratic participation, and rule of law; of careful decision making; of respect for local variation; and of long-term association with the land.

The Mao-era experience points toward another connection: the congruence between violence perpetrated between human beings and violence perpetrated toward the nonhuman world. China under Mao provides one of history's darkest stories. Political campaigns so distorted human relationships that family members were driven to denounce and beat each other, neighbors spied on neighbors, schoolchildren drove teachers to suicide, and the world was turned upside down for countless millions. Language was so manipulated and controlled that even private thoughts were made available for public scrutiny and modification. As we have seen, most, if not all, of the Mao-era political campaigns that victimized human beings also victimized nature. Mao and the Party thought little more of wrenching millions from their homes and families in mass relocations than they did of violating the face of nature beyond its ability to adjust. They gave little more consideration to destroying the dreams and lives of millions of individuals than they did to rejecting centuries of publicly stated ideals of harmonious accommodation to nature. The natural world was used and misused in extraordinary ways that defied logic and were catastrophic for human beings, as exemplified in most extreme fashion by the Great Famine that starved millions following the Great Leap Forward's widespread deforestation and agricultural experiments.

These patterns of linked environmental and human degradation share common origins: at their cores lies an authoritarian decision to discount the weak and voiceless. Just as individual lives had little value under Mao and people had little say in their own fates, so was nature unable to defend itself. Fostering the capacity for empathy – whether for humans who seem to have no immediate utility, or for nonhumans, or even, metaphorically, for ecosystems which cannot argue their own case – may provide hope both for the natural environment and for the resolution of China's current crisis of values. Respect for difference and a renewed sense of humility before nature may also provide China's people with spiritual sustenance. As attested by the contemporary renewal of interest in Buddhism, Christianity, and other religions, and the popularity of the Falungong sect, such sustenance appears to be in short supply during an era of crass materialism and a much-noted "crisis of faith."

THE LEGACY

Mao-era efforts to control humans in nature, and nature in humans, have set the scene for the current precarious environmental situation, which has deteriorated with China's post-Mao push to development. Explosive economic growth and the rush to industrialize are obvious sources of China's unfolding environmental crisis. However, the core dynamics explored in these pages are still at work, albeit in attenuated or altered form. Political repression still marginalizes intellectuals, including those who oppose the Three Gorges Dam, some of whom have been jailed or otherwise persecuted. Urgency still leads to rapid and unsustainable exploitation of natural resources, although now the urgency is to get rich rather than to achieve socialist utopia or continuous revolution. A centralized bureaucracy anxious about its ability to maintain control still promulgates decrees that are formalistically applied at local levels, often to ill effect. And China's people are still relocating en masse, sometimes forcibly, as in the case of the millions moved for the Three Gorges Dam, sometimes voluntarily, as they flood into cities in search of work, establishing makeshift settlement camps characterized by problems with waste disposal, lack of potable water, and the spread of disease. Less obviously, but also significantly, China's environmental problems are linked to the ideological bankruptcy and disillusionment left by the country's Maoist experiment.

After Mao's death in 1976, as we have noted, China passed out of its ultra-leftist phase. Cultural Revolution victims, including Deng

Xiaoping, the Number Two "capitalist roader" after Liu Shaoqi, emerged from exile and prison and began to institute profound economic reforms. They decollectivized the People's Communes, opened China to the outside world, and elevated long-suffering intellectuals from society's most distrusted stratum to become active participants in the modernization effort. The educated youth were allowed to return to the cities, and university entrance examinations were reinstated. For the first time in more than a decade, managers were expected to have skills.

Despite such positive developments, the failure of the revolution to deliver on its promises, and Mao's misuse of his vast reservoirs of popular support, had left generations of Chinese with a deep sense of betrayal and cynicism. The disjunction between public exhortations to "serve the people" and the reality of a "new class" of corrupt and incompetent leaders had caused many Chinese to become suspicious of state-promoted values in any form. Having sacrificed themselves, their families, their educations, and their physical comforts to the abstractions of the revolution, many now turned to individualism and materialism, attempting to advance themselves and those in their "relationship nets" through gifts and favors proffered "through the back door." The country's strong economic performance, attributed to "socialism with Chinese characteristics," shored up the Party's weakened grasp on political power. But in a country whose bankrupt leadership's fragile authority rested on improved living standards and shallow nationalism, materialism and greed came to dominate private and public life.

The Mao-era legacy of disillusionment, often called the "crisis of confidence" or "crisis of belief" [*xinxing weiji* or *xinyang weiji*], has exacerbated the negative environmental effects of industrial development and the huge population. Numerous issues affecting environmental protection can be linked to this legacy. These include the tendency of individuals to focus on short-term personal gain; corruption and information-hoarding among bureaucracies whose behavior affects the environment; a utilitarian approach to relationships and difficulty empathizing with strangers or, more broadly, caring about the nonhuman world; and deep mistrust of government campaigns and exhortations toward public goals, including environmental goals such as pollution control, moratoriums on logging, reforestation, and protection of endangered species. As a Chinese philosophy professor writes,

Down to this day there are many places in China where power is above the law, where leaders do what they like and the environmental departments don't dare to speak out. Moreover the operations of government are opaque and so it is impossible for the people and the media to supervise them.[7]

The Three Gorges Dam, which critics have called a last-gasp monument to the Communist Party, can be understood in the context of Maoist megaprojects that aimed both at mastery of nature and suppression of human freedoms. Jiang Zemin's statements at the completion of the cofferdam in November 1997 show that Mao-era motifs of conquest have not been abandoned:

> From old, the Chinese people have had a brave history of carrying out activities to conquer, open up, and utilize nature. The legends, Jingwei Fills the Seas[8] and The Foolish Old Man Who Removed the Mountains, and the story of Yu the Great harnessing the waters, express how, from ancient times, the Chinese people have had a strong struggle spirit of reforming nature, of "Man Must Conquer Nature."[9]

As geographer Richard Louis Edmonds writes, "the Sanxia [Three Gorges] Dam seems to be yet another attempt by China to catch up rapidly with developed nations and solve problems with a single grand project as occurred during the Great Leap Forward."[10] Other huge public works projects are going forward as well; high-rise cranes transform the landscape, a grandiose plan to transfer water from South to North China is being seriously considered, and a campaign to "develop the West" is in danger of causing grave environmental damage. The world's tallest, biggest, and longest constructions are being raced to completion as if to demonstrate to all the world that China has "face," it can still conquer nature. These phenomena are not, of course, merely Maoist in origin; they can be traced to an ancient tradition of ethnocentric pursuit of greatness in a world in which other countries are expected to pay court to the Middle Kingdom.

Other Mao-era legacies affecting the environment include China's devastating population burden of 1.3 billion, and continued ambiguities concerning land rights, and thus lack of incentive to protect land that is "leased" to its holders but nominally belongs to the state. Under socialism, a communal property system was established in which no one had real responsibility, promoting the confiscation of public resources for private purposes. This mentality lingers today. Furthermore, continued overexploitation of resources out of ignorance, poverty, and desperation stems in part from a low level of education in the countryside and from the significant gap in the ages of highly educated people, a lapse in skills created during Cultural Revolution chaos. Although the profound economic stagnation of the later Mao years delayed some of the industrial pollution and overharvesting of resources that arrived with the economic reforms, it also set back the development of technologies that might later have helped China to carry out more sustainable development policies.

Despite eloquent public rhetoric about sustainable development, an impressive roster of environmental laws, and the central government's apparently serious efforts to deal with China's enormous environmental problems, implementation and enforcement of environmental measures have been erratic. Much of Chinese society and leadership is convinced that it is now China's turn to enjoy all the benefits of development and that pollution remediation measures and cleanup are luxuries that the country cannot yet afford. Payoffs, emphasis on immediate gains, economic difficulties, and lack of governmental authority encourage local enterprises to circumvent regulations.[11] Efforts to implement rule of law have yet to overcome corruption and reliance on personal connections and backdoor negotiations over objective authority and legal confrontation. An overly centralized bureaucracy, a legacy of the imperial and Soviet systems, complicates enforcement efforts. Administratively parallel institutions, such as those charged with environmental protection and those that oversee manufacturing, communicate poorly with each other. Periodic Maoist efforts to decentralize have left personnel-stuffed bureaucracies that can also complicate implementation. Meanwhile, at the level of common public behavior, millions of Styrofoam containers are tossed indifferently into China's waterways and mountains of garbage accumulate on public streets.[12] Although many modern and modernizing societies struggle with such issues, in China such behavior is tied to lingering socialist notions that the government should be responsible for all public goods and to a values crisis which leaves the citizenry particularly hard pressed to arrive at a sense of shared responsibility or common concern.

Legal protections for nature reserves and endangered species have been particularly difficult to enforce in the face of indifference, poverty, and greed. Such problems were noted, for example, by giant panda specialist George Schaller in the early 1980s, when, in order to gain the cooperation of local bureaucrats in conservation efforts, the World Wide Fund for Nature was obliged to provide greedy local officials with high-tech laboratories that could not possibly have been useful in remote areas. Although Schaller found some Chinese conservators deeply committed to their work, he and his foreign colleagues often fought uphill battles to get others even to tag and monitor the pandas they were charged with protecting.[13] "Paper parks" that exist in name only are a common phenomenon in China, as they are in many other parts of the world.

In international environmental negotiations, China is legendary for its practice of driving hard bargains on global environmental problems, exacting technology transfers and economic subsidies in return for cooperation on global environmental issues such as stratospheric ozone depletion and climate change. True, such negotiating positions may stem not so much from cynicism and the values crisis as from genuine economic pressures and a legitimate desire to gain restitution for centuries of imperialism and exclusion, a history China is more than willing to bring up.[14] But in China's profit-driven atmosphere, development and environment policies are vulnerable to individuals who have elected to exploit the system and each other, and the natural world suffers accordingly.

Moreover, generations of policies mandated from the top have hindered development of popular checks on unsustainable or environmentally degrading activity, thus making the obstacles listed above even more daunting. Failure to implement deep political reforms has kept China's semicapitalistic economic system from producing the democracy and accountability that some associate with free market systems. In the West, nongovernmental organizations have proved essential to awakening the citizenry to environmental issues, lobbying for environmental protections, publicizing violations, and holding industry and government accountable. In China, however, suppression of grass-roots organizations has left the environmental bureaucracy poorly equipped to mobilize popular support for environmental protection on its own. Yet the Party continues to fear free expression and is reluctant to unleash the right to organize. Continued tight controls over freedom of information, despite inroads by fax machines and the Internet, make it difficult, at least in the short term, for China's citizens to reach across borders to participate in "global civil society." Mechanisms for citizen complaints against polluting industries are as yet underdeveloped.

In sum, many of China's difficulties in dealing with the negative environmental impacts of industrialization can be linked to the Mao years. Factors that contributed to environmental degradation under Mao remain in attenuated or altered form, stifling intellectual freedom and hindering wise policy-making. The post-Mao crisis of values has created an often-cynical society in which indifference to the public good has exacerbated problems with enforcement. Yet despite this difficult legacy, there are signs of hope.

CHINA'S ENVIRONMENTAL FUTURE

Environmental problems have become a genuine central concern of China's government, not least because policy-makers have recognized that they carry a high price in health and cleanup costs, increased erosion, flooding, desertification, and sandstorms. Many leaders are aware of studies showing that costs of environmental degradation through disease, lost productivity, and cleanup costs have effectively wiped out China's rapid economic growth rate, and there is eager acceptance of green technologies if they come at low cost and contribute to economic development.[15] More stringent emissions standards are being implemented, and heavily polluting factories are being shut down or, in an interesting echo of Mao-era solutions, are being moved into more remote areas. In 1998, the State Environmental Protection Administration was elevated to the level of Ministry in an effort to give it greater oversight authority, and there has been a significant increase in the environmental agencies' powers to enforce the strong environmental regulations that exist on paper. Although resources for enforcement remain limited and violations widespread, China's government seems determined to turn around the country's reputation for being one of the most polluted in the world.

In another promising development, despite government nervousness about the institutions of civil society, environmental nongovernmental organizations, quasi-nongovernmental organizations (GONGOs, or government-organized nongovernmental organizations), and student environmental clubs and activist groups are starting to flourish. These groups often share information and conduct joint projects with overseas environmental NGOs like the World Resources Institute and Resources for the Future, and draw support from Western foundations such as the Ford Foundation and WWF-Beijing. In Beijing, the well-known NGO Friends of Nature organizes public cleanups, tree-planting drives, and efforts to save endangered species. Global Village Beijing, whose founder, Sherri Liao Xiaoyi, was recently awarded a major international environmental prize, produces educational materials and television programs. A legal clinic, the Center for Legal Assistance to Pollution Victims, opened in 1999 and is swamped with requests for help. In China's interior, the Shaanxi Mothers Environmental Protection Association organizes cleanups, workshops, and children's art competitions. In Yunnan, quasi-academic umbrella groups such as the Center for Biodiversity and Indigenous Knowledge are studying the environmental values and sustainable practices of minority nationalities, including the Dai, Aini, Jinuo, Lahu, Bai, and Naxi. Meanwhile, student and neighborhood environmental groups throughout the country are beginning to protest and publicize violations by polluters and poachers and otherwise act as monitors and pressure groups. Ironically, high pollution levels have raised environmental consciousness and promoted environmental values. In autumn 1999 in Beijing, for example, the Communist Party's temporary shutdown of polluting industries so as to be able to show the world a glorious fiftieth anniversary of the P.R.C. reminded Beijingers what it was like to glimpse blue skies and created public pressure to make this a regular event.

On the biodiversity issue, courageous groups and individuals have acted to publicize the plight of the Tibetan antelope; one such activist was martyred by a poacher's bullet. A nationwide student campaign to save the Tibetan antelope, in collaboration with Friends of Nature, recently established a web site and is conducting environmental education workshops and putting on theatrical performances. Similar activism centers around a campaign to save the rare Yunnan snub-nosed monkey. The young leader, a photographer and filmmaker named Xi Zhinong, has become a local environmental hero. He first discovered that the monkey's Deqin County habitat was about to be logged when he was on assignment for China Central Television. Appealing to top environmental officials, he gained the state's intervention, but the logging resumed as soon as officials' backs were turned. He and his wife, Shi Lihong, a former *China Daily* reporter, have since established the Yunnan Plateau Research Institute, a nongovernmental organization devoted to the monkey's cause, and they have moved with their infant child to the region to work with poor villagers and local leaders to enlist them in the monkey's protection, help them find development alternatives, and monitor and publicize the situation.

China's youth, particularly those pursuing higher educations, yearn to join the world community, to become global citizens, and to link with their peers overseas. Many of them are deeply concerned about China's environmental health. Student environmental organizations (formed under the aegis of the Communist Youth League, their activities approved by its leadership) have undertaken a wide range of activities. In Shenyang, for example, Northeast University's "Green Power" publishes a magazine and has adopted the Liao River, educating people who live along the riverbanks about fertilizer and pesticide use. Sichuan University's Green River Environmental Conservation and Protection Society has adopted Chengdu's waterways, while other groups are linking to protect and clean up the Yangzi, including a desperate effort to protect the highly endangered white river dolphin, which is likely to become extinct in the wild when the Three Gorges Dam is completed. Other groups organize "green camping" outings in a sort of student-based ecotourism, arrange Earth Day activities, and otherwise try to spread their environmental messages. These activities are on the whole supported by the universities and virtually every major Chinese university has one of these clubs.

Inspiration and hope for a better environmental future also lie in the nostalgia of China's elderly for the deep forests in which they once played and the clear waters in which they once swam, and in their memories of wild animals, large fish, and the songs of numerous birds. One such older-generation Chinese, a writer named Tang Xiyang, has written a sort of environmental rallying cry for China in his book, *A Green World Tour,* an account of his ecotour of the world's nature reserves. He explicitly links his environmental awareness and compassion to his own victimization during the Cultural Revolution.

In sum, if China's leaders can see their way toward loosening controls on public participation, a government may yet evolve that is environmentally responsible and responsive, backed by citizen awareness of environmental issues and support for strong environmental enforcement. Notwithstanding the arguments of some scholars who believe that authoritarian governments should be in a better position to regulate and control pollution than freer societies, in China, at least, top-down regulation has not thus far been successful on its own in dictating significantly better environmental behavior.

Significant citizen support for sound environmental practices must come from an informed base of knowledge, for ecological literacy has a critical role in propelling action and shaping environmental values and behavior. As we have seen, Mao systematically suppressed intellectuals and scientific knowledge, supplanting scientific warnings concerning objective limitations with his own preferences and desires, in accordance with his vision of the capabilities of a mobilized society. China is still compensating for those decades of lost expertise and training. Ecological literacy and basic environmental education are now critical, yet few ordinary Chinese citizens understand about watersheds, food chains, toxic materials that they cannot see, smell, or taste, not to speak of the consequences of transnational problems like ozone layer depletion and climate change. China's environmental future thus rests in part on its ability to integrate environmental education into the curriculum and convey basic scientific knowledge to its citizens. Fortunately, the central government and educators recognize this, and they have taken dramatic steps to integrate environmental sciences and awareness of environmental issues into the curriculum at all levels. In some universities, a course in such issues is already mandatory for all students, and there is a laudable plan to make this a nationwide requirement. On a recent lecture tour, I found Chinese college students as well if not better informed than some of their Western counterparts about basic environmental problems, and very receptive to learning about how nongovernmental institutions have promoted environmental values and policy in other parts of the world. Moreover, when asked why we should care about the environment, a surprising number responded that we should care about nature because we are an integral part of it, a philosophical approach to the human–nature relationship that is best described as "deep green."

THE ROLE OF TRADITIONAL CHINESE PHILOSOPHY

Any citizen support for environmental policy measures, even that based on compelling scientific information about the human impact on the earth's infrastructure, will have a more solid foundation if it draws on a cultural philosophy or an environmental ethic. Whether China's indigenous traditions can help guide the country out of its environmental problems, and if so, which traditions will be of most help, is a question that some Chinese environmentalists have begun to consider. This debate is linked to a larger discussion of the appropriate role of traditional Chinese culture in a modernizing nation, a conversation that is at least as old as the crumbling of the Qing dynasty in 1911; ideological struggles during the Republican era often revolved around it. The debate over uses of China's cultural and political traditions was revived after the disillusionment with Maoism during the course of the 1966–76 Cultural Revolution, particularly in the form of arguments over why China is "backward," and whether formerly dominant Confucian values – such as social harmony based on hierarchy and duty, enlightened paternal leadership, and so forth – are constraining and "feudal," or worth reviving. The discussion goes to the heart of a struggle for a modern identity following the collapse of the imperial system, foreign exploitation, decades of civil war and Japanese invasion, and the devastating Mao years.[16]

Citizens of other countries awakening to their environmental problems have often sought counsel and inspiration in their roots. American environmentalists, for example, have drawn on the romance of the wilderness, the Transcendental movement, and Native American wisdom, and the broader public tends also to value the possibility of an unfettered experience of wild nature.[17] Although Chinese confronting environmental problems will find little guidance in the Mao years, their Confucian, Buddhist, and Daoist traditions may be useful in helping to crystallize a modern environmental consciousness or cultural philosophy.

As mentioned in the introduction to this volume, Confucianism, the dominant traditional philosophy, is an anthropocentric ethic that espouses harmony with nature but understands nature primarily as a resource for human beings, to be shaped to human desires, though in accordance with its own laws. Buddhism, a biocentric tradition, stresses reverence for the divine spark of life in all living beings, while Daoism, arguably an ecosystem-centered, or ecocentric, philosophy, equates humans with nature and espouses human alignment with nature's flow of energy or "way."[18] Such traditions construct an understanding of nature in which humans stand not in opposition to nature but as part of it. China's great medieval poets Li Bai and Tao Yuanming often wrote of their reverence for nature. Brush-painted scrolls often depict tiny humans climbing towering mountains, although constructions like tea pavilions and stone stairways ritualize and control nature for human enjoyment, Confucian-style. None of these traditions advocates human mastery and reconfiguration of the natural world to the degree that the Communist Party attempted, much less a war against it.

Interestingly, China's three major traditions mirror the philosophical approaches of Western environmentalism. These have inspired differing strategies for "saving the earth" and appeal to different constituencies. Broadly sketched, the anthropocentric Judeo-Christian notion of human stewardship over the natural world appeals to a sense of duty to conserve the resources on which humans depend; the biocentric animal rights orientation leads followers to advocate for the sanctity and integrity of all living forms; and the "deep ecology" movement sees sustainability as conditional upon an understanding of human beings as humble members of interdependent ecosystems comprising living and nonliving elements.

When asked about environmental issues, Chinese from all walks of life and age groups mention China's traditions, most often citing the phrase, *Tian Ren Heyi* [Harmony between the Heavens and Humankind] as a reproach to the Maoist slogan, *Ren Ding Sheng Tian* [Man Must Conquer Nature]. They thereby demonstrate that such values have not been destroyed despite Maoism's best efforts to create a radical break with tradition. Although discussion of the strengths and weaknesses of various Chinese philosophical traditions with respect to nature is just beginning within China,[19] overseas Chinese scholars and Western environmentalists have been actively examining Chinese traditions as part of an effort to formulate a contemporary environmental ethic. In their debate, Confucianism has been seen alternately as a source of sustainable agricultural practices and as irredeemably anthropocentric, utilitarian, and exploitative of nature. The Confucian emphasis on human society, and on nature as a resource that should be conserved because it sustains that society, resonates for anthropocentric environmentalists. However, it troubles "deep" ecologists who believe human beings must entirely rethink our efforts to dominate, control, and reshape nature if we are to avoid destroying the earth.[20]

In my view, Confucianism's pragmatism, by far the dominant tradition in China, might be well tempered through incorporating a Daoist sense of humility and understanding of humans as part of nature, an approach articulated by a surprising number of educated young Chinese. It is unlikely, however, that Daoism will reemerge to guide China, for Daoism emphasizes government by inaction and represents too radical an alternative to the Communist Party's statist tradition of remolding nature. Seeing human beings as organic components of a natural process would be a major stretch of the imagination for China's current leadership.[21]

Buddhism, with its vegetarian traditions and reverence for life, also has much to contribute to a society infamous for traditional medicines that rely on body parts of endangered species and cruel practices like bear-bile farming. China has some of the world's most inhumane zoos, and consumption of rare wildlife as a form of wealth-display and novelty-seeking is increasing. Moreover, China's transition to a meat-based diet is a worry for those concerned about food security and public health, for meat requires many times more energy to produce than plants and brings with it a host of cardiovascular and other diseases. In reaction, some Chinese are organizing to combat inhumane animal practices, and others are developing synthetic substitutes for medicinal ingredients. International pressure is also playing an educative role. The International Fund for Animal Welfare (IFAW) has a strong Chinese presence, and TRAFFIC, a grass-roots organization that monitors the Convention on International Trade in Endangered Species (CITES), has a Hong Kong office. However, utilitarian attitudes toward animals are deeply entrenched in Chinese culture, and while there are a few vegetarian restaurants attached to temples, the Buddhist revival in China does not seem to be having much effect on attitudes or behavior toward the nonhuman world.

To conclude, China's environmental problems today must be understood in the context of a complex legacy. Value systems, national identity, and government legitimacy have remained unstable since the Mao years. Widespread indifference to the public good stems from the betrayal of Maoist exhortations to consider "the people" at all costs. Yet heavily anthropocentric attitudes toward the natural world, coupled with a legacy of decades of repression of intellectuals and disdain for scientific knowledge, hinder environmentally aware policy-makers and citizens who are attempting to effect profound policy and behavior shifts. Until China confronts its uneasy Maoist legacy, it may struggle fruitlessly to achieve a sustainable relationship with the natural world. On the other hand, the country's difficult past offers a window of hope. The crisis of values has created an openness to new ideas and philosophies and a reevaluation of Chinese traditions. This openness – together with industrial pollution's impact on public health, improved scientific education, public awareness campaigns, and publicity over links among floods, deforestation, and land reclamation – has created unprecedented receptivity to environmentalism among the Chinese people. If the human–nature relationship and the relationship among human beings are indeed intimately linked, as I have argued, then renewed concern about the human–nature relationship may also help the Chinese to chart a more just and tolerant approach to relationships in the human world.

NOTES

INTRODUCTION

1. Quoted in *Rand-McNally Illustrated Atlas of China* (New York: Rand-McNally, 1972), frontispiece. No other bibliographic information available.
2. See, for example, the writings of the "deep ecologists," particularly Arne Naess, in George Sessions, ed., *Deep Ecology for the Twenty-first Century* (Boston: Shambhala, 1995) and the influential land ethic movement inspired by Aldo Leopold's *A Sand County Almanac* (New York: Oxford University Press, 1949). For environmentalists belonging to the school of "deep ecology" (also called biocentric or ecocentric ecology), unhealthiness in contemporary human–nature interactions can be traced to a socially constructed gulf that is both destructive to humans (not to speak of nature) and false, and a healthier ethic depends on shifting or dissolving the dividing line between humans and nature. The "deep ecology" movement is based on the effort to shift attitudes so that humans see themselves as included in nature rather than as standing in opposition to it.
3. For a discussion of voluntarism, see Kenneth Lieberthal, *Governing China: From Revolution through Reform* (New York: W.W. Norton, 1995), pp. 63–80. For general background on Mao and Maoism, see Jonathan D. Spence, *Mao Zedong* (New York: Viking, 1999); Philip Short, *Mao: A Life* (New York: Henry Holt, 2000); Li Zhisui, *The Private Life of Chairman Mao: The Memoirs of Mao's Personal Physician,* translated by Tai Hung-chao, with the editorial assistance of Anne F. Thurston (New York: Random House, 1996); and Stuart Schram, *The Thought of Mao Tse-tung* (New York: Cambridge University Press, 1989).
4. See examples in Lester Ross and Mitchell Silk, *Environmental Law and Policy in the People's Republic of China* (New York: Quorum Books, 1987), pp. 13–14.

5. See, for example, Joseph Needham, *Science and Civilisation in China,* vol. 4, part III, *Civil Engineering and Nautics* (New York: Cambridge University Press, 1971), pp. 235–236, for a description of the Daoist–Confucian debate over hydraulics.

6. Peter Perdue's elegant phrase describes environmental degradation in Hunan province. See Peter Perdue, *Exhausting the Earth: State and Peasant in Hunan, 1500–1850* (Cambridge, MA: Council on East Asian Studies, Harvard University, 1987). See also Mark Elvin and Liu Ts'ui-jung, eds., *Sediments of Time: Environment and Society in Chinese History* (New York: Cambridge University Press, 1997) and Robert B. Marks, *Tigers, Rice, Silk, and Silt* (New York: Cambridge University Press, 1997).

7. "The Dykes of the Yangtze River," translated by Mark Elvin and quoted on p. 513 in Mark Elvin, "The *Bell of Poesy:* Thoughts on Poems as Information on Late-imperial Chinese Environmental History," in S.M. Carletti, M. Sacchetti, and P. Santangelo, eds., *Studi in Onore di Lionello Lanciotti* (Napoli: Istituto Universitario Orientale, 1996), Vol. 1 (of 3), pp. 497–523.

8. Robert B. Marks, "Commercialization without Capitalism: Processes of Environmental Change in South China," *Environmental History,* Vol. 1, No. 2 (April 1996), p. 74.

9. See Purdue, *Exhausting,* for a sense of how these problems played out in Ming-Qing China in Hunan province.

10. Zhou Enlai is said to have supported China's early efforts at starting a birth control campaign, seeing it as a protection for women and children and a way of promoting national health and prosperity. See Zongli Tang and Bing Zuo, *Maoism and Chinese Culture* (New York: Nova Science Publishers, 1996), pp. 347–348. Marshal Peng Dehuai's courageous opposition to the Leap at the 1959 Lushan Plenum, and his purge by Mao, are well known.

11. When land was allocated to families in the economic reforms, it was "contracted" to them but still officially belonged to the state. Especially in the first few years after this semiprivatization of land, there was great uncertainty about the terms of use. Many farmers had little confidence in the future and rushed to exploit the land. Although the length of contracts has been extended, there is still officially no right to own land. An active Chinese discussion of the issue promotes the view that one of the main obstacles to sustainable development in China is a collective property system that encourages everyone to exploit resources. In 1984, for example, one scholar argued, "Although we may say that contracting the forests among households will result in their being cut down, leaving no one responsible for the forests will lead everyone to cut them down, which is

far worse" (Zhu Zanping, "Discussing the Internal Motivation to Cultivate Forests in the Collective Forest Areas of South China" (*Nongye jingji wenti,* No. 11 [1984], pp. 36–39), translated in Ross and Silk, *Environmental Law,* p. 194. See also Zheng Yisheng and Qian Yihong, *Shendu youhuan: Dangdai Zhongguo de kechixu fazhan wenti* [Deep Hardships: Problems of Sustainable Development in China] (Beijing: Jinri Zhongguo chubanshe, 1998) for an expression of this view.

12. See Yvonne Guerrier, Nicholas Alexander, Jonathan Chase, and Martin O'Brien, eds., *Values and the Environment: A Social Science Perspective* (New York: John Wiley & Sons, 1995) and, for a typology of environmental values that inform behavior, see Stephen R. Kellert, *The Value of Life: Biological Diversity and Human Society* (Washington, DC: Island Press, 1996). For a cautionary argument about not equating attitudes and behavior, see Ole Bruun and Arne Kalland, "Images of Nature: An Introduction to the Study of Man–Environment Relations in Asia," in Ole Bruun and Arne Kalland, eds., *Asian Perceptions of Nature: A Critical Approach* (Richmond, Surrey: Curzon Press, 1995), pp. 1–24.

13. *Beijing Review,* No. 29 (1982), p. 6, cited in David M. Lampton, "The Implementation Problem in Post-Mao China," in David M. Lampton, ed., *Policy Implementation in Post-Mao China* (Berkeley: University of California Press, 1987), p. 161.

14. Qu Geping and Li Jinchang, *Population and the Environment in China,* translated by Jiang Baozhong and Gu Ran (Boulder, CO: Lynne Rienner Publishers, 1994), p. 149.

15. See, for example, Lieberthal, *Governing China,* p. 282.

16. Richard Louis Edmonds points out that pollution was already serious in the 1950s; an early effort to promote "environmental hygiene" based on the Soviet model foundered with the Great Leap Forward's emphasis on rapid development. See his *Patterns of China's Lost Harmony: A Survey of the Country's Environmental Degradation and Protection* (New York: Routledge, 1994), pp. 228–229. See also, on air and water pollution during the Mao years, Bernard Glaeser, *Environment, Development, Agriculture* (Armonk, NY: M. E. Sharpe, 1995), pp. 87–88, and, on early emphasis on industry, see Lieberthal, *Governing China,* pp. 280–282.

17. See, for example, Vaclav Smil, *China's Environmental Crisis: An Inquiry into the Limits of National Development* (Armonk, NY: M.E. Sharpe, 1993); Mark Hertsgaard, "Our Real China Problem," *Atlantic Monthly,* Vol. 280, No. 5 (November 1997), pp. 97–112; Nicholas Kristof, "Asian Pollution Is Widening Its Deadly Reach," *The New York Times,* November 29, 1997, p. 1 and "Across Asia, A Pollution Disaster Hovers," *The New York Times,* November 28, 1997, p. 1; He Baochuan, *China on the Edge: The Crisis of*

Ecology and Development (San Francisco, CA: China Books and Periodicals, 1991).

18. Some argue that the debate is unwinnable and counterproductive. See, for example, Jeffrey C. Ellis, "On the Search for a Root Cause: Essentialist Tendencies in Environmental Discourse," in William Cronon, ed., *Uncommon Ground: Toward Reinventing Nature* (New York: W.W. Norton, 1995), pp. 256–268.

19. See, for example, Barry Commoner, *The Closing Circle: Nature, Man, and Technology* (New York: Bantam Books, 1972).

20. P. R. Ehrlich and J. P. Holdren, "Impact of Population Growth," in *Science*, Vol. 171 (March 26, 1971), pp. 1212–1217. See also P. R. Ehrlich and A. H. Ehrlich, *The Population Explosion* (New York: Simon and Schuster, 1990).

21. Robert Repetto et al., *Wasting Assets: Natural Resources in the National Income Accounts* (Washington, DC: World Resources Institute, 1989); Herman E. Daly and John B. Cobb, Jr., *For the Common Good: Redirecting the Economy Toward Community, the Environment, and a Sustainable Future* (Boston: Beacon Press, 1989).

22. Donald Worster, *The Wealth of Nature: Environmental History and the Ecological Imagination* (New York: Oxford University Press, 1993).

23. Lynn T. White, Jr., "The Historical Roots of our Ecologic Crisis," *Science*, Vol. 155 (March 10, 1967), pp. 1203–1207. Murray Bookchin argues in, for example, *Ecology of Freedom* (Palo Alto, CA: Cheshire Books, 1982) and *Philosophy of Social Ecology: Essays on Dialectical Naturalism* (Montreal: Black Rose Books, 1990), that inequality among human beings, and the desire to dominate other humans, is the source of the desire to dominate nature. See also Michael Painter and William H. Durham, eds., *The Social Causes of Environmental Destruction in Latin America* (Ann Arbor: University of Michigan Press, 1995) for arguments linking the concentration of land resources in the hands of the Latin American elite and Latin America's status on the periphery of the world economy to environmental degradation, and Piers Blaikie, *The Political Economy of Soil Erosion in Developing Countries* (London: Longman, 1985), for a statement of political ecology.

24. James C. Scott, *Weapons of the Weak: Everyday Forms of Peasant Resistance* (New Haven: Yale University Press, 1985).

25. Marc Blecher and Vivienne Shue, *Tethered Deer: Government and Economy in a Chinese County* (Stanford, CA: Stanford University Press, 1996). The phrase "Communist neo-traditionalism" has been used to describe patterns of clientelism and patronage, alliances, and networks in a more nuanced understanding of Mao-era political life. See Andrew G. Walder, *Communist Neo-traditionalism: Work and Authority in Chinese Industry*

(Berkeley: University of California Press, 1986). See also Edward Friedman, Paul Pickowicz, and Mark Selden, with Kay Ann Johnson, *Chinese Village, Socialist State* (New Haven: Yale University Press, 1991), who argue that to see China as totalitarian "obscures how local power "spread, entrenched itself, and defended parochial interests," p. 268.

26. James C. Scott, *Seeing Like a State: How Certain Schemes to Improve the Human Condition Have Failed* (New Haven: Yale University Press, 1998), pp. 4–5.

27. See, for example, Worster, *Wealth of Nature*. On environmental destruction in the Soviet Union, by contrast, see Douglas R. Weiner, *Models of Nature: Ecology, Conservation, and Cultural Revolution in Soviet Russia* (Bloomington: Indiana University Press, 1988). There is also an argument that socialism as it has been thus far practiced does not reflect socialism's potential for promoting environmentally sustainable practices. See, for example, Natalia Mirovitskaya and Marvin S. Soroos, "Socialism and the Tragedy of the Commons: Reflections on Environmental Practice in the Soviet Union and Russia," *Journal of Environment and Development,* Vol. 4, No. 1 (Winter 1995), pp. 77–110.

28. Garrett Hardin, "The Tragedy of the Commons" (*Science,* December 13, 1968), makes the famous argument that overexploitation becomes rational when resource ownership is not established.

29. Some environmental historians implicitly or explicitly criticize the capitalist system and raise the possibility that a socialist solution might resolve problems with land management, the "tragedy of the commons," and short-sighted greed. On a related tack, several influential environmentalists have warned that the very premises on which Western societies are built are inadequate to meet global environmental challenges. Robert Heilbroner, for example, has argued that the collapse of Soviet-style command economies and the triumph of free market economies will not delay the coming confrontation with global environmental limits. See *An Inquiry into the Human Prospect, Updated and Reconsidered for the Nineteen Nineties,* 2nd rvsd. ed. (New York: W.W. Norton, 1996). William Ophuls and A. Stephen Boyan, Jr. claim that "liberal democracy as we know it ... is doomed." See their *Ecology and the Politics of Scarcity Revisited: The Unraveling of the American Dream* (San Francisco, CA: W.H. Freeman, 1992), p. 3. In their view, the Enlightenment ideology of modernity and the core belief in the value of individualism are simply not viable in an age of ecological scarcity. These views contrast with those of mainstream Western development economists who point to economic growth and industrialization as a source of short-term degradation only. As growth promotes the capitalization of wealth, funds become available for cleanup, and degradation is reversed. See, for example, Gene Grossman and Alan Krueger, "Economic Growth and the

Environment," *Quarterly Journal of Economics* (May 1995), pp. 353–377, for a typical statement of this view. Developing countries, including China under "market socialism," have used this argument to resist environmental measures that they see as intended to hold them back from the levels of development enjoyed in the industrialized North.

CHAPTER ONE

1. *Bitter Love* is the name of a film script by the writer Bai Hua, much criticized in 1981 and later made into a film in Taiwan. The theme was expressed by a question mark that a dying artist's footprints left in the snow: "You love the motherland, but does the motherland love you?" See Bai Hua and Peng Ning, "Kulian" [Bitter Love], *Shiyue* (March 1979), pp. 140–171, 248.

2. T. R. Malthus, *An Essay on the Principle of Population* (New York: Cambridge University Press, 1993). In his introduction, Donald Winch provides another reason for Malthus' unpopularity with socialist thinkers as well: "He opposed all schemes based on common property, communal provision, and compulsory social insurance that held out a promise of equal security and plenty for all, regardless of merit or effort." See Donald Winch, "Introduction," p. xix.

3. *Marx and Engels on the Population Bomb: Selections from the Writings of Marx and Engels Dealing with the Theories of Thomas Robert Malthus,* edited by Ronald L. Meek and translated by Dorothea L. Meek and Ronald L. Meek (London: Ramparts Press, 1953).

4. Mao Zedong, *Mao Zedong xuanji* [Selected Works of Mao Zedong], Vol. 4 (Beijing: Renmin chubanshe, 1967), p. 1400.

5. See Zhang Ying, ed., *Zhou Enlai yu wenhua mingren* [Zhou Enlai and Famous Cultural People] (Nanjing: Jiangsu jiaoyu chubanshe, 1998), pp. 134–147.

6. I have retained the romanized Chinese to avoid confusion with the Three Gorges Dam.

7. Shang Wei, "A Lamentation for the Yellow River: The Three Gate Gorge Dam *(Sanmenxia),*" in Dai Qing, *The River Dragon Has Come! The Three Gorges Dam and the Fate of China's Yangtze River and Its People* (Armonk, NY: M. E. Sharpe, 1998), p. 155.

8. Huang Wanli is less famous in China than Ma Yinchu, but those who know his story hold him in high esteem, and many mention the two men in the same breath as examples of people whose lost contribution has cost China dearly.

9. A Chinese woman wrote to me, for example, about her father's uncle, an economist: "I remember that he wept when Ma was criticized, and

repeated Ma's theories as correct. He suffered for his whole life, too, for being loyal to Ma."

10. The precise figure is impossible to determine, as some victims of the movement, like Ma Yinchu, were never formally given "rightist" labels, while others were labeled "right opportunists" or members of "counterrevolutionary cliques" in secondary movements. Frederick C. Teiwes cites a figure of 550,000; see Frederick C. Teiwes, "The Establishment and Consolidation of the New Regime, 1949–1957," in Roderick MacFarquhar, ed., *The Politics of China, 1949–1989* (New York: Cambridge University Press, 1993), p. 82. Merle Goldman states that between 400,000 and 700,000 lost their positions and were sent to the countryside, reflecting a quota of 5 percent of the workers in all work units. See Merle Goldman, "The Party and the Intellectuals," in Roderick MacFarquhar and John King Fairbank, eds., *The Cambridge History of China,* Vol. 14: *The People's Republic, Part I: The Emergence of Revolutionary China, 1949–1965* (New York: Cambridge University Press, 1987), p. 257. Maurice Meisner states that by the end of the purges in 1958, a million Party members had been "expelled, put on probation, or reprimanded." See Maurice Meisner, *Mao's China and After: A History of the People's Republic,* 3rd ed. (New York: Free Press, 1999), p. 188.

11. Suzanne Pepper, *Civil War in China: The Political Struggle, 1945–1949* (Berkeley: University of California Press, 1978), esp. pp. 132–198 on disillusionment with the Guomindang.

12. Marxist theory made class distinctions paramount. When intellectuals were reclassified as "mental workers" after the death of Mao, it meant sudden elevation in status from the depths to the heights.

13. See, for example, Immanuel C. Y. Hsu, *The Rise of Modern China,* 5th ed. (New York: Oxford University Press, 1995), p. 647.

14. For details, see Laurence A. Schneider, "Learning from Russia: Lysenkoism and the Fate of Genetics in China, 1950–1986," in Denis Fred Simon and Merle Goldman, eds., *Science and Technology in Post-Mao China* (Cambridge, MA: Council on East Asian Studies, Harvard University, 1989), pp. 45–68.

15. Ibid., pp. 53–54; Zhang Wenhe and Li Yan, eds., *Kouhao yu Zhongguo* [Slogans and China] (Beijing: Zhonggong dangshi chubanshe, 1998), pp. 104–105.

16. Zhang and Li, *Slogans,* p. 106.

17. See, for example, Hualing Nieh, editor and co-translator, *Literature of the Hundred Flowers. Vol I: Criticism and Polemics,* and *Vol. II: Poetry and Fiction* (New York: Columbia University Press, 1981).

18. Liu Binyan, *A Higher Kind of Loyalty: A Memoir by China's Foremost Journalist,* translated by Zhu Hong (New York: Pantheon, 1990), pp. 69–91.

19. Qu Geping and Li Jinchang, *Population and the Environment in China,* translated by Jiang Baozhong and Gu Ran (Boulder, CO: Lynne Rienner Publishers, 1994), p. 7.

20. Zhang Chunyuan, "Xu" [Introduction], in Ma Yinchu, *Xin renkoulun* [New Demography] (Changchun: Jilin renmin chubanshe, 1997), p. 9.

21. Dai Qing, *Yangtze! Yangtze!* (Toronto: Earthscan Publications, 1994), p. 225. The first quotation refers to the slogan, *Ren Duo, Liliang Da, Reqi Gao,* translated in this study as "With Many People, Strength is Great, and Enthusiasm is High."

22. Zhang Chunyuan, "'Xin renkou lun' xin zai shenme difang?" [What Is New about 'New Demography'?], in Ma Yinchu, *Xin renkoulun,* p. 67.

23. *Jingji yanjiu,* November 1958 and *Xin jianshe,* December 1956, quoted in Zhang Chunyuan, ibid., p. 67.

24. Li Yong, ed., *"Wenhua dageming' zhong' de mingren zhi you"* [The Troubles of Famous People during the Cultural Revolution] (Beijing: Zhongyang minzu xueyuan chubanshe, 1994), p. 328.

25. Ibid.

26. H. Yuan Tien, *China's Strategic Demographic Initiative* (New York: Praeger, 1991), pp. 20–21.

27. Ibid., pp. 8–12. The institution of registration requirements after 1723 may also have contributed to an apparent increase.

28. Tien, *Demographic Initiative,* p. 9. Qu and Li, *Population and Environment,* pp. 173–174.

29. A former Communist Youth League instructor once told me he thought Mao's views on population were shaped by the loss of three of his sons – he effectively lost all three of his sons by his first wife, Yang Kaihui, as one disappeared in Shanghai, one suffered permanent brain damage in a police beating, and one died in the Korean War.

30. "The Bankruptcy of the Idealist Conception of History," *Selected Works of Mao Tse-tung,* Vol. 4 (Beijing: Foreign Languages Press, 1967), p. 453.

31. "Intraparty Correspondence, March 15, 1959, at Wuchang," in *Miscellany of Mao Tse-tung Thought (1949–1968). Part I* (Arlington, VA: Joint Publications Research Service, February 1974) [hereafter cited as JPRS], p. 219. Mao goes on to acknowledge that too many children are no good either.

32. Li Zhisui, *The Private Life of Chairman Mao: The Memoirs of Mao's Personal Physician,* translated by Tai Hung-chao, with the editorial assistance of Anne F. Thurston (New York: Random House, 1996), p. 125.

33. *Khrushchev Remembers: The Last Testament,* translated and edited by Strobe Talbott (Boston: Little, Brown, 1974), p. 255.

34. Li Zhisui, *Private Life,* p. 125.

35. Liu Binyan, *Loyalty,* p. 38.

36. Qu and Li, *Population and Environment,* pp. 174–175. Vaclav Smil estimates that in 1949 there were 540 million on the mainland, with birthrates at six children per family in the 1950s and 1960s. Vaclau Smil, *China's Environmental Crisis: An Inquiry into the Limits of National Development* (Armonk, NY: M.E. Sharpe, 1993).

37. Tien, *Demographic Initiative,* p. 21.

38. Qu and Li, *Population and Environment,* pp. 174–175.

39. I am indebted to geographer Richard Louis Edmonds for this insight and figure.

40. Tien, *Demographic Initiative,* p. 27.

41. Zongli Tang and Bing Zuo, *Maoism and Chinese Culture* (New York: Nova Science Publishers, 1996), p. 348.

42. Judith Banister, *China's Changing Population* (Stanford, CA: Stanford University Press, 1987), pp. 148–149.

43. Quoted in Tien, *Demographic Initiative,* p. 25.

44. Mao Zedong, "Speech at the Conference of Heads of Delegations to the Second Session of the 8th Party Congress (18 May 1958)," JPRS, p. 123.

45. Banister, *Changing Population,* p. 149.

46. Ibid., p. 150.

47. Mao Zedong, "Some Interjections at a Briefing of the State Planning Commission Leading Group (11 May 1964)," JPRS, p. 349.

48. Banister, *Changing Population,* p. 150.

49. Smil, *China's Environmental Crisis,* p. 19.

50. Ibid., p. 14.

51. Tien, *Demographic Initiative,* p. 30.

52. Unless otherwise stated, the details of Ma's life are drawn from Li Yong, *Troubles,* pp. 323–341; Tian Xueyuan, ed., *Ma Yinchu renkou wenji* [Ma Yinchu's Essays on Population] (Hangzhou: Zhejiang renmin chubanshe, 1997); Yang Jianye, *Ma Yinchu* (Hebei: Huashan wenyi chubanshe, 1997); Shengxian Zhengxie and Wenshi Ziliao Weiyuanhui, eds., *Ma Yinchu zai guxiang* [Ma Yinchu in his Homeland] (Hangzhou: Hangzhou daxue chubanshe, 1995). The best English-language account of Ma's life remains that of Kenneth R. Walker, "A Chinese Discussion of Planning for Balanced Growth: A Summary of the Views of Ma Yinchu and his Critics," in Robert Ash, ed., *Agricultural Development in China, 1949–1989: The Collected Papers of Kenneth R. Walker (1931–1989)* (New York: Oxford University Press, 1998), pp. 333–334. See also Tang and Zuo, *Maoism,* pp. 343–362.

53. Xie Mian, *Yongyuan de xiaoyuan* [The Eternal Campus] (Beijing: Beijing daxue chubanshe, 1997), p. 37.

54. Quoted in Zhang and Li, *Slogans,* p. 120.
55. Quoted in Tien, *Demographic Initiative,* p. 24. See also Walker, "A Chinese Discussion," p. 335.
56. Zhang Chunyuan, "What Is New?" pp. 71, 65.
57. Li Yong, *Troubles,* p. 329.
58. Walker, "A Chinese Discussion," p. 347.
59. Zhang Chunyuan, "Introduction" p. 6.
60. Winch, "Introduction," p. xiv.
61. Quoted in Zhang Chunyuan, "Introduction," p. 78.
62. Quoted in Walker, "A Chinese Discussion," p. 350.
63. Zhang Chunyuan, "What Is New?" p. 68.
64. You Yuwen, "Ma Yinchu and His Theory of Population," *China Reconstructs,* December 1979, pp. 28–30.
65. Li Yong, *Troubles,* p. 329.
66. Ibid., p. 330.
67. Walker, "A Chinese Discussion," p. 353. Liu may have been following Mao, who complained that Ma focused on the mouth rather than the hands. This view has its modern exponent in the work of Julian Simon, for whom people are "the ultimate resource." See Julian Simon, *The Ultimate Resource* (Princeton, NJ: Princeton University Press, 1986) and *The Ultimate Resource 2* (Princeton, NJ: Princeton University Press, 1996).
68. Li Yong, *Troubles,* p. 330.
69. Quoted in Zhang Chunyuan, "Introduction," p. 7.
70. Li Yong, *Troubles,* p. 331.
71. Ibid., p. 332.
72. Quoted in Zhang Chunyuan, "Introduction," p. 6
73. Quoted in Zhang Chunyuan, "What is New?" p. 80.
74. Malthus added the "preventive check" of moral restraint, which affected birth rates, to his 1803 *Essay on Population* after critics berated him for including only the "positive checks" of vice and misery, which affected death rates, in the first essay published in 1798. Winch, "Introduction," pp. 20, 36.
75. Zhang Chunyuan, "What Is New?" p. 81.
76. Li Yong, *Troubles,* pp. 330–336; Xie Mian, *Eternal Campus,* p. 40.
77. Tian Xueyuan, ed., *Ma Yinchu's Collected Essays,* p. 143.
78. For example, Shengzhou Youeryuan Renkou yu Huanjing Jiaoyu Keyan Xiaozu, ed., *Youeryuan renkou yu huanjing jiaoyu huodong zhinan* [Primary School Population and Environment Education Activities] (Zhejiang: Zhejiang sheng, Shengzhoushi jiaoyu ju, 1996).
79. Zhang Chunyuan, "What Is New?" p. 70.

80. Judith Banister argues, for example, that had the government encouraged fertility control and provided contraceptives throughout the country beginning in the 1950s, fertility decline could have been gradual and noncompulsory. Judith Banister, "Population, Public Health and the Environment in China," *China Quarterly,* No. 156 (December 1998), p. 988.

81. Li Yong, *Troubles,* p. 328.

82. Qu and Li, *Population and Environment,* p. 174.

83. Yuan Weishi, "Why Did the Chinese Environment Get So Badly Messed Up?" *Nanfang zhoumo* [Southern Weekend], February 25, 2000, p. 13. Translated by David Cowhig.

84. Karl Wittfogel, *Oriental Despotism: A Comparative Study of Total Power* (New Haven: Yale University Press, 1957).

85. Sun Yat-sen, *The International Development of China* (New York: G.P. Putnam's Sons, 1929). For an entertaining look at Sun's plans, see Simon Winchester, *The River at the Centre of the World: A Journey up the Yangtze, and Back in Chinese Time* (London: Penguin Books, 1996), p. 225.

86. Rhoads Murphey argues that it is *the* distinctive characteristic. See Rhoads Murphey, "Man and Nature in China," *Modern Asian Studies,* Vol. 1, No. 4 (1967), pp. 313–333, especially pp. 313–314.

87. Shang Wei, "Lamentation," p. 143.

88. Smil, *China's Environmental Crisis,* pp. 44, 47; S. D. Richardson, *Forests and Forestry in China* (Washington, DC: Island Press, 1990), p. 8.

89. Shang Wei, "Lamentation," p. 170.

90. See Joseph Needham, *Science and Civilisation in China,* vol. 4, part III, *Civil Engineering and Nautics* (New York: Cambridge University Press, 1971), pp. 235–236. Similar debates over dam height, reservoir level, siltation issues, and costs were underway at the same time over the proposed Three Gorges Dam on the Yangzi. For a detailed discussion of this parallel debate, which resulted in the Three Gorges Dam being postponed until the contemporary era, see Kenneth Lieberthal and Michel Oksenberg, *Policy Making in China: Leaders, Structures, and Processes* (Princeton, NJ: Princeton University Press, 1988), pp. 269–338.

91. Shang Wei, "Lamentation," p. 144.

92. Li Zhisui, *Private Life,* p. 122.

93. Shang Wei, "Lamentation," pp. 143–153.

94. Ibid., pp. 154–155.

95. Ibid., p. 150.

96. Dai Qing, *Yangtze! Yangtze!,* p. 163.

97. Shang Wei, "Lamentation," p. 151.

98. Ibid., pp. 151, 153.

99. Huang Wanli, "Zhihe yonghuai" [Feelings on River Management], mimeographed document.

100. E Chun, "Gan dui 'shangdi' shuo bu de ren" [The Person Who Dared Say No to "God"], *Jilinsheng wenyi bao,* 1997 (month/day n.a.), p. 23.

101. See also Mao Zedong, "Remarks at the Spring Festival, 13 February 1964," in Stuart Schram, ed., *Chairman Mao Talks to the People: Talks and Letters: 1956–1971* (New York: Pantheon, 1974), p. 201.

102. For a poetic and moving account of the wasted lives of intellectuals in such camps, see Yang Jiang, *Six Chapters from My Life "Downunder"* (Seattle: University of Washington Press, 1983).

103. Shi Weimin, "Ji shi Zhengxie weiyuan Huang Wanli" [A Remembrance of City Consultative Committee Member Huang Wanli], *Beijing zhengxie,* Vol. 6 (December 1991), p. 17.

104. See Liu Changmin, "Environmental Issues and the South-North Water Transfer Scheme," *China Quarterly,* No. 156 (December 1998), pp. 899–910.

105. Dai Qing, *Yangtze! Yangtze!,* pp. 167–168.

106. This account of the tribulations of Yellow River relocatees is drawn from Leng Meng, "Battle of Sanmenxia: Population Relocation During the Three Gate Gorge Hydropower Project," translated by Ming Yi, *Chinese Sociology and Anthropology,* Vol. 31, No. 3 (Spring 1999). See also Jing Jun, *The Temple of Memories: History, Power and Morality in a Chinese Village* (Stanford, CA: Stanford University Press, 1998); Dai Qing, *The River Dragon Has Come!* for additional information on relocations for big dams.

107. Quoted in Leng Meng, "The Battle of Sanmenxia," p. 37.

108. See, for example, William K. Stevens, "Will Dam Busting Save Salmon? Maybe Not," *The New York Times,* October 5, 1999, p. D1, and John McPhee, "Farewell to the Nineteenth Century: The Breeching of the Edwards Dam," *The New Yorker,* September 27, 1999, pp. 44–53.

109. Leng Meng, "Battle of Sanmenxia," p. 11; Shang Wei, "Lamentation," p. 154; Vaclav Smil, *The Bad Earth: Environmental Degradation in China* (Armonk, NY: M.E. Sharpe, 1984), pp. 45–46.

110. Cao Yingwang, *Zhou Enlai yu shishui,* cited in Shang Wei, "Lamentation," p. 155.

111. Smil, *Bad Earth,* p. 46; Leng Meng, "Battle of Sanmenxia," p. 12.

112. Rena Singer, "China's Yellow River, Now a Trickle, Poses New Threat," *Philadelphia Inquirer,* February 1, 1999; Leng Meng, "Battle of Sanmenxia," p. 12.

113. Ma Fuhai, "Zai jinian Sanmenxia shuili shuniu gongcheng jianshe sanshi-nian dahuishang de jianghua" [Speech at the Meeting Commemorating the

Construction of the Three Gate Gorge Project], quoted in Shang Wei, "Lamentation," p. 156.

114. Ibid., pp. 30–31.

115. Yi Si, "The World's Most Catastrophic Dam Failures: The August 1975 Collapse of the Banqiao and Shimantan Dams," in Dai Qing, *River Dragon*, p. 25; Human Rights Watch/Asia, *The Three Gorges Dam in China: Forced Resettlement, Suppression of Dissent and Labor Rights Concerns* (New York: Human Rights Watch, February 1995), especially pp. 497–523.

116. Shui Fu, "A Profile of Dams in China," in Dai Qing, *River Dragon*, pp. 22–23. See also Jean-Luc Domenach, *The Origins of the Great Leap Forward: The Case of One Province*, translated by A.M. Berrett (Boulder, CO: Westview Press, 1995), for discussion of dams in Henan province.

117. Quoted in Shui Fu, "Profile," p. 23.

118. World Bank, "China: Xiaolangdi Resettlement Project," Report No. 12527-CHA, 1993, p. 3.

119. Jiang Zemin, "Zai Sanxia gongcheng da jiang zhailiu yishi shang de jianghua" [Speech at the Ceremony for Diverting the Great River at the Three Gorges Construction Site], *Renmin ribao*, November 9, 1997.

120. See, for example, Zhuan Fang, [no title available], *Beijing zhengxie*, December 6, 1991, p. 17. In conversations, other Chinese have also drawn the comparison.

CHAPTER TWO

1. Domenach comments "That a reasonable and rather skeptical people allowed itself to be drawn into one of the wildest adventures seen in this century may be because it had no choice. Protest had been crushed; people were being shot in sports arenas; one had to keep one's head down." Jean-Luc Domenach, *The Origins of the Great Leap Forward: The Case of One Chinese Province*, translated by A. M. Berrett (Boulder, CO: Westview Press, 1995), p. 129. See Edward Friedman, Paul G. Pickowicz, and Mark Selden, with Kay Ann Johnson, *Chinese Village, Socialist State* (New Haven: Yale University Press, 1991), p. 223, for an example of political persecution of a Leap opponent in Hebei. An alternative view is that the Chinese were understandably eager to develop and that the Leap was intensely popular, at least at first. See Frederick C. Teiwes, with Warren Sun, "The Politics of an 'Un-Maoist' Interlude: The Case of Opposing Rash Advance, 1956–1957," in Timothy Cheek and Tony Saich, eds., *New Perspectives on State Socialism in China* (Armonk, NY: M. E. Sharpe, 1997), pp. 151–190.

2. Shui Fu, "A Profile of Dams in China," in Dai Qing, *The River Dragon Has Come! The Three Gorges Dam and the Fate of China's Yangtze River and Its People* (Armonk, NY: M. E. Sharpe, 1998), p. 22.

3. Kenneth Lieberthal, *Governing China: From Revolution through Reform* (New York: W. W. Norton, 1995), pp. 63–64.

4. For a discussion of this slogan, see Zhang Wenhe and Li Yan, eds., *Kouhao yu Zhongguo* [Slogans and China] (Beijing: Zhonggong dangshi chubanshe, 1998), p. 244.

5. I am grateful to Dai Qing for her recollection of this Great Leap Forward song. See also Anna Louise Strong, *The Rise of the Chinese People's Communes* (Beijing: New World Press, 1959), frontispiece.

6. Mao Zedong, "Speeches at the Second Session of the Eighth Party Congress (8–23 May 1958)," The First Speech (8 May 1958), in Joint Publications Research Service, *Miscellany of Mao Zedong Thought (1949–1968). Part I* (Arlington, VA: 1974) (hereafter cited as JPRS), p. 96.

7. "Talks with Directors of Various Cooperative Areas," (30 November 1958), JPRS, p. 136.

8. "Critique of Stalin's 'Economic Problems of Socialism in the Soviet Union' 1959 (?)" [sic], JPRS, p. 192.

9. Simon Winchester, *The River at the Centre of the World: A Journey Up the Yantgze, and Back in Chinese Time* (London: Viking Press, 1997), p. 199.

10. Jasper Becker, *Hungry Ghosts: Mao's Secret Famine* (New York: Free Press, 1996), p. 308.

11. Li Rui, "'Da Yuejin' shibai de jiaoxun hezai?" in *Li Rui lunshuo wenxuan* [Selections from Li Rui's Writings and Talks] (Beijing: Zhongguo shehui kexue chubanshe, 1998), pp. 217 and 233.

12. Domenach, *Origins,* p. 148.

13. Jurgen Domes, *Socialism in the Chinese Countryside: Rural Societal Policies in the People's Republic of China, 1949–1979,* translated by Margitta Wendling (London: C. Hurst & Co., 1980), pp. 26–27.

14. Roderick MacFarquhar, Timothy Cheek, and Eugene Wu, eds., *The Secret Speeches of Chairman Mao: From the Hundred Flowers to the Great Leap Forward* (Cambridge, MA: Council on East Asian Studies, Harvard University, 1989), p. 427.

15. Domenach, *Origins,* p. 143.

16. Becker, *Hungry Ghosts,* p. 78.

17. Cited on p. 111 in Mou Mo and Cai Wenmei, "Resettlement in the Xin'an River Power Station Project," in Dai Qing, *River Dragon,* pp. 104–123. Mou and Cai argue, p. 106, that the many negative impacts of the power station include inundation of fertile land, submersion of antiquities, and enduring poverty for the local county.

Notes

18. Friedman et al., *Chinese Village*, p. 219. Note that if there is no common humanity, then it is even less likely that there can be commonality between humans and nature, as in the Daoist tradition.

19. Teiwes, with Sun, "Politics of an 'Un-Maoist' Interlude," esp. pp. 173 and 178.

20. Urgency was characteristic throughout the Mao years. The rapid transformation of individual consciousness, society, and nature was also a strong emphasis during the Cultural Revolution, when Mao returned to the peak of his power and his vision of continuing revolution held sway.

21. Other common translations include "adventurism," "bold advances," and Roderick MacFarquhar's "reckless advance," in *The Origins of the Cultural Revolution 2: The Great Leap Forward, 1958–1960* (London: Oxford University Press, 1983). I prefer the more informal "rushing ahead," which has the connotation of heedlessness.

22. The literature on *yundong* is extensive. See, for example, Gordon Bennett, "*Yundong:* Mass Campaigns in Chinese Communist Leadership" (Berkeley, CA: Center for Chinese Studies, China Research Monograph No. 12, 1976); Lester Ross, *Environmental Policy in China* (Bloomington: Indiana University Press, 1988), pp. 104–107; Lieberthal, *Governing China*, p. 66; Ezra Vogel, *Canton under Communism: Programs and Policies in a Provincial Capital, 1949–1968* (Cambridge, MA: Harvard University Press, 1969), pp. 167–168; and Lynn T. White III, *Policies of Chaos: The Organizational Causes of Violence in China's Cultural Revolution* (Princeton, NJ: Princeton University Press, 1989), p. 18.

23. Michael Schoenhals, "Political Movements, Change, and Stability: The Chinese Communist Party in Power," *China Quarterly*, No. 159 (September 1999), p. 597.

24. Teiwes and Sun argue that the two-line struggle is basically a Cultural Revolution interpretation that influenced Western analysts and that, rather, Mao was preoccupied with international matters during the *fanmaojin* period but never lost his position at the center of power. See Teiwes, with Sun, "Politics of an 'Un-Maoist' Interlude," p. 313.

25. For background concerning intra-Party disagreements in the pre-Leap period, see ibid. See also MacFarquhar, *Origins 2;* David Bachman, *Bureaucracy, Economy, and Leadership in China: The Institutional Origins of the Great Leap Forward* (New York: Cambridge University Press, 1991); and Kenneth Lieberthal, "The Great Leap Forward and the Split in the Yenan Leadership," in Roderick MacFarquhar and John King Fairbank, eds., *The Cambridge History of China*, Vol. 14: *The People's Republic, Part 1: The Emergence of Revolutionary China, 1949–1965,* (New York: Cambridge University Press, 1987), pp. 293–359.

26. Li Rui, "'Da Yuejin' shibai de jiaoxun hezai?" p. 212.

27. Mao once complained that the "Central Line" slogans, "'Go all out, aim high, and achieve greater, faster, better, and more economical results' are not easily understood by foreigners. They don't seem to make sense, as there are no subjects... The 600 million people are the subject." "Fourth Speech, 23 May 1958," JPRS, p. 117.

28. It built on Zhou Enlai's 1955–56 mention of the first three elements. Li Fuchun is said to have added the *sheng* element. See Li Rui, "'Da Yuejin' shibai de jiaoxun hezai?" p. 212.

29. For an excellent discussion of the language of speed, see Michael Schoenhals, *Saltationist Socialism: Mao Zedong and the Great Leap Forward 1958* (doctoral dissertation, University of Stockholm, 1987), Skrifter utgivna av Föreningen for Orientaliska Studier, 19, pp. 5–22 and *passim*.

30. Domenach, *Origins*, p. 143.

31. See Teiwes, with Sun, "The Politics of an 'Un-Maoist' Interlude," *passim*, for a discussion of Zhou Enlai's prominent role in the *fanmaojin* episode, which, the authors argue, was the last time he went out on a limb to oppose Mao.

32. "Talks at the Nan-ning Conference," 13 January 1958, in JPRS, p. 83. The translation uses "bold advances" rather than "rushing ahead."

33. Schoenhals, *Saltationist Socialism*, p. 6.

34. Zhang and Li, *Slogans*, p.183.

35. Teiwes, with Sun, "Politics of an 'Un-Maoist' Interlude," p. 174.

36. "Second Speech, 17 May 1958," JPRS, p. 106.

37. "Speech at the Conference of Heads of Delegations to the Second Session of the Eighth Party Congress," 18 May 1958, JPRS, p. 123.

38. Dali Yang, *Calamity and Reform in China: State, Rural Society, and Institutional Change Since the Great Leap Famine* (Stanford, CA: Stanford University Press, 1996), p. 34. See also MacFarquhar, *Origins 2*, pp. 91–116, for a description of the euphoric "high tide" of the Leap in October–November 1958.

39. Li Rui, "'Da Yuejin' shibai de jiaoxun hezai?" p. 224. Interestingly, Li Rui points out on p. 223 that Ma Yinchu weighed in on the question of population and speed, writing in one of his last published works, "If we want speed, then having many people is a burden."

40. Mao continued these remarks with a military metaphor: "The two 'encirclement and suppression' campaigns in Kiangsu [sic] involved five battles in two sleepless weeks, but it was only a short-term surprise attack. We must not push too hard" ("Speech at the Conference of Heads of Delegations to the Second Session of the Eighth Party Congress," 18 May 1958, JPRS, p. 122). Another issue was the propriety of achieving socialism before the Soviet

Union. "Even if it is possible for us to be the first, we should not do so. The October Revolution was Lenin's cause. Are we not emulating Lenin? So, what's the need of hurrying?... If we rush, we may possibly commit errors in international matters" ("Speech at the Sixth Plenum of the Eighth Central Committee," 19 December 1958, JPRS, p. 145).

41. "Speech at the Sixth Plenum of the Eighth Central Committee," 19 December 1958, JPRS, pp. 141–142.

42. See Penny Kane, *Famine in China, 1959–61: Demographic and Social Implications* (New York: St. Martin's Press, 1988); and Dali Yang, "Surviving the Great Leap Famine: The Struggle over Rural Policy, 1958–1962," in Cheek and Saich, eds., *New Perspectives,* pp. 262–302.

43. Becker, *Hungry Ghosts* pp. 64, 74–75, and 102; U.S. Embassy-Beijing, "Grassland Degradation in Tibetan Regions of China – Possible Recovery Strategies" (September 1996), p. 2.

44. Friedman et al., *Chinese Village,* p. 221.

45. A recent outspoken book points to the waste arising from a collective system in which no one exercises property rights as a major obstacle to sustainable development. See Zheng Yisheng and Qian Yihong, *Shenju youhuan: Dangdai Zhongguo de kechixu fazhan wenti* [Deep Hardships: Problems of Sustainable Development in China] (Beijing: Jinri Zhongguo chubanshe, 1998). An alternative perspective on the "tragedy of the commons" is expressed by Pamela Leonard in "The Political Landscape of a Sichuan Village" (unpublished doctoral dissertation, Cambridge University, 1994), where the argument is made that good governance as well as clear private property rights are fundamental to sustainability. See especially pp. 205–206.

46. An innovation of Chayashan, the first People's Commune, as a technique for boosting yields, wiping away illiteracy, and achieving communization through 24-hour mass efforts. See a good description of this in Becker, *Hungry Ghosts,* pp. 121–122.

47. See Li Choh-ming, *The Statistical System of Communist China* (Berkeley: University of California Press, 1962), especially pp. 83–108, "The Statistical Fiasco of 1958."

48. See MacFarquhar et al., *Secret Speeches,* p. 450, and Friedman et al., *Chinese Village,* p. 222.

49. Becker, *Hungry Ghosts,* p. 72.

50. Friedman et al., *Chinese Village,* p. 229.

51. Becker, *Hungry Ghosts,* pp. 67 and 73. See also p. 163 for stories about 10,000-*jin* fields.

52. Wang Dongfu, "1958 nian de Wenjiang diwei fushuji" [Wenjiang's District Vice-Party Secretary of 1958], *Chengdu zhoumo,* May 13, 2000.

53. Zhang and Li, *Slogans,* p. 238.

54. Becker, *Hungry Ghosts,* pp. 69–70.

55. See Jim Harkness, "Forestry and Conservation of Biodiversity in China," *China Quarterly,* No. 156 (December 1998), p. 914. In areas where coal was available, the industrial activity led, of course, to an increase in air pollution and, presumably, intensified extraction of coal from earth-damaging small mines.

56. Qin Chaoyang, *Village Sketches,* quoted in Becker, *Hungry Ghosts,* p. 60, no citation information given.

57. Zhang and Li, *Slogans,* pp. 206–207; Friedman et al., *Chinese Village,* p. 227.

58. Zhang Yimou, Director, *Huozhe* [To Live], Shanghai Film Studios, 1994.

59. Qu Geping and Li Jinchang, *Population and the Environmnet in China,* translated by Jiang Baozhong and Gu Ran (Boulder, CO: Lynne Rienner Publishers, 1994), p. 57; David M. Lampton, ed., *Policy Implementation in Post-Mao China* (Berkeley: University of California Press, 1987); p. 163; He Bochuan, *China on the Edge: The Crisis of Ecology and Development* (San Francisco, CA: China Books and Periodicals, 1991), pp. 28–29.

60. S. D. Richardson, *Forests and Forestry in China* (Washington, DC: Island Press, 1990), p. 89.

61. Ibid., p. 89.

62. Ibid., pp. 96–97.

63. Wang Hongchang, "Deforestation and Dessication in China: A Preliminary Study," in *An Assessment of the Economic Losses Resulting from Various Forms of Environmental Degradation in China.* Occasional Papers of the Project in Environmental Scarcities, State Capacity, and Civil Violence. (Cambridge, MA: American Academy of Arts and Sciences and the University of Toronto, 1997), p. 11.

64. See, for example, Leonard, "Political Landscape," p. 197.

65. See also ibid., p. 198, for other stories of opposition to the cutting.

66. Friedman et al., *Chinese Village,* p. 234.

67. "Speech at the Sixth Plenum of the Eighth Central Committee," 19 December 1958, JPRS, p. 147.

68. Li Zhisui, *The Private Life of Chairman Mao: The Memoirs of Mao's Personal Physician,* translated by Tai Hung Chao, with editorial assistance of Anne F. Thurston (New York: Random House, 1996), p. 313.

69. See, for example, He Qingshi speech in *Hongqi,* May 13, 1957, "The Workers Must Become Masters of Culture," quoted in Zhang and Li, *Slogans,* pp. 188–189.

70. Mass attacks on "pests" were not Mao-era inventions. Indeed, early twentieth-century Christian missionaries were known to encourage simi-

lar campaigns. See Shirley Garret, *Social Reformers in Urban China: The Chinese Y.M.C.A., 1895–1926* (Cambridge, MA: Harvard University Press, 1970). However, Maoist implementation and coordination exceeded prior efforts and spectacularly misjudged the ecosystem.

71. "Speech at the Conference of Heads of Delegations," JPRS, p. 123.

72. I am indebted to David Barrett for this information.

73. In Villiams' three-thirds system, one-third was planted, one-third planted with trees or grass, and one-third allowed to lie fallow. Friedman et al., *Chinese Village*, p. 222.

74. For information on the people's reaction to the growing famine, and the state's response, see Friedman et al., *Chinese Village*, pp. 230–234, 262–266; and Becker, *Hungry Ghosts*, pp. 94–95, 114–118, and 154–157.

75. See Li Rui, *Lushan huiyi shilu* [True Record of the Lushan Plenum] (Beijing: Chunqiu chubanshe, 1989).

76. MacFarquhar, *Origins 2*, p. 11.

77. See, for example, Zhang Xianliang's mordant memoir, *Grass Soup*, translated by Martha Avery (Boston: David R. Godine, 1994).

78. Becker, *Hungry Ghosts*, p. 2.

79. Friedman et al., *Chinese Village*, p. 233.

80. Domenach, *Origins*, p. 128.

81. Dai Qing, *River Dragon*, p. 10.

82. Domenach, *Origins*, pp. 160–161.

83. Roderick MacFarquhar argues that Mao always called the shots, merely biding his time and making a tactical retreat; he launched the Cultural Revolution to reinvigorate the revolution rather than merely to regain political power. *The Origins of the Cultural Revolution 3: The Coming of the Cataclysm, 1961–1966* (New York: Columbia University Press, 1997), p. 469.

84. "1959 (?)" [*sic*], JPRS, pp. 202–203.

85. Yi Si, "The World's Most Catastrophic Dam Failures: The August 1975 Collapse of the Banqiao and Shimantan Dams," in Dai Qing, *River Dragon*, p. 38. For a discussion of the impact of hasty planning and slip-shod construction during the "war-preparation" years, see also Barry Naughton, "The Third Front: Defence Industrialization in the Chinese Interior," *China Quarterly*, No. 115 (September 1988), pp. 363–364.

CHAPTER THREE

1. Dazhai's elevation to model status actually began as early as 1960 but failed to take off because of the catastrophic results of the Leap.

2. Zhang Wenhe and Li Yan, eds., *Kouhao yu Zhongguo* [Slogans and China] (Beijing: Zhonggong dangshi chubanshe, 1998), pp. 316–321.

3. Jonathan D. Spence, *The Search for Modern China* (New York: W. W. Norton, 1990), p. 594. The full slogan went, "In Agriculture, Learn from Dazhai, In Industry, Learn from Daqing" (a model oilfield).

4. Li Zhisui, who often went swimming with Mao, scoffs that Mao merely "floated on his back, his giant belly buoying him like a balloon, carried down the river by the current." See Li Zhisui, *The Private Life of Chairman Mao: The Memoirs of Mao's Personal Physician* translated by Tai Hung-chai, with editorial assistance of Anne F. Thurston (New York: Random House, 1996), p. 463.

5. "Chairman Mao Teaches Us: In Agriculture, learn from Tachai," *China Pictorial*, January 1968, p. 27.

6. Liang Heng and Judith Shapiro, *After the Nightmare* (New York: Alfred A. Knopf, 1986), p. 222; Kenneth Lieberthal, *Governing China: From Revolution through Reform* (New York: W. W. Norton, 1995), pp. 652–653.

7. Richard Louis Edmonds writes, "Almost every Chinese source blames mismanagement during the Great Leap Forward, the Cultural Revolution, and the efforts under Mao Zedong to make all regions self-sufficient in grain as responsible for failure to stem soil erosion during the 1960s and 1970s." See Richard Louis Edmonds, *Patterns of China's Lost Harmony* (New York: Routledge, 1994), p. 71.

8. Roderick MacFarquhar, *The Origins of the Cultural Revolution 3: The Coming of the Cataclysm, 1961–1966* (New York: Columbia University Press, 1997), p. 424.

9. Liang and Shapiro, *After the Nightmare*, pp. 214–216; Simon Leys, *Chinese Shadows* (New York: Penguin Books, 1978), pp. 74–75.

10. Judith Shapiro and Liang Heng, *Cold Winds, Warm Winds* (Middletown, CT: Wesleyan University Press, 1986), pp. 44–45.

11. Chen Guoji and Cui Jiansheng eds., *Jianguo yilai da shiji shi* [History of Great Events Since the Founding of the Country] (Huhehot: Neimenggu renmin chubanshe, 1998), p. 379.

12. Chin Chi, "Flowering of the Tachai Spirit," *China Pictorial*, February 1966, p. 2.

13. Chen and Cui, *Great Events*, pp. 378–379.

14. Indeed, questions about Dazhai's production figures were raised, and suppressed, as early as late 1964. See Spence, *Search*, p. 594.

15. David Zweig, *Agrarian Radicalism in China, 1968–1981* (Cambridge, MA: Harvard University Press, 1989), p. 40.

16. Ibid., p. 40.

17. Jiang Hong, Peiyuan Zhang, Du Zheng, and Fenghui Wang [Names as published], "The Ordos Plateau of China," in Jeanne X. Kasperson, Roger

E. Kasperson, and B.L. Turner II, eds., *Regions at Risk: Comparisons of Threatened Environments* (Tokyo: United Nations University Press, 1995), p. 450.

18. Shi Weimin and He Gang, *Zhiqing beiwanglu: Shangshan xiaxiang yundong zhong de shengchan jianshe bingtuan* [Educated Youth Memoirs: The Construction-Production Army Corps Rustification Movement] (Beijing: Zhongguo shehui kexue chubanshe, 1996), p. 87.

19. Anthony Saich, correspondence.

20. See, for example, Jean Oi, *State and Peasant in Contemporary China: The Political Economy of Village Government* (Berkeley: University of California Press, 1989), pp. 98–99.

21. "New People, New Land, New Scenes," *China Pictorial,* January 1967, p. 37.

22. Ching Nung, "Hard Work Conquers Nature," *China Pictorial,* February 1966, p. 7.

23. Mao Zedong, "In Memory of Norman Bethune," December 21, 1939, *Selected Works,* Vol. II, (Beijing: Foreign Languages Press, 1967), pp. 337–338; "Serve the People," September 8, 1944, *Selected Works,* Vol. III (Beijing: Foreign Languages Press, 1967), p. 227; "The Foolish Old Man Who Removed the Mountains," June 11, 1945, *Selected Works,* Vol. III, p. 322.

24. In Mao's essay, the people's labor evokes pity from "old man Heaven" [*tian*], who intercedes to lift the mountains away, a detail apparently lost on those whose dogmatic imitation of the old man's labors permitted no outside help, or perhaps was used to rationalize the army's assistance.

25. "The 'Foolish Old Men' of Today: Members of the Shashihyu Brigade Perform Heroic Feats in Changing Nature," *China Pictorial,* July 1967, p. 39.

26. Spence, *Search,* p. 697.

27. Stefan Landsberger, *Chinese Propaganda Posters: From Revolution to Modernization* (Armonk, NY: M. E. Sharpe, 1995), p. 27.

28. Zhang and Li, *Slogans,* p. 334.

29. Jasper Becker, *Hungry Ghosts: Mao's Secret Famine* (New York: Free Press, 1996), p. 251.

30. "Peasant Paintings," *China Pictorial,* October 1966, p. 36.

31. "'Foolish Old Men' of Today," *China Pictorial,* p. 39.

32. Liang and Shapiro, *After the Nightmare,* pp. 223–224.

33. "'Foolish Old Men' of Today," *China Pictorial,* p. 41.

34. Zhang and Li, *Slogans,* pp. 330–331.

35. "New All-round Leap for China's National Economy," *China Pictorial,* March 1967, p. 12.

36. Chin Chi, "Flowering," p. 2.

37. Spence, *Search,* p. 697.

38. Quoted in Zhang and Li, *Slogans,* p. 330.

39. For a discussion of the origin of the slogan, see ibid., p. 326.

40. Zhang and Li, *Slogans,* p. 332.

41. Ibid., p. 331.

42. Chen and Cui, *Great Events,* pp. 378–379.

43. Qu Geping and Li Jinchang, *Population and the Environment in China,* translated by Jiang Baozhong and Gu Ran (Boulder, CO: Lynne Rienner Publishers, 1994), p. 61.

44. Vaclav Smil, *The Bad Earth: Environmental Degradation in China* (Armonk, NY: M. E. Sharpe, 1984), p. 16.

45. See, for example, Yang Xiguang and Susan McFadden, *Captive Spirits* (New York: Oxford University Press, 1997); Harry Wu and Carolyn Wakeman, *Bitter Winds: A Memoir of My Years in China's Gulag* (New York: John Wiley, 1994).

46. Zhang Xianliang, *Half of Man Is Woman,* translated by Martha Avery (New York: W. W. Norton, 1986), pp. 270–271.

47. "Xue Dazhai ren, zou Dazhai lu, wei geming kaishan zaotian" [Learn from the Dazhai People, Go the Dazhai Road, Open the Mountains to Create Farmland for the Revolution], *Yunnan ribao,* April 25, 1970.

48. Ibid.

49. Ibid.

50. Ibid.

51. U. S. Embassy-Beijing, "Grassland Degradation in Tibetan Regions of China – Possible Recovery Strategies" (September 1996).

52. Oi, *State and Peasant,* pp. 98–99.

53. See, for example, Anne Osborne, "Economy and Ecology of the Lower Yangzi," in Mark Elvin and Liu Ts'ui-jung, eds., *Sediments of Time: Environment and Society in Chinese History* (New York: Cambridge University Press, 1997), pp. 208–209, and Peter C. Perdue, *Exhausting the Earth: State and Peasant in Hunan, 1500–1850* (Cambridge, MA: Council on East Asian Studies, Harvard University, 1987), pp. 205–211.

54. Smil, *Bad Earth,* p. 63. See also Eduard B. Vermeer, "Population and Ecology on the Frontier," in Elvin and Liu, *Sediments,* pp. 264–266, for a description of intensified reclamations during the late Ming and Qing dynasties.

55. A Chinese scholar of the Yangzi area land reclamation argues that the encroachments along the middle Yangzi were primarily intended to help combat schistosomiasis, a parasitic disease transmitted by paddy field snails, rather than to create farmland. See Lu Guonian, *Changjiang zhongliu*

hupeng shang sanjiao zhou de xingcheng yu yanbian ji dimao de zaixian yu moni [The Central Yangzi River Basin Fan Delta's Formation and Changes and Landforms'. Reappearance and Modeling] (Beijing: Cihui chubanshe, 1991), pp. 121–126.

56. Zhang and Li, *Slogans,* p. 332.

57. Yunnan Gaoyuan Hupo Ziyuan Bu Heli Kaifa Liyong de Shengtai Houguo Diaoyan Keti Zu [Survey and Research Group on the Ecological Results of the Unsuitable Opening and Development of the Yunnan Plateau], *Yunnan gaoyuan 'sihu' de shengtai wenti yu shengtai houguo* [Yunnan Plateau 'Four Lakes' Ecological Problems and Ecological Consequences] (Kunming: Yunnan keji chubanshe, 1987). Hereafter cited as YNGY.

58. *China: A Lonely Planet Travel Survival Kit* (Hawthorne, Victoria, Australia: Lonely Planet Books, 1996), pp. 736–737. See also Patrick R. Booz, *Yunnan.* 3rd. ed. (Chicago, IL: Passport Books, 1997), pp. 47–57.

59. YNGY, p. 34.

60. Kaocha Keti Zu [Investigation Topic Committee], *Dianchi diqu: Shengtai huanjing yu jingji zonghe kaocha baogao* [Dianchi District: Ecological Environment and Economy Summary Investigation Report] (Kunming: Yunnan keji chubanshe, 1988), p. 194. Hereafter cited as DCDQ.

61. YNGY, p. 50.

62. Ibid., p. 21.

63. "Qian qing cang hai bian lu zhou: Ji Kunming diqu junmin weihai zaotian de yingxiong shi ji" [One Thousand *Qing* of Blue Sea Become Green Land, Commemorate the Kunming District Army and People's *Weihai Zaotian* Heroic Deeds], *Yunnan ribao* August 17, 1970.

64. "Weihai zaotian chuan jie bao: Wanmu xin tian zhaicha mang" [*Weihai zaotian* Victory News: 10,000 *mu* of New Farmland Busy with Planting], *Yunnan ribao,* May 13, 1970.

65. "Kunming Haigeng 'wuqi' nongchang yansheng" [Kunming Haigeng's May 7th Agricultural Farm is Born], *Yunnan ribao,* May 8, 1970.

66. Project description and quotations are from the August 17 *Yunnan ribao* article.

67. YNGY, p. 34.

68. DCDQ, p. 194.

69. YNGY, p. 34.

70. *Yunnan ribao,* August 17, 1970.

71. Ibid.

72. Ibid.

73. Ibid.

74. Ibid.

75. *Yunnan ribao,* May 8, 1970.

76. Ibid., May 13, 1970.
77. YNGY, pp. 63–67.
78. DCDQ, pp. 191–192.
79. Ibid., p. 194.
80. Ibid., p. 193.
81. YNGY, p. 36.
82. Ibid., p. 33.
83. Ibid., p. 37.
84. Ibid., p. 48.
85. Ibid., p. 48.
86. Comparing forest cover figures for 1959 and 1981, for example, we find that the area of vegetation cover remained the same, but mature wood was halved during the period.
87. YNGY, p. 49.
88. DCDQ, p. 194.
89. At Lake Tai, for example, I was told that a similar effort to create grain-fields during the Cultural Revolution joined a small island to the mainland, slowing down currents and exacerbating present-day water pollution problems.
90. Zhang and Li, *Slogans,* p. 335.

CHAPTER FOUR

1. My debt here should be obvious – James C. Scott's categories are administrative reorganization and weak civil society. See James C. Scott, *Seeing Like a State: How Certain Schemes to Improve the Human Condition Have Failed* (New Haven: Yale University Press, 1998).
2. Friedman, Selden, and Pickowicz have drawn the comparison between Beijing's extraction of regional resources and "world economy" theories of center-periphery relations. See Edward Friedman, Paul G. Pickowicz, and Mark Selden, with Kay Ann Johnson, *Chinese Village, Socialist State* (New Haven: Yale University Press, 1991), p. 175.
3. Liu Binyan, *A Higher Kind of Loyalty: A Memoir by China's Foremost Journalist,* translated by Zhu Hong (New York: Pantheon, 1990); Wu Ningkun. *A Single Tear: A Family's Persecution, Love and Endurance in Communist China* (New York: Atlantic Monthly Press, 1993). See also Zhang Xianliang, *Grass Soup,* translated by Martha Avery (Boston: David R. Godine, 1994).
4. Shi Weimin and He Gang, *Zhiqing beiwanglu: Shangshan xiaxiang yundong zhong de shengchan jianshe bingtuan* [Educated Youth Memoirs: The

Production-Construction Army Corps in the Rustification Movement] (Beijing: Zhongguo shehui kexue chubanshe, 1996), p. 81.

5. A third kind of Cultural Revolution dislocation involved the May 7th Cadre Schools into which hundreds of thousands of officials and intellectuals were sent to engage in agricultural production and public works projects while receiving political reeducation. Since most of these were situated in areas already converted to arable land, this is not a focus of this chapter.

6. Alfred Crosby, *Ecological Imperialism: The Biological Expansion of Europe, 900–1900* (New York: Cambridge University Press, 1986), pp. 89–90.

7. Barry Naughton calls the Third Front "a military metaphor with economic resonance" ("Industrial Policy," p. 157). He explains that the Third Front referred variously to the investment program, the geographic area, and the period (1965–71) during which investment was a national focus. See Naughton, "The Third Front: Defence Industrialization in the Chinese Interior," *China Quarterly,* No. 115 (September 1988), pp. 355–356.

8. The official figure is 17 million. A scholar of the Educated Youth movement told me that an additional 2 million were sent before the Cultural Revolution and another million went to the countryside with their parents. In his opinion, the sometimes-cited figure of 30 million would have to include students originally from the countryside who were sent back home from their urban schools. For the greater figure, see Wang Mingjian, ed., *Shangshan xiaxiang – yichang jueding 3000 wan Zhongguo ren mingyun de yundong zhi mi* [Up to the Mountains and Down to the Countryside – The Conundrum of a Movement that Determined the Fate of 30 Million Chinese] (Beijing: Guangming ribao chubanshe, 1998).

9. For an example, see Jiang Hong, Peiyuan Zhang, Du Zheng, and Fenghui Wang, "The Ordos Plateau of China," in Jeanne X. Kasperson, Roger E. Kasperson and B. L. Turner II, eds., *Regions at Risk: Comparisons of Threatened Environments* (Tokyo: United Nations University Press, 1995), p. 442.

10. Naughton explains that the Third Front was not in itself irrational, but the scale on which it was pursued certainly caused China long-term economic damage and setbacks. (See Naughton, "The Third Front," p. 373.)

11. Barry Naughton, "Industrial Policy during the Cultural Revolution: Military Preparation, Decentralization, and Leaps Forward," in William A. Joseph, Christine P. W. Wong and David Zweig, eds., *New Perspectives on the Cultural Revolution* (Cambridge, MA: Council on East Asian Studies, Harvard University, 1991), p. 157.

12. Zhang Wenhe and Li Yan, eds., *Kouhao yu Zhongguo* [Slogans and China] (Beijing: Zhonggong dangshi chubanshe, 1998), pp. 349–354; Barbara Barnouin and Yu Changgen, *Chinese Foreign Policy During the Cultural Revolution* (London and New York: Kegan Paul International, 1998), pp. 85–97.

13. *Guanyu daji xianxing fangeming pohuai huodong de zhishi* [Directive on Attacking the Destructive Activities of Counterrevolutionaries], quoted in Shi and He, *Memoirs*, p. 161.

14. Barnouin and Yu, *Foreign Policy*, p. 90; Zhang and Li, *Slogans*, p. 351.

15. Naughton, "Industrial Policy," p. 157.

16. Zhang and Li, *Slogans*, p. 343.

17. "Talk on the Third Five-year Plan," in Joint Publications Research Service, *Miscellany of Mao Tse-tung Thought (1949–1968). Part I* (Arlington, VA: February 1974), (hereafter cited as JPRS), p. 354. On May 11, at a meeting of the State Planning Commission, Mao held that agriculture was the rear-end ("Some Interjections at a Briefing of the State Planning Commission Leading Group," JPRS, p. 349). His emphasis on the Third Front may have intensified in just a few weeks, or he may have misspoken.

18. Naughton, "The Third Front," p. 354.

19. Zhang and Li, *Slogans*, pp. 340–341. See also Barnouin and Yu, *Foreign Policy*, pp. 92–93.

20. Zhang and Li, *Slogans*, pp. 344–345.

21. Panzhihua Shiwei Dangshi Yanjiu Shi, eds., *Cong shenmi zou xiang huihuang* [From Mysterious to Glorious: The Story of the Construction of Panzhihua] (Beijing: Hongqi chubanshe, 1997), p. 51.

22. Naughton, "Industrial Policy," p. 158. See also Naughton, "The Third Front," pp. 374–375.

23. Naughton, "Industrial Policy," pp. 159–160.

24. Shi and He, *Memoirs*, p. 161.

25. Naughton, "Industrial Policy," p. 168.

26. Information Office of Sichuan Provincial People's Government, "Panxi: A Land Richly Endowed by Nature" (Chengdu: Sichuan meishu chubanshe, n. d.), pp. 32–33.

27. In addition to the works cited, this section draws on two other hagiographic works, Jinse de Panzhihua Bianweihui, eds., *Jinse de Panzhihua* [Golden Panzhihua] (Chengdu: Sichuan kexue jishu chubanshe, 1990), and Zhonggong Panzhihua Shiwei Dangshi Yanjiushi, eds., *Panzhihua kaifa jianshe shi da shiji* [Great Events in the History of Opening Up Panzhihua] (Chengdu: Chengdu keji daxue chubanshe, 1994).

28. Dukou's name was officially changed to Panzhihua in 1987, although both names had been used freely, and it is the only city in China named after a flower. See brochure from the Foreign Investment Office, Panzhihua Municipal Government, "A Guide to Investment in Panzhihua (no publisher or date)," p. 12.

29. Sichuansheng Panzhihuashi Zhi Bianxuan Weiyuanhui, *Panzhihuashi zhi* [Panzhihua City Record] (Chengdu: Sichuan kexue jishu chubanshe, 1994), pp. 8–9.

30. Foreign Investment Office, Panzhihua Municipal Government, "A Guide to Investment in Panzhihua," (already cited), pp. 14–16.

31. *Panzhihua Record,* p. 3. Mao was in fact a famous insomniac. See Li Zhisui, *The Private Life of Chairman Mao: The Memoirs of Mao's Personal Physician,* translated by Tai Hung-chao, with editorial assistance of Anne F. Thurston (New York: Random House, 1996), pp. 97, 180, 203, and *passim.*

32. *From Mysterious,* p. 102.

33. According to one of the Panzhihua hagiographies, "Some leading comrades wondered whether there shouldn't be less emphasis on construction, more emphasis on the question of the masses' food, clothing, and consumer goods." But after Mao spoke, they were persuaded that there should be no further delays. *Golden Panzhihua,* p. 59. See also Naughton, "The Third Front," p. 332.

34. *Panzhihua Record,* p. 3.

35. *Richly Endowed,* p. 34.

36. *From Mysterious,* p. 49.

37. Ibid., p. 51.

38. Ibid., pp. 59–60.

39. While some Third Front industries were being built underground, the cities were excavating air-raid shelters, particularly in the summer and fall of 1969. By mid-December, the cities and towns of Hunan province had already built enough shelters to house half their residents. In Fujian's Nan'an County on the middle reaches of the Pu River, people built elaborate trenches and fox holes, opened gun holes in the walls of homes, and dug networks of underground tunnels (Shi and He, *Memoirs,* p. 355). Some of this activity had negative environmental consequences. I was told that when a tunnel was built in Yantong Mountain in Kunming, for example, it interrupted one of the underground springs supplying Cui Lake, interfering with water volume and current. In Chengdu, a major river, the Yu, which once bisected the city, disappeared entirely. The water was diverted, the riverbed was covered over, and underground springs were converted into air-raid shelters; a massive central square was

erected over parts of the river where people used to swim. Today, in People's Park, a "subway" amusement park ride can be taken through a stretch of the old riverbed. Meanwhile, on the frontiers, educated youths were made to dig tunnels beneath their living quarters, which sometimes collapsed, causing injury, erosion, and landslides. See ibid., pp. 162–164.

40. *Panzhihua Record,* p. 131. There is no explanation given for the extremely high death rate in 1965, although we can easily imagine the numerous deadly accidents, infectious diseases, and limited medical facilities. The decrease in subsequent years is attributed to an improvement in health care and social welfare measures.

41. Naughton, "The Third Front," p. 357.

42. *From Mysterious,* p. 87.

43. *Panzhihua Record,* p. 129.

44. Ibid., pp. 130–131. The 1982 Third Census showed 3,308,546 people living in Panzhihua, 99.2 percent of them originally from elsewhere, and 38.3 percent from beyond Sichuan province. Of these, the largest number were from far northeast provinces of Liaoning (with 28,337 people, probably reflecting the large numbers transferred from the Angang steel plant), and Shandong (with 15,646). One can only imagine the difficulties they must have had adapting to the very different Sichuan climate.

45. Ibid., pp. 89–90.

46. Ibid., p. 101.

47. Naughton points out, however, that steel production was not regularized until 1978. "Industrial Policy," p. 168.

48. Wan Yongru, "Xiujian Cheng-Kun lu, jianshe Panzhihua: Lu Zhengcao jiangjun fangwen ji" [Building the Chengdu-Kunming Railroad, Constructing Panzhihua: An Interview with General Lu Zhengcao], in *Golden Panzhihua,* pp. 141–142. See also Naughton, "The Third Front," pp. 357–358.

49. *Golden Panzhihua,* pp. 157–158.

50. Ibid., pp. 328–330.

51. *Panzhihua Record,* pp. 131 and 331.

52. Ibid., p. 329.

53. Benzene (C_6H_6) is an extremely toxic carcinogen that affects the central nervous system. When sufficient quantities are inhaled or ingested, it can cause tremors, convulsions, paralysis, and death. Symptoms may occur several months or years after prolonged exposure. Decomposition is hazardous, as it creates carbon monoxide and carbon dioxide. Recommended disposal is by controlled burning, an after-burner, and scrubber.

54. *Richly Endowed,* p. 54.

55. Qu Geping and Li Jinchang, *Population and Environment,* translated by Jiang Baozhong and Gu Ran (Boulder, CO: Lynne Rienner Publishers, 1994), p. 40.

56. Naughton points out that the huge investments in the Southwest caused a tremendous drain on the rest of the country. Railroads in the East were neglected for almost ten years, creating bottlenecks and long-term distortions in China's investment structure. See "Industrial Policy," pp. 179–180.

57. Naughton, "The Third Front," p. 383.

58. Liang Heng and Judith Shapiro, *After the Nightmare,* (New York: Alfred A. Knopf, 1986), p. 181; Naughton, "The Third Front," pp. 356 and 377.

59. See, for example, Liang Heng and Judith Shapiro, *Son of the Revolution,* (New York: Alfred A. Knopf, 1983), pp. 40–127.

60. "Educated Youth Go to the Countryside," *China Reconstructs,* May 1965, p. 2. In Chinese, directional terminology is used to refer to a change in administrative levels, so that one goes "up" to a larger village, town, or city and "down" to a smaller one.

61. Normally, one child per family was permitted to remain home to care for aging parents. Other exemptions could sometimes be obtained for medical reasons or through political connections.

62. As has been noted, there are many ways to calculate this figure. Many statistics do not include youths who went to the countryside but remained within their home provinces, for example. The official figure is 17 million. For a discussion of the difficulty of ascertaining reliable figures, see Thomas A. Bernstein, *Up to the Mountains and Down to the Villages: The Transfer of Youth from Urban to Rural China* (New Haven: Yale University Press, 1977), pp. 21–32.

63. Shi and He, *Memoirs,* p. i. They cite a figure of 2,229,000 from 1966 to 1976. Figures would be different based on other calculations. This figure is probably low, given that Shi and He cite a conservative total figure of 14,030,000.

64. The relationship between Red Guard factional struggle and the war preparation campaign is laid out in a Central Committee directive of August 28, 1969, which called on the people rapidly to develop war preparation work, mobilize for war, and stop internal armed fighting and factional fighting. Study of this directive became a component of the war preparation campaign, which was soon to reach its peak. See Zhang and Li, *Slogans,* p. 353.

65. See, for example, the opening pages of *Blood Red Sunset: A Memoir of the Chinese Cultural Revolution* by Ma Bo, translated by Howard Goldblatt (New York: Viking, 1995).

66. Anniversaries were celebrated according to when groups were sent down, but most fell in 1994.
67. Shi and He, *Memoirs,* p. i.
68. Ibid., pp. 58–59.
69. Quoted in ibid., p. 60.
70. The Heilongjiang youth stayed longer than almost any others and were given the nickname *heshang tuan* [monk regiment] because there were few women. When women were finally imported, it was the end of their war responsibility (ibid., p. 166).
71. Ibid., p. 166.
72. Shan Weijian and Judith Shapiro, unpublished memoir of Shan's years in the Great Northern Wilderness.
73. Shi and He, *Memoirs,* p. 82.
74. Quoted in ibid., p. 83.
75. Ibid., pp. 81–85, 141, 168–169.
76. Ma Bo, *Blood Red Sunset,* p. 187.
77. Ibid., p. 195.
78. Ibid., p. 351.
79. Ibid., pp. 352–353.
80. Ibid., p. 368.
81. Qu and Li, *Population and Environment,* p. 74.
82. Shi and He, *Memoirs,* p. 141.
83. This description of the Sanjiang Plain comes from "Sanjiang Wetland Conservation in the Context of Agricultural Development," an unpublished manuscript by Ma Zhong prepared in November 1999 for the Carnegie Council on Ethics and International Affairs.
84. For a detailed discussion of the growth, structure, and numbers in the Heilongjiang Production-Construction Army Corps, see Shi and He, *Memoirs,* pp. 12–14. Division Six, where the next interviewee was based, is said to have expanded 980,000 *mu* of arable land into 3,420,000 *mu* by filling in wetlands.
85. In September 1969, the State Council and Central Military Commission issued a war transport construction directive (*Jiaotong zhanbei jianshe zhishi*) that called for road-building in the "Three North" [*san bei*] area, to be begun in 1970 and completed within three years. See Shi and He, *Memoirs,* p. 352.
86. Ma Zhong, "Sanjiang Wetland Conservation." Since the late 1970s, the World Bank and Japanese transnational corporations have invested about $200 million U.S. dollars in reclaiming wetlands in the area. In 1997–2000, the Japan Overseas Economic Cooperation Fund invested an additional $200 million in an "Integrated Agricultural

Development Project for State Farms in the Heilongjiang Reclamation Area."

87. Lester Brown, *Who Will Feed China? Wake-up Call for a Small Planet* (Washington, DC: Worldwatch Institute, 1995).

88. John Mackinnon, Meng Sha, Catherine Cheung, Geoff Carey, Zhu Xiang and David Melville, *A Biodiversity Review of China*, Geoff Carey, ed. (Hong Kong: World Wide Fund for Nature International, 1996), pp. 281–284. "Xishuangbanna" means "land of 12,000 rice paddies." The Dai share linguistic and religious roots with their Thai neighbors.

89. Yunnan Society of Ecological Economics, Xishuangbanna Nature Reserve Administration, and Yunnan Forestry Investigation and Plan Institute, eds., *Xishuangbanna: A Nature Reserve of China* (Beijing: China Forestry Publishing House, 1992), pp. 22–24.

90. Mackinnon et al., *A Biodiversity Review of China*, p. 284.

91. It also runs through Burma, Guangdong, Guangxi, Southern Taiwan, and other verdant regions, and over a great deal of ocean.

92. *Xishuangbanna: A Nature Reserve of China*, p. 94.

93. "Xishuangbanna ziran baohuqu zhenxi zhiwu he jingji zhiwu" [Rare and Economic Plants in the Xishuangbanna Nature Reserves] in Xishuangbanna Ziran Baohuqu Zonghe Kaochatuan, *Xishuangbanna ziran baohuqu zonghe kaocha baogao ji* [Summary Investigation Report on Xishuangbanna Protected Area] (Kunming: Yunnan keji chubanshe, 1987), p. 197.

94. "Xishuangbanna zhenxi shoulei shuliang fenbu ji qi baohu" [Quantitative Distribution and Protection of Rare Animals in Xishuangbanna] in Xishuangbanna Ziran Baohuqu Zonghe Kaochatuan, *Xishuangbanna ziran baohuqu zonghe kaocha baogao ji*, p. 325.

95. Ibid., p. 330.

96. The Army Corps also undertook rubber cultivation on Hainan Island, China's primary rubber base, and Guangdong; some of the dynamics described in this section occurred there as well. In Guangdong, for example, high production figures concealed problems with overharvesting and lack of protection of trees. According to Shi and He, the "red attitude" meant that local knowledge was useless. "Many soldiers and local-level cadres raised many objections to this [overharvesting] method, but leading cadres didn't listen, saying ... management is a means, tapping is the goal." From 1969 to 1974, the Guangzhou Army Corps "opened the wilderness" to grow 2,190,000 *mu* of rubber; they had to replant 1,500,000 *mu*, but only 1,130,000 *mu* remained, with a survival rate of only 30.6 percent. Shi and He, *Memoirs*, p. 129.

97. Quoted in Yang Rungao, "Xishuangbanna senlin jianshao de chengyin ji dui ziran dili huanjing de yingxiang de fenxi yanjiu" [Causes of Reduction of Forest in Xishuangbanna and Analytical Analysis of its Impact on the Natural Geographic Environment], unpublished doctoral dissertation (Kunming: Yunnan Normal University, 1998), p. 7.

98. *Yunnan sheng zhi,* Vol. 71, *Renkou zhi* [Yunnan Province Records, Vol. 71, Population Records] (Kunming: Yunnan sheng chubanshe, 1998), pp. 88 and 99.

99. *Yunnan sheng zhi,* Vol. 39, *Nongken zhi* [Yunnan Province Records, Vol. 39, State Farm and Agricultural Records] (Kunming: Yunnan sheng chubanshe, 1998), p. 817.

100. Quoted in Shi and He, *Memoirs,* p. 119.

101. State Planning Commission, Materials Ministry Revolutionary Committee, Finance Ministry Revolutionary Committee, and State Farm and Reclamation Ministry's Military Representatives, "Linked Directive Concerning Certain Questions about Rubber Reclamation Areas after Going Down," cited in ibid., p. 119.

102. Quoted in ibid., p. 119.

103. Deng Xian, quoted in ibid., pp. 120–121.

104. Four reserves were established in Xishuangbanna in 1958, with an area of 57,000 hectares, but by the 1980s, the protected area had decreased to 4,500 hectares. Yang Rungao, "Causes," p. 8. Today, however, protected areas officially cover 240,000 hectares. *Xishuangbanna: A Nature Reserve,* p. 7.

105. Deng Xian, quoted in Shi and He, *Memoirs,* pp. 122–123.

106. Interpretations of what actually happened or didn't happen during the Lin Biao Incident are myriad. Was the plane blown up or did it run out of fuel? Was the body even in the plane? Who was conspiring against whom? See, for example, Yao Mingle, *The Conspiracy and Death of Lin Biao* (New York: Alfred A. Knopf, 1983) for a "wild history" [*yeshi*]. The critical point here, and for most Chinese, is that it was suddenly revealed that there was deep enmity between Mao and the man responsible for the Mao cult.

107. See a similar story in Yang Xiguang and Susan McFadden, *Captive Spirits: Prisoners of the Cultural Revolution* (New York: Oxford University Press, 1997), pp. 207–209.

108. *Summary Investigation Report on Xishuangbanna,* p. 325.

109. Yang Rungao, "Causes," p. 7.

110. Ibid., p. 116.

111. Shi and He, *Memoirs,* p. 129.

112. Zhao Songqiao, *Physical Geography of China* (Beijing: Science Press; New York: John Wiley & Sons, 1986), pp. 152–154.

113. For details of the return home movement, see Shi and He, *Memoirs,* pp. 407–416, and Liu Wenjie, *Jiyang yu cuotuo* [Encouragement and Idleness] (Zhengzhou: Henan renmin chubanshe, 1994), pp. 210–222.
114. See text of Wang Zhen's speech in Shi and He, *Memoirs,* pp. 410–411.
115. Cited in Shi and He, *Memoirs,* p. 422.
116. Kong Jiesheng, *Da lin mang* [The Vast Forest] (Guangzhou: Huacheng chubanshe, 1985).
117. Quoted in Shi and He, *Memoirs,* p. 130.
118. Ibid., p. 121.
119. Yang Rungao, "Causes," p. 15.
120. There is a Chinese debate over whether or not rubber plantations should be counted as forest cover. Although technically the amount of forest cover has not changed, there is more rubber and less rainforest.
121. Aldo Leopold, *A Sand County Almanac* (New York: Oxford University Press, 1949), p. 224.
122. Zhang and Li, *Slogans,* p. 356.
123. Li Zhisui, *Private Life,* esp. pp. 547–625. Mao was thought for many years to have had parkinson's disease.
124. Qu and Li, *Population and Environment,* p. 3.
125. Jian Xie, "Humanity and Nature: A Review of Development and Environmental Degradation of Contemporary China," available on the Professional Association for China's Environment web site, *www. chinaenviro.net.*

CHAPTER FIVE

1. Donald Worster, *The Wealth of Nature: Environmental History and the Ecological Imagination* (New York: Oxford University Press, 1993); Donald Worster, ed., *The Ends of the Earth: Perspectives on Modern Environmental History* (New York: Cambridge University Press, 1988). See also, for example, Marc Reisner, *Cadillac Desert: The American West and its Disappearing Water* (New York: Penguin Books, 1993) and Patricia Nelson Limerick, *Legacy of Conquest: The Unbroken Past of the American West* (New York: W.W. Norton, 1987).
2. Boris Komarov, *The Destruction of Nature in the Soviet Union* (White Plains, NY: M. E. Sharpe, 1980), p. 10.
3. F. W. Carter and David Turnock, eds., *Environmental Problems in Eastern Europe* (New York: Routledge, 1993); Ze'ev Wolfson [Boris Komarov], *The Geography of Survival: Ecology in the Post-Soviet Era* (Armonk, NY: M. E. Sharpe, 1994); Murray Feshbach, *Ecocide in the USSR: Health and Nature Under Siege* (New York: Basic Books, 1992).

4. Douglas R. Weiner, *Models of Nature: Ecology, Conservation, and Cultural Revolution in Soviet Russia* (Bloomington: Indiana University Press, 1988), p. 234.

5. Komarov, *Destruction,* p. 16.

6. Sergio Diaz-Briquets and Jorge Pérez-López, *Conquering Nature: The Environmental Legacy of Socialism in Cuba* (Pittsburgh, PA: Pittsburgh University Press, 2000).

7. Yuan Weishi, "Why Did the Chinese Environment Get So Badly Messed Up?" *Nanfang zhoumo* [Southern Weekend], February 25, 2000, p. 13. Translated by David Cowhig. E-mail communication, March 7, 2000.

8. A mythical beast who filled in the ocean by dropping in one pebble at a time.

9. Jiang Zemin, "Zai Sanxia gongcheng da jiang zhailiu yishi shang de jianghua" [Speech at the Ceremony for Diverting the Great River at the Three Gorges Construction], *Renmin ribao,* November 9, 1997.

10. Richard Louis Edmonds, *Patterns of China's Lost Harmony* (New York: Routledge, 1994), p. 86.

11. David M. Lampton, "The Implementation Problem in Post-Mao China," in David M. Lampton, ed., *Policy Implementation in Post-Mao China* (Berkeley: University of California Press, 1987), pp. 3–24.

12. Patrick E. Tyler, "When It Comes to Trash, Chinese Just Say Throw," *The New York Times,* December 8, 1996.

13. George B. Schaller, *The Last Panda* (Chicago, IL: University of Chicago Press, 1993), pp. 36–44.

14. See, for example, Scott D. Seligman, *Dealing with the Chinese* (New York: Warner Books, 1989), pp. 143–144.

15. See, for example, the World Bank, *Clear Water, Blue Skies: China's Environment in the New Century* (Washington, DC: World Bank, 1997), and Vaclav Smil, "Environmental Problems in China: Estimates of Economic Costs" (Honolulu, HI: East-West Center Special Reports, No. 5, April 1996).

16. See, for example, Germaine A. Hoston, *The State, Identity, and the National Question in China and Japan* (Princeton, NJ: Princeton University Press, 1994), esp. pp. 3–42.

17. See, for example, J. Baird Callicott, "Traditional American Indian and Traditional Western European Attitudes toward Nature: An Overview," in Robert Elliot and Arran Gare, eds., *Environmental Philosophy* (St. Lucia, Queensland: Open University Press, 1983), pp. 231–250.

18. There are, of course, huge gaps between philosophical Daoism and religious Daoism, known for alchemy, the pursuit of immortality, and a wide range of folk practices.

19. Exceptions include Wenhui Hou, "Reflections on Chinese Traditional Ideas of Nature," *Environmental History,* Vol. 2, No. 4 (October 1997), pp. 482–492.
20. See, for example, J. Baird Callicott and Roger Ames, *Nature in Asian Traditions of Thought* (Albany, NY: SUNY Press, 1989); Tu Weiming, "Beyond the Enlightenment Mentality," in Mary Evelyn Tucker and John A. Grim, eds., *Worldviews and Ecology: Religion, Philosophy, and the Environment* (Maryknoll, NY: Orbis Books, 1994), pp. 19–29; Mary Tucker, "Ecological Themes in Taoism and Confucianism," in Tucker and Grim, *Worldviews,* pp. 150–162.
21. I am indebted to John Israel for this insight.

BIBLIOGRAPHY

BOOKS IN ENGLISH

Bachman, David. *Bureaucracy, Economy, and Leadership in China: The Institutional Origins of the Great Leap Forward.* New York: Cambridge University Press, 1991.

Banister, Judith. *China's Changing Population.* Stanford, CA: Stanford University Press, 1987.

Barnouin, Barbara and Yu Changgen. *Chinese Foreign Policy During the Cultural Revolution.* London and New York: Kegan Paul International, 1998.

Becker, Jasper. *Hungry Ghosts: Mao's Secret Famine.* New York: Free Press, 1996.

Bernstein, Thomas A. *Up to the Mountains and Down to the Villages: The Transfer of Youth from Urban to Rural China.* New Haven: Yale University Press, 1977.

Blaikie, Piers. *The Political Economy of Soil Erosion in Developing Countries.* London: Longman, 1985.

Blecher, Marc and Vivienne Shue. *Tethered Deer: Government and Economy in a Chinese County.* Stanford, CA: Stanford University Press, 1996.

Bookchin, Murray. *The Ecology of Freedom.* Palo Alto, CA: Cheshire Books, 1982.

———. *Philosophy of Social Ecology: Essays on Dialectical Naturalism.* Montreal: Black Rose Books, 1990.

Booz, Patrick R. *Yunnan.* 3rd ed. Chicago, IL: Passport Books, 1997.

Brown, Lester A. *Who Will Feed China? Wake-up Call for a Small Planet.* Washington, DC: Worldwatch Institute, 1995.

Callicott, J. Baird and Roger Ames. *Nature in Asian Traditions of Thought.* Albany, NY: SUNY Press, 1989.

Cannon, Terry and Alan Jenkins, eds. *The Geography of Contemporary China.* New York: Routledge, 1990.

Carter, F.W. and David Turnock, eds. *Environmental Problems in Eastern Europe.* New York: Routledge, 1993.

Bibliography

China: A Lonely Planet Travel Survival Kit. Hawthorne, Victoria, Australia: Lonely Planet Books, 1996.

Commoner, Barry. *The Closing Circle: Nature, Man, and Technology.* New York: Bantam Books, 1972.

Cronon, William, ed. *Uncommon Ground: Toward Reinventing Nature.* New York: W.W. Norton, 1995.

Crosby, Alfred W. *Ecological Imperialism: The Biological Expansion of Europe, 900–1900.* New York: Cambridge University Press, 1986.

Dai Qing. *The River Dragon Has Come! The Three Gorges Dam and the Fate of China's Yangtze River and Its People.* Armonk, NY: M. E. Sharpe, 1998.

———. *Yangtze! Yangtze!* Toronto: Earthscan Publications, 1994.

Daly, Herman E. and John B. Cobb, Jr. *For the Common Good: Redirecting the Economy toward Community, the Environment, and a Sustainable Future.* Boston: Beacon Press, 1989.

Diaz-Briquets, Sergio and Jorge Pérez-López. *Conquering Nature: The Environmental Legacy of Socialism in Cuba.* Pittsburgh, PA: University of Pittsburgh Press, 2000.

Domenach, Jean-Luc. *The Origins of the Great Leap Forward: The Case of One Chinese Province.* Translated by A.M. Berrett. Boulder, CO: Westview Press, 1995.

Domes, Jurgen. *Socialism in the Chinese Countryside: Rural Societal Policies in the People's Republic of China, 1949–1979.* Translated by Margitta Wendling. London: C. Hurst & Co., 1980.

Edmonds, Richard Louis. *Patterns of China's Lost Harmony: A Survey of the Country's Environmental Degradation and Protection.* New York: Routledge, 1994.

Ehrlich, P.R. and A.H. Ehrlich. *The Population Explosion.* New York: Simon & Schuster, 1990.

Elvin, Mark and Liu Ts'ui-jung, eds. *Sediments of Time: Environment and Society in Chinese History.* New York: Cambridge University Press, 1997.

Feshback, Murray. *Ecocide in the USSR: Health and Nature under Siege.* New York: Basic Books, 1992.

Friedman, Edward, Paul G. Pickowicz and Mark Selden, with Kay Ann Johnson. *Chinese Village, Socialist State.* New Haven: Yale University Press, 1991.

Garrett, Shirley. *Social Reformers in Urban China: The Chinese Y.M.C.A., 1895–1926.* Cambridge, MA: Harvard University Press, 1970.

Glaeser, Bernhard. *Environment, Development, Agriculture.* Armonk, NY: M. E. Sharpe, 1995.

———, ed. *Learning from China? Development and Environment in Third World Countries.* London: Allen & Unwin, 1987.

Bibliography

He Bochuan. *China on the Edge: The Crisis of Ecology and Development.* San Francisco, CA: China Books and Periodicals, 1991.

Heilbroner, Robert L. *An Inquiry into the Human Prospect, Updated and Reconsidered for the Nineteen Nineties.* 2nd rvsd. ed. New York: W.W. Norton, 1996.

Hsu, Immanuel C. Y. *The Rise of Modern China.* 5th ed. New York: Oxford University Press, 1995.

Human Rights Watch/Asia. *The Three Gorges Dam in China: Forced Resettlement, Suppression of Dissent and Labor Rights Concerns.* New York: Human Rights Watch, February 1995.

Jing Jun. *The Temple of Memories: History, Power and Morality in a Chinese Village.* Stanford, CA: Stanford University Press, 1996.

Kane, Penny. *Famine in China, 1959–61: Demographic and Social Implications.* New York: St. Martin's Press, 1988.

Kasperson, Jeanne X., Roger E. Kasperson and B.L. Turner II, eds. *Regions at Risk: Comparisons of Threatened Environments.* Tokyo: United Nations University Press, 1995.

Kelliher, Daniel. *Peasant Power in China: The Era of Rural Reform, 1979–1989.* New Haven: Yale University Press, 1992.

Khrushchev, Nikita. *Khrushchev Remembers: The Last Testament.* Translated and edited by Strobe Talbott. Boston: Little, Brown, 1974.

Komarov, Boris. *The Destruction of Nature in the Soviet Union.* White Plains, NY: M. E. Sharpe, 1980.

Landsberger, Stefan. *Chinese Propaganda Posters: From Revolution to Modernization.* Armonk, NY: M. E. Sharpe, 1995.

Leopold, Aldo. *A Sand County Almanac.* New York: Oxford University Press, 1949.

Leys, Simon [Pierre Rykmans]. *Chinese Shadows.* New York: Penguin Books, 1978.

Li Choh-ming. *The Statistical System of Communist China.* Berkeley: University of California Press, 1962.

Li Zhisui. *The Private Life of Chairman Mao: The Memoirs of Mao's Personal Physician.* Translated by Tai Hung-chao. With the editorial assistance of Anne F. Thurston. New York: Random House, 1996.

Liang Heng and Judith Shapiro. *Son of the Revolution.* New York: Alfred A. Knopf, 1983.

———. *After the Nightmare.* New York: Alfred A. Knopf, 1986.

Lieberthal, Kenneth. *Governing China: From Revolution through Reform.* New York: W.W. Norton, 1995.

Lieberthal, Kenneth and Michel Oksenberg. *Policy Making in China: Leaders, Structures, and Processes.* Princeton, NJ: Princeton University Press, 1988.

Limerick, Patricia Nelson. *Legacy of Conquest: The Unbroken Past of the American West.* New York: W.W. Norton, 1987.

Little, Daniel. *Understanding Peasant China: Case Studies in the Philosophy of Social Science.* New Haven: Yale University Press, 1989.

Liu Binyan. *A Higher Kind of Loyalty: A Memoir by China's Foremost Journalist.* Translated by Zhu Hong. New York: Pantheon, 1990.

Ma Bo. *Blood Red Sunset: A Memoir of the Chinese Cultural Revolution.* [*Xuese Huanghun*] Translated by Howard Goldblatt. New York: Viking, 1995.

MacFarquhar, Roderick. *The Origins of the Cultural Revolution 2: The Great Leap Forward, 1958–1960.* New York: Columbia University Press, 1983.

———. *The Origins of the Cultural Revolution 3: The Coming of the Cataclysm, 1961–1966.* New York: Columbia University Press, 1997.

Mackinnon, John, Meng Sha, Catherine Cheung, Geoff Carey, Zhu Xiang and David Melville. *A Biodiversity Review of China.* Edited by Geoff Carey. Hong Kong: World Wide Fund for Nature International, 1996.

———. *An Essay on the Principle of Population.* Selected and introduced by Donald Winch. Text of the 1803 edition. New York: Cambridge University Press, 1993.

———. *An Essay on the Principle of Population or a View of its Past and Present Effects on Human Happiness.* 9th ed. London: Reeves and Turner, 1888.

Malthus, Thomas R. *On Population.* Edited and introduced by Gertrude Himmelfarb. First published 1798. New York: Modern Library, 1960.

———. *Chairman Mao Talks to the People: Talks and Letters: 1956–1971.* Edited by Stuart Schram. New York: Pantheon, 1974.

———. *Miscellany of Mao Tse-tung Thought (1949–1968). Part I.* Arlington, VA: Joint Publications Research Service, February 1974.

———. *The Secret Speeches of Chairman Mao: From the Hundred Flowers to the Great Leap Forward.* Edited by Roderick MacFarquhar, Timothy Cheek, and Eugene Wu. Cambridge, MA: Council on East Asian Studies, Harvard University, 1989.

Mao Zedong. *Selected Works of Mao Zedong,* Vols. 1–4. Beijing: Foreign Languages Press, 1967.

Marks, Robert B. *Tigers, Rice, Silk, and Silt.* New York: Cambridge University Press, 1997.

Marx, Karl and Friedrich Engels. *Marx and Engels on the Population Bomb: Selections from the Writings of Marx and Engels Dealing with the Theories of Thomas Robert Malthus.* Edited by Ronald L. Meek and translated by Dorothea L. Meek and Ronald L. Meek. London: Ramparts Press, 1953.

Meisner, Maurice. *Mao's China and After: A History of the People's Republic.* 3rd ed. New York: Free Press, 1999.

Bibliography

Miller, H. Lyman. *Science and Dissent in Post-Mao China: The Politics of Knowledge.* Seattle: University of Washington Press, 1996.

Needham, Joseph. *Science and Civilisation in China,* Vol. 4, Part III: *Civil Engineering and Nautics.* New York: Cambridge University Press, 1971.

Nieh, Hualing, ed. and co-trans. *Literature of the Hundred Flowers, Vol. 1: Criticism and Polemics.* New York: Columbia University Press, 1981.

———. *Literature of the Hundred Flowers, Vol. II: Poetry and Fiction.* New York: Columbia University Press, 1981.

Oi, Jean. *State and Peasant in Contemporary China: The Political Economy of Village Government.* Berkeley: University of California Press, 1989.

Ophuls, William and A. Stephen Boyan, Jr. *Ecology and the Politics of Scarcity Revisited: The Unraveling of the American Dream.* San Francisco, CA: W. H. Freeman, 1992.

Painter, Michael and William H. Durham, eds. *The Social Causes of Environmental Destruction in Latin America.* Ann Arbor: University of Michigan Press, 1995.

Pepper, Suzanne. *Civil War in China: The Political Struggle, 1945–1949.* Berkeley: University of California Press, 1978.

Purdue, Peter. *Exhausting the Earth: State and Peasant in Hunan, 1500–1850.* Cambridge, MA: Council on East Asian Studies, Harvard University, 1987.

Qu Geping and Li Jinchang. *Population and the Environment in China.* Translated by Jiang Baozhong and Gu Ran. Boulder, CO: Lynne Rienner Publishers, 1994.

Reisner, Marc. *Cadillac Desert: The American West and its Disappearing Water.* Revised and updated. New York: Penguin Books, 1993.

Richardson, S.D. *Forests and Forestry in China.* Washington, DC: Island Press, 1990.

Ross, Lester. *Environmental Policy in China.* Bloomington: Indiana University Press, 1988.

——— and Mitchell A. Silk. *Environmental Law and Policy in the People's Republic of China.* New York: Quorum Books, 1987.

Schaller, George B. *The Last Panda.* Chicago, IL: University of Chicago Press, 1987.

Schmidt, Alfred. *The Concept of Nature in Marx.* Translated by Ben Fowkes. London: New Left Books, 1971.

Schram, Stuart. *The Thought of Mao Tse-tung.* New York: Cambridge University Press, 1989.

Scott, James C. *Seeing Like a State: How Certain Schemes to Improve the Human Condition Have Failed.* New Haven: Yale University Press, 1998.

———. *Weapons of the Weak: Everyday Forms of Peasant Resistance.* New Haven: Yale University Press, 1985.

Bibliography

Seligman, Scott. *Dealing with the Chinese.* New York: Warner Books, 1989.

Sessions, George, ed. *Deep Ecology for the Twenty-first Century.* Boston: Shambhala, 1995.

Shapiro, Judith and Liang Heng. *Cold Winds, Warm Winds: Intellectual Life in China Today.* Middletown, CT: Wesleyan University Press, 1987.

Short, Philip. *Mao: A Life.* New York: Henry Holt, 2000.

Simon, Julian. *The Ultimate Resource.* Princeton, NJ: Princeton University Press, 1986.

———. *The Ultimate Resource 2.* Princeton, NJ: Princeton University Press, 1996.

Sinkule, Barbara J. and Leonard Ortolano, eds. *Implementing Environmental Policy in China.* Westport, CT: Praeger, 1995.

Smil, Vaclav. *The Bad Earth: Environmental Degradation in China.* Armonk, NY: M. E. Sharpe, 1984.

———. *China's Environmental Crisis: An Inquiry into the Limits of National Development.* Armonk, NY: M. E. Sharpe, 1993.

Spence, Jonathan D. *Mao Zedong* (Penguin Lives). New York: Viking, 1999.

———. *The Search for Modern China.* New York: W. W. Norton, 1990.

Stone, Christopher. *Should Trees Have Standing?* Los Altos, CA: William Kaufmann, 1974.

Sun Yat-sen. *The International Development of China.* New York: G. P. Putnam's Sons, 1929.

Tang Zongli and Bing Zuo [names as published]. *Maoism and Chinese Culture.* New York: Nova Science Publishers, 1996.

Tien, H. Yuan. *China's Strategic Demographic Initiative.* New York: Praeger, 1991.

Van Slyke, Lyman P. *Yangtze: Nature, History, and the River.* New York: Addison-Wesley, 1988.

Vogel, Ezra. *Canton under Communism: Programs and Politics in a Provincial Capital, 1949–1968.* Cambridge, MA: Harvard University Press, 1969.

Walder, Andrew J. *Communist Neo-traditionalism: Work and Authority in Chinese Industry.* Berkeley: University of California Press, 1986.

Weiner, Douglas R. *Models of Nature: Ecology, Conservation, and Cultural Revolution in Soviet Russia.* Bloomington: Indiana University Press, 1988.

White, Lynn T. III. *Policies of Chaos: The Organizational Causes of Violence in China's Cultural Revolution.* Princeton, NJ: Princeton University Press, 1989.

Winch, Donald. *Malthus.* New York: Oxford University Press, 1987.

Winchester, Simon. *The River at the Centre of the World: A Journey up the Yangtze, and Back in Chinese Time.* London: Viking, 1997.

Wittfogel, Karl. *Oriental Despotism: A Comparative Study of Total Power.* New Haven: Yale University Press, 1957.

Bibliography

Wolfson, Ze'ev [Boris Komarov]. *The Geography of Survival: Ecology in the Post-Soviet Era.* Armonk, NY: M. E. Sharpe, 1994.

World Bank. *Clear Water, Blue Skies: China's Environment in the New Century.* Washington, DC: World Bank, 1997.

Worster, Donald. *The Wealth of Nature: Environmental History and the Ecological Imagination.* New York: Oxford University Press, 1993.

————, ed. *The Ends of the Earth: Perspectives on Modern Environmental History.* New York: Cambridge University Press, 1988.

Wu, Harry and Carolyn Wakeman. *Bitter Winds: A Memoir of My Years in China's Gulag.* New York: John Wiley, 1994.

Wu Ningkun. *A Single Tear: A Family's Persecution, Love and Endurance in Communist China.* New York: Atlantic Monthly Press, 1993.

Yang, Dali. *Calamity and Reform in China: State, Rural Society, and Institutional Change Since the Great Leap Famine.* Stanford, CA: Stanford University Press, 1996.

Yang Jiang. *Six Chapters from my Life "Downunder."* Translated by Howard Goldblatt. Seattle: University of Washington Press, 1983.

Yang Xiguang and Susan McFadden. *Captive Spirits: Prisoners of the Cultural Revolution.* New York: Oxford University Press, 1997.

Yao Mingle. *The Conspiracy and Death of Lin Biao.* New York: Alfred A. Knopf, 1983.

Yunnan Society of Ecological Economics, Xishuangbanna Nature Reserve Administration, and Yunnan Forestry Investigation and Plan Institute, eds. *Xishuangbanna: A Nature Reserve of China.* Beijing: China Forestry Publishing House, 1992.

Zhang Xianliang. *Grass Soup.* Translated by Martha Avery. Boston: David R. Godine, 1994.

————. *Half of Man is Woman.* Translated by Martha Avery. New York: W.W. Norton, 1986.

Zhao Songqiao. *Physical Geography of China.* Beijing: Science Press, 1986.

Zweig, David. *Agrarian Radicalism in China, 1968–1981.* Cambridge, MA: Harvard University Press, 1989.

ARTICLES AND BOOK CHAPTERS IN ENGLISH

Banister, Judith. "Population, Public Health and the Environment in China," *China Quarterly,* No. 156 (December 1998), pp. 988–1014.

Bennett, Gordon. *"Yundong:* Mass Campaigns in Chinese Communist Leadership." Berkeley, CA: Center for Chinese Studies, China Research Monograph #12, 1976.

Bruun, Ole and Arne Kalland. "Images of Nature: An Introduction to the Study of Man–Environment Relations in Asia," in Ole Bruun and Arne Kalland, eds., *Asian Perceptions of Nature: A Critical Approach.* Richmond, Surrey: Curzon Press, 1995, pp. 1–24.

Callicott, J. Baird. "Traditional American Indian and Traditional Western European Attitudes Toward Nature: An Overview," in Robert Elliot and Arran Gare, eds., *Environmental Philosophy.* St. Lucia, Queensland: Open University Press, 1983, pp. 231–250.

Chin Chi. "Flowering of the Tachai Spirit," *China Pictorial,* February 1966, p. 2.

———. "The 'Foolish Old Men' of Today: Members of the Shashihyu Brigade Perform Heroic Feats in Changing Nature," July 1967, pp. 39–41.

———. "New All-round Leap for China's National Economy," March 1967, pp. 11–17.

———. "New People, New Land, New Scenes," January 1967, pp. 37–39.

China Pictorial. "Peasant Paintings," October 1966, p. 36.

Ching Nung. "Hard Work Conquers Nature," *China Pictorial,* February 1966, pp. 4–7.

Cullet, Phillipe. "Definition of an Environmental Right in a Human Rights Context," *Netherlands Quarterly of Human Rights,* Vol. 13 (January 1995), pp. 25–41.

Dai Qing. "Resettlement in the Three Gorges Project," in Dai Qing, *Yangtze! Yangtze!* Toronto: Earthscan Publications, 1994, pp. 225–228.

———. "Never Dam the Three Gorges. An Interview with Professor Huang Wanli," in Dai Qing, *Yangtze! Yangtze!* Toronto: Earthscan Publications, 1994, pp. 163–170.

Durham, William H. "Political Ecology and Environmental Destruction in Latin America," in Michael Painter and William H. Durham, eds., *The Social Causes of Environmental Destruction in Latin America.* Ann Arbor: University of Michigan Press, 1995, pp. 249–264.

Ehrlich, P. R. and J. P. Holdren, "Impact of Population Growth," *Science,* Vol. 171 (March 26, 1971), pp. 1212–1217.

Ellis, Jeffry C. "On the Search for a Root Cause: Essentialist Tendencies in Environmental Discourse," in William Cronon, ed., *Uncommon Ground: Toward Reinventing Nature.* New York: W.W. Norton, 1995, pp. 256–268.

Elvin, Mark. "The *Bell of Poesy:* Thoughts on Poems as Information on Late-Imperial Chinese Environmental History," in S. M. Carletti, M. Sacchetti, and P. Santangelo, eds., *Studi in Onore di Lionello Lanciotti* (Napoli: Istituto Universitario Orientale, 1996), Vol. 1 (of 3), pp. 497–523.

Foreign Investment Office, Panzhihua Municipal Government. "A Guide to Investment in Panzhihua" (brochure), no publisher or date.

Bibliography

Goldman, Merle. "The Party and the Intellectuals," in Roderick MacFarquhar and John King Fairbank, eds., *The Cambridge History of China*, Vol. 14: *The People's Republic, Part I: The Emergence of Revolutionary China, 1949–1965*. New York: Cambridge University Press, 1987, pp. 218–258.

Grossman, Gene and Alan Krueger. "Economic Growth and the Environment," *Quarterly Journal of Economics* (May 1995), pp. 353–377.

Hardin, Garrett. "The Tragedy of the Commons," *Science*, December 13, 1968.

Harkness, James. "Recent Trends in Forestry and Conservation of Biodiversity in China," *China Quarterly*, No. 156 (December 1998), pp. 911–934.

Hertsgaard, Mark. "Our Real China Problem," *Atlantic Monthly*, Vol. 280, No. 5 (November 1997), pp. 97–112.

Hou, Wenhui. "Reflections on Chinese Traditional Ideas of Nature," *Environmental History*, Vol. 2 No. 4 (October 1997), pp. 482–492.

Information Office of Sichuan Provincial People's Government. "Panxi: A Land Richly Endowed by Nature" (Pamphlet). Chengdu: Sichuan meishu chubanshe, 1997.

Jiang Hong, Peiyuan Zhang, Du Zheng and Fenghui Wang [names as published]. "The Ordos Plateau of China," in Jeanne X. Kasperson, Roger E. Kasperson and B.L. Turner II, eds., *Regions at Risk: Comparisons of Threatened Environments*. Tokyo: United Nations University Press, 1995, pp. 420–458.

Kristof, Nicholas. "Asian Pollution is Widening its Deadly Reach," *The New York Times*, November 29, 1997, p. 1.

———. "Across Asia, A Pollution Disaster Hovers," *The New York Times*, November 28, 1997, p. 1.

Lampton, David M. "The Implementation Problem in Post-Mao China," in David M. Lampton, ed., *Policy Implementation in Post-Mao China*. Berkeley: University of California Press, 1987, pp. 3–24.

Leonard, Pamela. "The Political Landscape of a Sichuan Village." Doctoral dissertation. Cambridge University, 1994.

Lieberthal, Kenneth. "The Great Leap Forward and the Split in the Yenan Leadership," in Roderick MacFarquhar and John King Fairbank, eds., *The Cambridge History of China*, Vol. 14: *The People's Republic, Part 1: The Emergence of Revolutionary China, 1949–1965*. New York: Cambridge University Press, 1987, pp. 293–359.

Liu Changming. "Environmental Issues and the South-North Water Transfer Scheme," *China Quarterly*, No. 156 (December 1998), pp. 889–910.

Ma Zhong. "Sanjiang Wetland Conservation in the Context of Agricultural Development." Paper prepared for the Carnegie Council on Ethics and International Affairs, November 1999.

Marks, Robert B. "Commercialization without Capitalism: Processes of Environmental Change in South China," *Environmental History*, Vol. 1, No. 2 (April 1996), pp. 56–82.

Bibliography

McPhee, John. "Farewell to the Nineteenth Century: The Breeching of the Edwards Dam," *The New Yorker,* September 27, 1999, pp. 44–53.

Meng Leng. "The Battle of Sanmenxia: Population Relocation During the Three Gate Gorge Hydropower Project." Translated by Ming Yi. *Chinese Sociology and Anthropology,* Vol. 31, No. 3 (Spring 1999), entire.

Mills, J.A., T.S. Kang, S. [sic], K.H. Lee, R. Parry-Jones and M. Phipps. "Market for Gall Bladders in Asia," *Traffic Bulletin,* Vol. 16, No. 3 (March 1997), pp. 107–112.

Mirovitskaya, Natalia and Marvin S. Soroos. "Socialism and the Tragedy of the Commons: Reflections on Environmental Practice in the Soviet Union and Russia," *Journal of Environment and Development,* Vol. 4, No. 1 (Winter 1995), pp. 77–110.

Mou Mou and Cai Wenmei. "Resettlement in the Xin'an River Power Station Project," in Dai Qing, *The River Dragon Has Come! The Three Gorges Dam and the Fate of China's Yangtze River and Its People.* Armonk, NY: M. E. Sharpe, 1998, pp. 104–123.

Murphey, Rhoads. "Man and Nature in China," *Modern Asian Studies,* Vol. 1, No. 4 (1967), pp. 313–333.

Naughton, Barry. "Industrial Policy during the Cultural Revolution: Military Preparation, Decentralization, and Leaps Forward," in William A. Joseph, Christine P. W. Wong and David Zweig, eds., *New Perspectives on the Cultural Revolution.* Cambridge, MA: Council on East Asian Studies, Harvard University, 1991, pp. 153–187.

———. "The Third Front: Defence Industrialization in the Chinese Interior," *China Quarterly,* No. 115 (September 1988), pp. 351–386.

Osborne, Anne. "Economy and Ecology of the Lower Yangzi," in Mark Elvin and Liu Ts'ui-jung, eds., *Sediments of Time: Environment and Society in Chinese History.* New York: Cambridge University Press, 1997, pp. 203–234.

Repetto, Robert et al. *Wasting Assets: Natural Resources in the National Income Accounts.* Washington, DC: World Resources Institute, 1989.

Sachs, Aaron. "Eco-Justice: Linking Human Rights and the Environment," *Worldwatch Paper,* No. 127. Washington, DC: Worldwatch Institute, 1995.

Schoenhals, Michael. "Political Movements, Change, and Stability: The Chinese Communist Party in Power," *China Quarterly,* No. 159 (September 1999), pp. 595–605.

———. "Saltationist Socialism: Mao Zedong and the Great Leap Forward." Doctoral dissertation. Skrifter utgivna av Föreningen for Orientaliska Studier, University of Stockholm, 1987.

Schram, Stuart. "Mao Tse-tung's Thought from 1949 to 1976," in Roderick MacFarquhar and John King Fairbank, eds., *The Cambridge History of*

China, Vol. 15: *The People's Republic, Part 2: Revolutions within the Chinese Revolution, 1966–1982.* pp. 1–106.

Shan Weijian and Judith Shapiro. Unpublished recollections of Shan's years in the Great Northern Wilderness.

Shang Wei. "A Lamentation for the Yellow River: The Three Gate Gorge Dam (*Sanmenxia*)," in Dai Qing, *The River Dragon Has Come! The Three Gorges Dam and the Fate of China's Yangtze River and Its People.* Armonk, NY: M. E. Sharpe, 1998, pp. 143–159.

Shui Fu. "A Profile of Dams in China," in Dai Qing, *The River Dragon Has Come! The Three Gorges Dam and the Fate of China's Yangtze River and Its People.* Armonk, NY: M. E. Sharpe, 1998, pp. 18–24.

Singer, Rena. "China's Yellow River, Now a Trickle, Poses New Threat," *The Philadelphia Inquirer,* February 1, 1999.

———. "Environmental Problems in China: Estimates of Economic Costs," *East–West Center Special Reports,* No. 5 (April 1996).

Smil, Vaclav. "Land Degradation in China: An Ancient Problem Getting Worse," in Piers Blaikie and Harold Brookfield, *Land Degradation and Society.* New York: Methuen, 1987, pp. 214–220.

Stevens, William K. "Will Dam Busting Save Salmon? Maybe Not," *The New York Times,* October 5, 1999, p. D1.

Teiwes, Frederick C. with Warren Sun. "The Politics of an 'Un-Maoist' Interlude: The Case of Opposing Rash Advance, 1956–1957," in Timothy Cheek and Tony Saich, eds., *New Perspectives on State Socialism in China.* Armonk, NY: M. E. Sharpe, 1997, pp. 151–190.

Teiwes, Frederick C. "The Establishment and Consolidation of the New Regime, 1949–1957," in Roderick MacFarquhar, ed., *The Politics of China, 1949–1989.* New York: Cambridge University Press, 1993, pp. 5–86.

Tu Weiming. "Beyond the Enlightenment Mentality," in Mary Evelyn Tucker and John A. Grim, eds., *Worldviews and Ecology: Religion, Philosophy, and the Environment.* Maryknoll, NY: Orbis Books, 1994, pp. 19–29.

Tucker, Mary. "Ecological Themes in Taoism and Confucianism," in Mary Evelyn Tucker and John A. Grim, eds., *Worldviews and Ecology: Religion, Philosophy, and the Environment.* Maryknoll, NY: Orbis Books, 1994, pp. 150–162.

Tyler, Patrick. "When It Comes to Trash, Chinese Just Say Throw," *The New York Times,* December 8, 1996.

U.S. Embassy-Beijing. "Grassland Degradation in Tibetan Regions of China – Possible Recovery Strategies," September 1996.

Vermeer, Eduard B. "Population and Ecology on the Frontier," in Mark Elvin and Liu Ts'ui-jung, eds., *Sediments of Time: Environment and Society in*

Chinese History. New York: Cambridge University Press, 1997, pp. 235–279.

Walker, Kenneth R. "A Chinese Discussion of Planning for Balanced Growth: A Summary of the Views of Ma Yinchu and his Critics," in Robert Ash, ed., *Agricultural Development in China, 1949–1989: The Collected Papers of Kenneth R. Walker (1931–1989).* New York: Oxford University Press, 1998, pp. 333–355.

Wang Hongchang. "Deforestation and Dessication in China: A Preliminary Study," in *An Assessment of the Economic Losses Resulting from Various Forms of Environmental Degradation in China.* Occasional Papers of the Project in Environmental Scarcities, State Capacity, and Civil Violence. Cambridge, MA: American Academy of Arts and Sciences and the University of Toronto, 1997.

Weiner, Douglas R. "The Changing Face of Soviet Conservation," in Donald Worster, ed., *The Ends of the Earth: Perspectives on Modern Environmental History.* New York: Cambridge University Press, 1988, pp. 252–276.

White, Lynn T., Jr. "The Historical Roots of our Ecologic Crisis," *Science,* Vol. 155 (March 10, 1967), pp. 1203–1207.

Winch, Donald. "Introduction," in T. R. Malthus, *An Essay on the Principle of Population.* Selected and introduced by Donald Winch. New York: Cambridge University Press, 1993, pp. vii–xxiii.

World Bank. "China: Xiaolangdi Resettlement Project," Report No. 12527-CHA. Washington, DC: 1993.

Xie Jian. "Humanity and Nature: A Review of Development and Environmental Degradation of Contemporary China." Published electronically on web page: www.chinaenvironment.net (December 1999).

Yang Dali. "Surviving the Great Leap Famine: The Struggle over Rural Policy, 1958–1962," in Timothy Cheek and Tony Saich, eds., *New Perspectives on State Socialism in China.* Armonk, NY: M. E. Sharpe, 1997, pp. 262–302.

Yi Si. "The World's Most Catastrophic Dam Failures: The August 1975 Collapse of the Banqiao and Shimantan Dams," in Dai Qing, *The River Dragon Has Come! The Three Gorges Dam and the Fate of China's Yangtze River and Its People.* Armonk, NY: M. E. Sharpe, 1998, pp. 25–38.

You Yuwen. "Ma Yinchu and his Theory of Population," *China Reconstructs,* December 1979, pp. 28–30.

Yuan Weishi. "Why Did the Chinese Environment Get So Badly Messed Up?" *Nanfang zhoumo* [Southern Weekend], February 25, 2000. Translated by David Cowhig. E-mail communication, March 7, 2000.

Zhu Zanping. "Discussing the Internal Motivation to Cultivate Forests in the Collective Forest Areas of South China," *Nongye jingji wenti,* No. 11 (1984), pp. 36–39. Translated in Lester Ross and Mitchell A. Silk,

Environmental Law and Policy in the People's Republic of China. New York: Quorum Books, 1987, pp. 189–196.

BOOKS AND MONOGRAPHS IN CHINESE

Chen Guoji and Cui Jiansheng, eds. *Jianguo yilai da shiji shi* [History of Great Events since the Founding of the Country]. Huhehot: Neimenggu renmin chubanshe, 1998.

Deng Xian. *Zhongguo zhiqing meng* [Dream of a Chinese Educated Youth]. Beijing: Guofang daxue chubanshe, 1996.

Jinse de Panzhihua bianweihui, eds. *Jinse de Panzhihua* [Golden Panzhihua]. Chengdu: Sichuan kexue jishu chubanshe, 1990.

Kaocha keti zu [Investigation Topic Committee]. *Dianchi diqu: Shengtai huanjing yu jingji zonghe kaocha baogao* [Dianchi District: Ecological Environment and Economy Summary Investigation Report]. Kunming: Yunnan keji chubanshe, 1988.

Kong Jiesheng. *Da lin mang* [The Vast Forest]. Guangzhou: Huacheng chubanshe, 1985.

Li Rui. *Lushan huiyi shilu* [True Record of the Lushan Plenum]. Beijing: Chunqiu chubanshe, 1989.

Li Yong, ed. *'Wenhua Dageming' zhong de mingren zhi you* [The Troubles of Famous People during the Cultural Revolution]. Beijing: Zhongyang minzu xueyuan chubanshe, 1994.

Liu Wenjie. *Jiyang yu cuotuo* [Encouragement and Idleness]. Zhengzhou: Henan renmin chubanshe 1994.

Lu Guonian. *Changjiang zhongliu hupeng shang sanjiao zhou de xingcheng yu yanbian ji dimao de zaixian yu moni* [The Central Yangzi River Basin Fan Delta's Formation and Changes and Landforms' Reappearance and Modeling]. Beijing: Cihui chubanshe, 1991.

Ma Yinchu. *Ma Yinchu renkou wenji* [Ma Yinchu's Collected Essays on Population], edited by Tian Xueyuan. Hangzhou: Zhejiang renmin chubanshe, 1997.

———. *Xin renkoulun* [New Demography]. Changchun: Jilin renmin chubanshe, 1997.

Mao Zedong. *Mao Zedong xuanji* [Selected Works of Mao Zedong], Vols. 1–4. Beijing: Renmin chubanshe, 1960.

Panzhihua shiwei dangshi yanjiu shi, eds. *Cong shenmi zou xiang huihuang: Panzhihua kaifa jianshe shihua* [From Mysterious to Glorious: The Story of the Construction of Panzhihua]. Beijing: Hongqi chubanshe, 1997.

Shengxian zhengxie wenshi ziliao weiyuanhui, eds. *Ma Yinchu zai guxiang* [Ma Yinchu in his Homeland]. Hangzhou: Hangzhou daxue chubanshe, 1995.

Shengzhou youeryuan renkou yu huanjing jiaoyu keyan xiaozu, eds. *Youeryuan renkou yu huanjing jiaoyu huodong zhinan* [Primary School Population and Environment Education Activities]. Zhejiang: Zhejiang sheng, Shengzhoushi jiaoyu ju, 1996.

Shi Weimin and He Gang. *Zhiqing beiwanglu: Shangshan xiaxiang yundong zhong de shengchan jianshe bingtuan* [Educated Youth Memoirs: The Production-Construction Army Corps in the Rustification Movement]. Beijing: Zhongguo shehui kexue chubanshe, 1996.

Sichuansheng Panzhihuashi zhi bianxuan weiyuanhui. *Panzhihuashi zhi* [Panzhihua City Record]. Chengdu: Sichuan kexue jishu chubanshe, 1994.

Wang Mingjian, ed. *Shangshan xiaxiang – Yichang jueding 3000 wan Zhongguoren mingyun de yundong zhi mi* [Up to the Mountains and Down to the Countryside – The Conundrum of a Movement that Determined the Fate of 30 Million Chinese]. Beijing: Guangming ribao chubanshe, 1998.

Xie Mian. *Yongyuan de xiaoyuan* [The Eternal Campus]. Beijing: Beijing daxue chubanshe, 1997.

Xishuangbanna ziran baohuqu zonghe kaochatuan. *Xishuangbanna ziran baohuqu zonghe kaocha baogao ji* [Summary Investigation Report on Xishuangbanna Protected Area]. Kunming: Yunnan keji chubanshe, 1987.

Yang Jianye. *Ma Yinchu*. Shijiazhuang: Huashan wenyi chubanshe, 1997.

Yunnan gaoyuan hupo ziyuan bu heli kaifa liyong de shengtai houguo diaoyan keti zu [Survey and Research Group on the Ecological Results of the Unsuitable Opening and Development of the Yunnan Plateau]. *Yunnan gaoyuan 'sihu' de shengtai wenti yu shengtai houguo* [Yunnan Plateau 'Four Lakes' Ecological Problems and Ecological Consequences]. Kunming: Yunnan keji chubanshe, 1987.

Yunnan sheng zhi, Vol. 39, *Nongken zhi* [Yunnan Province Records, Vol. 39, State Farm and Reclamation Records]. Kunming: Yunnan sheng chubanshe, 1998.

Yunnan sheng zhi, Vol. 71, *Renkou zhi* [Yunnan Province Records, Vol. 71, Population Records]. Kunming: Yunnan sheng chubanshe, 1998.

Zhang Wenhe and Li Yan, eds. *Kouhao yu Zhongguo* [Slogans and China]. Beijing: Zhonggong dangshi chubanshe, 1998.

Zhang Ying, ed. *Zhou Enlai yu wenhua mingren* [Zhou Enlai and Famous Cultural People]. Nanjing: Jiangsu jiaoyu chubanshe, 1998.

Zheng Yisheng and Qian Yihong. *Shendu youhuan: Dangdai Zhongguo de kechixu fazhan wenti* [Deep Hardships: Problems of Sustainable Development in China]. Beijing: Jinri Zhongguo chubanshe, 1998.

Zhonggong Panzhihua shiwei dangshi yanjiushi, eds. *Panzhihua kaifa jianshe shi da shiji* [Great Events in the History of Opening Panzhihua]. Chengdu: Chengdu keji daxue chubanshe, 1994.

Bibliography

ARTICLES IN CHINESE

Bai Hua and Peng Ning. "Kulian" [Bitter Love], *Shiyue* (March 1979), pp. 140–171, 248, film script.

E Chun. "Gan dui 'shangdi' shuo bu de ren" [The Person Who Dared Say No to "God"]. Jilinsheng wenyi bao, no month/day avail., 1997, pp. 18–24.

Huang Wanli. "Zhi shui ying cao" [Feelings on Harnessing the Waters]. Mimeographed collection of poems, June 1991.

———. "Zhi he yonghuai" [Feelings on River Management]. Mimeographed essay.

Jiang Zemin. "Zai Sanxia gongcheng da jiang zhailiu yishi shang de jianghua" [Speech at the Ceremony for Diverting the Great River at the Three Gorges Construction], *Renmin ribao,* November 9, 1997.

Li Rui. "'Da Yuejin' shibai de jiaoxun hezai?" in *Li Rui lunshuo wenxuan* [Selections from Li Rui's Writings and Talks]. Beijing: Zhongguo shehui kexue chubanshe, 1998, pp. 207–234.

Ma Fuhai. "Zai jinnian Sanmenxia shuili shuniu gongcheng jianshe sanshinian dahuishang de jianghua" [Speech at the Meeting Commemorating the Construction of the Three Gate Gorge Project], quoted in Shang Wei, "A Lamentation for the Yellow River: The Three Gate Gorge Dam *(Sanmenxia),"* in Dai Qing, *The River Dragon Has Come! The Three Gorges Dam and the Fate of China's Yangtze River and Its People.* Armonk, NY: M. E. Sharpe, 1998, p. 156.

Shi Weimin. "Ji shi zhengxie weiyuan Huang Wanli" [A Remembrance of City Consultative Committee Member Huang Wanli], *Beijing zhengxie,* No. 6 (December 1991).

Wan Yongru. "Xiujian Cheng-Kun lu, jianshe Panzhihua: Lu Zhengcao jiangjun fangwen ji" [Building the Chengdu-Kunming Railroad, Constructing Panzhihua: Interview with General Lu Zhengcao], in Jinse de Panzhihua bianweihui, eds., *Jinse de Panzhihua* [Golden Panzhihua]. Chengdu: Sichuan kexue jishu chubanshe, 1990, pp. 138–145.

Wang Dongfu. "1958 nian de Wenjiang diwei fushuji," [Wenjiang's District Vice-Party Secretary of 1958], *Chengdu zhoumo,* May 13, 2000.

Yang Rungao. "Xishuangbanna senlin jianshao de chengyin ji dui ziran dili huanjing de yingxiang de fenxi yanjiu" [Causes of Reduction of Forest in Xishuangbanna and Analytical Analysis of its Impact on the Natural Geographic Environment]. Unpublished doctoral dissertation. Kunming: Yunnan shifan daxue, 1998.

———. "Kunming Haigeng 'wuqi' nongchang yansheng" [Kunming Haigeng's May 7th Agricultural Farm is Born]. *Yunnan ribao,* May 8, 1970.

Bibliography

————. "Qian qing cang hai bian lu zhou: Ji Kunming diqu junmin weihai zaotian de yingxiong shi ji" [One Thousand Qing of Blue Sea Become Green Land, Commemorate the Kunming District Army and People's Weihai Zaotian Heroic Deeds]. *Yunnan ribao,* August 17, 1970.

————. "Weihai zaotian chuan jie bao: Wanmu xin tian zhaicha mang" [Weihai Zaotian Victory News: 10,000 Mu of New Farmland Busy with Planting]. *Yunnan ribao,* May 13, 1970.

Yunnan ribao. "Xue Dazhai ren, zou Dazhai lu, wei geming kaishan zaotian" [Learn from the Dazhai People, Go the Dazhai Road, Open the Mountains to Create Farmland for the Revolution]. *Yunnan ribao,* April 25, 1970.

Zhang Chunyuan, "'Xin renkoulun' xin zai shenme difang?" [What is New about 'New Demography'?], in Ma Yinchu, *Xin renkoulun.* Changchun: Jilin renmin chubanshe, 1997, pp. 65–82.

Zhang Chunyuan, "Xu" [Introduction], in Ma Yinchu, *Xin renkoulun.* Changchun: Jilin renmin chubanshe, 1997.

Zhang Yimou, director. *Huozhe* [To Live]. Shanghai Film Studios, 1994.

INDEX